Beginning Ada Programming

From Novice to Professional

Andrew T. Shvets

Apress®

Beginning Ada Programming: From Novice to Professional

Andrew T. Shvets
Providence, RI, USA

ISBN-13 (pbk): 978-1-4842-5427-1
https://doi.org/10.1007/978-1-4842-5428-8

ISBN-13 (electronic): 978-1-4842-5428-8

Managing Director, Apress Media LLC: Welmoed Spahr
Acquisitions Editor: Steve Anglin
Development Editor: Matthew Moodie
Editorial Operations Manager: Mark Powers

Cover designed by eStudioCalamar

Cover image designed by Freepik (www.freepik.com)

Distributed to the book trade worldwide by Springer Science+Business Media New York, 233 Spring Street, 6th Floor, New York, NY 10013. Phone 1-800-SPRINGER, fax (201) 348-4505, e-mail orders-ny@springer-sbm.com, or visit www.springeronline.com. Apress Media, LLC is a California LLC and the sole member (owner) is Springer Science + Business Media Finance Inc (SSBM Finance Inc). SSBM Finance Inc is a **Delaware** corporation.

For information on translations, please e-mail editorial@apress.com; for reprint, paperback, or audio rights, please email bookpermissions@springernature.com.

Apress titles may be purchased in bulk for academic, corporate, or promotional use. eBook versions and licenses are also available for most titles. For more information, reference our Print and eBook Bulk Sales web page at http://www.apress.com/bulk-sales.

Any source code or other supplementary material referenced by the author in this book is available to readers on GitHub via the book's product page, located at www.apress.com/9781484254271. For more detailed information, please visit http://www.apress.com/source-code.

Printed on acid-free paper

*I wrote this book in honor of my wonderful family,
wife Tanya and sons Thaddaeus and David.
I love you all very much.*

Table of Contents

About the Author

Ever since beginning programming, **Andrew T. Shvets** was very interested in writing software that could be proven to be correct, without having to test every possible outcome or pray that extra bugs won't show up. Upon discovering SPARK/Ada, it became clear that his calling was answered.

About the Technical Reviewer

Germán González-Morris is a polyglot software architect/engineer with 20+ years in the field, with knowledge in Java(EE), Spring, Haskell, C, Python, and JavaScript, among others. He works with web distributed applications. Germán loves math puzzles (including reading Knuth) and swimming. He has tech-reviewed several books, including an application container book (WebLogic), as well as titles covering various programming languages (Haskell, TypeScript, WebAssembly, Math for coders, and regexp). You can find more details at his blog site (https://devwebcl.blogspot.com/) or Twitter account (@devwebcl).

Acknowledgments

As in any effort, there are those who have contributed to its success that are not directly visible. This section gives credit where it's due.

I would like to thank Jean Ichbiah for being the first to get the ball rolling on this wonderful language. Without Ada 83, this book would have been written about a much different language.

Since then, Tucker Taft has been the main designer for Ada 95, 2005, and 2012. He has worked hard to modernize and develop this language so that it can keep up with the future developments in languages. This is not an easy effort and I am glad that he has gone to the lengths that he did to make this possible.

AdaCore (`www.adacore.com/`) is a great company that has worked to keep the flame of the Ada programming language burning bright. This is the go-to place for Ada compilers and other development tools. Their dev tools can be obtained for just about any runtime environment. You can get started here: `http://libre.adacore.com/`.

Rosetta Code deserves a mention as well. This is a web site (`http://rosettacode.org/wiki/Rosetta_Code`) that has thousands of code examples about even the most mundane tasks that need to be done in a particular programming language (and believe me, there are many languages out there!). The page that talks about Ada can be found here: `http://rosettacode.org/wiki/Ada`. The entire project is run by volunteers contributing their time to create simple snippets of code to accomplish a particular task, although some are very complex. I am grateful to those wonderful people for doing such good work. Without these examples, finishing this book would be that much more difficult.

PART I

Introductory Topics

CHAPTER 1

Introduction

What You Will Get Out of This Book

Whenever you buy a book, you should know its benefits. This is what this book will do for you:

> It will teach a beginner how to write code in Ada in the shortest amount of time possible by focusing on the most important parts of the language.

Now, this book will not cover every possible topic in Ada. That is not in the scope of this book, for that you would do better to read through the *Ada 2012 Reference Manual*.

If you are wondering why Ada and not Python, Go, C#, Java, Scala, and so on, then read on. There are many new and shiny languages that come out each year and only one that is still trusted to run the systems on a major airliner, satellites, and rockets. There are good reasons for this.

The Current State of Software Development

In the world of software development, there is a dark and nasty secret. Despite new languages, frameworks, and development methodologies, few new applications are genuinely more secure or reliable. You will hear about the latest features of Swift, C#, Go, and so on and how amazing they are (to be fair, those languages do have their strong points). However, when it comes to building a reliable and secure application, their results are a mixed bag at best.

To put this another way, everyone wants to try the latest Lamborghini. This is an exciting car; who would not want to drive one around town? However, when you actually get into this car, you find that while the clutch is amazing, the steering is flawed and difficult to control or it might have a very powerful engine, but that engine breaks down after driving just a few miles. As a result, while you have a very shiny tool, it is worthless if you want a very reliable and secure program.

3

© Andrew T. Shvets 2020
A. T. Shvets, *Beginning Ada Programming*, https://doi.org/10.1007/978-1-4842-5428-8_1

The buffer overruns, dangling pointers, ill-defined types, and so on. After years of break-neck development of new languages and libraries in order to bring new features, there is a ton of code that is very unstable. New features are slapped on top of existing bugs and problems. At best, your app on your smartphone crashes and it is an inconvenience. At worst, a program that controls the acceleration of your car does not respond to further inputs and you are stuck barreling on the highway with no way to stop.

It must be said that there have been major improvements. The string object is a huge benefit for C++ that made string handling much more secure and less error prone. But as for C? This has been a less than ideal ride. Sure, C is fast, since it easily translates to assembler and runs very quickly. This is a benefit in some instances where performance is paramount. But most programs need to be reliable and secure; shaving 50 milliseconds off of an operation is often a miniscule benefit at best. If your video game crashes every hour, your driver creates a BSOD (Blue Screen of Death), or your word processor wipes out hours of work, it is understandable why people might be a *little* upset. This problem becomes exponentially worse when human lives or millions of dollars depend on having your software work correctly and without any potential for problems.

Why is this field such a disaster? There are many reasons, and these are some:

1) Poor documentation that does not fully describe what a particular piece of code does or does so in an unclear manner. As a result, developers go forward writing code on top of the existing software while unaware of the underlying problems. In time, problems arise from the earlier code, and those maintaining the code base are gifted with hours of frustration while trying to understand the problem at hand.

   It has been said that poor documentation is better than no documentation. However, if the documentation misleads the reader and does more harm, then it should have not been used at all.

2) Poor design that was done on the back of a napkin, implemented quickly as a prototype, and then built on top of. The difference between this example and the preceding one is that the original developers know that this will be a problem and are either too

lazy to take the proper corrective action (re-design) or are over-ruled by their superiors in order to "save time and money." In time, more software is piled on until the original code needs to be refactored in order to make anything work.

3) Poor communication makes it difficult to have large software projects where all of the required components fit together in a seamless fashion. This is due to poorly understood requirements, and teams think they know what needs to be done, but make assumptions along the way that are not relayed in a clear manner until integration.

4) Ever-shifting requirements are the bane of every software engineer. The customer comes to you and says that he has a specification. Your team (or you) is happy since the customer knows what he is doing. However, over time (often right before the end of the project) the scope begins to change. Either a new developer is writing the maintenance code or you have completely forgotten the underlying assumptions that you made in the past, which is an easy task to do unless you just happen to have photographic memory. As you struggle to stuff these new requirements into the existing code base, about as easy as trying to put a round peg through a triangle hole, all sorts of problems arise: your code starts to crash when it worked before, performance degrades, or the program behaves in unexpected ways without going down in flames completely.

Of course, having a complete re-write would be the sane solution, but that is rarely something you will have as an option since most projects/tasks have budgetary constraints to work within.

5) Development tools that do not check for some of the most obvious errors. Some of these features can be turned on via compiler flags (if they exist), but this is rarely done. And this is assuming that these features have been documented or work as advertised.

And many of the errors are very easy to resolve, whether it is checking to see if a variable has been initialized or if the input is a value that is completely unexpected.

So, now that you know why your OS crashes or game malfunctions, what can one do to improve on this? That is what the next section is for.

The Benefits That Ada Brings to the Table

At this point you know the disaster that is modern-day software development. Many of you have seen your games malfunction or other applications crash. What can Ada do to help?

1) The Ada language is very well documented and an international standard. It is remarkable how well the docs are maintained. The *Ada Reference Manual* (*ARM*) is the bible for all things related to the language. There is no ambiguity about what is meant in this documentation. The Web is also full of examples, tutorials, articles, blogs, source code, explanations, mailing lists, and so on.

   The latest version of the ARM can be obtained from this web site. You have the option of getting either the PDF, large text file, or HTML version:
   `www.ada-auth.org/arm.html`

2) When it comes to thoroughly thinking through your applications, Ada can help with this as well. Unlike C, where anything can be possible as long as it gets past the compiler, there are barriers that prevent the introduction of certain types of shoddy code. For example, a compiled Ada application has bounds checking that will cause the application to throw an exception if limits are exceeded. This requires a more patient and better thought-out approach, forcing the developer to spend more time thinking of the more intricate internal details and sidestepping potential design pitfalls. In the end, the number of errors is significantly reduced.

3) The strict typing in Ada makes it easier to understand how your project will work with another application. For example, if you and your friend are working on a game, having a clear understanding of what the different parts of it are saying is crucial. If you want

to have a maximum of 16 players in your game, you can create a custom type that is from 1 to 16 (more on this later in the book). Then, when it comes time to sharing this information, there is no ambiguity as to what the limit is. You and your friend can look up the limits of the custom type and know immediately what assumptions were made. Then, you both can make the decision whether the maximum is correct or not.

4)   This is similar to the preceding point about Ada's specification of so many details. By being specific with certain types, it will reduce the number of times that you need to check whether a value is within limits and clarity will be improved. As more limits are placed inside the application during the first development period, when it comes time to add features in the future – after the code is long forgotten by any of the developers – you will know whether some limit has been exceeded and which decisions were made in the past. You will save time by not debugging obscure bugs that are the result of an incorrect maximum value that has been inputted.

Doing the same application in C is much more tricky. Your code seems to be working fine, but after running the program for some time, you begin to notice odd bugs (files not be saved correctly, features working intermittently, etc.); you are not sure why and your compiler most likely compiled the code just fine with only minor warnings (if any). In the C scenario, long nights and caffeine await you. In the Ada example, the compiler would instantly inform you if anything is amiss, giving the programmer a chance to correct it long before the problem even crops up in an obscure bug or undefined behavior.

Software development need not be an annoying whack-a-mole game where one bug fix (or addition of a feature) necessitates a fix for another problem that crops up. Unless you have a limitless budget or simply enjoy this unproductive game, Ada can help you reduce or eliminate such a problem.

There are many other reasons. For example, the company (AdaCore) that maintains an implementation of an Ada compiler does not make a release every year. This gives you a chance to catch up on the internals of how the latest compiler works.

Also, the Ada compiler runs a static analysis tool during the compilation process to check for the most common trip ups. This is very valuable since there are many ways that you can make mistakes without realizing. Look at it as a friendly reminder in the beginning so that you do not have to waste hours of your life tracking down an obscure bug (the author has had these experiences and never liked them).

How Did This Language Get Its Name?

Each language has a name and there is a story behind why it acquired that name. For example, Python was named after the comedy show called *Monty Python's Flying Circus.*

Ada was named after the woman Augusta Ada King-Noel, Countess of Lovelace. She is considered by some to be the first programmer after reviewing and correcting some of the "code" that Charles Babbage wrote for his mechanical computer. You can learn more about her at

```
https://en.wikipedia.org/wiki/Ada_Lovelace
```

Why Write This Book

Whenever one begins a task, there is usually at least one compelling reason to keep going with this effort. These are the top reasons:

1) The primary reason is because there is a lack of introductory Ada 2012 programming books. There are many excellent pieces of literature on Ada, but almost all of them assume that you have experience writing code in another programming language, are looking to develop in an older version of the language, or have programmed in Ada before. These are excellent books, but if you are either making Ada your first programming language or coming with experience with another language, it makes sense to have a very gentle and guided introduction. In order to make this language more popular, this is an essential requirement.

It is very discouraging when a completely different programming language is the prerequisite for the one that you really want to learn. Look at it this way; let's say you pick up a book about Python and in the introduction it says that if you want to learn how to write code in this language, you will first need to learn how to write code in C or C++. This is a poor approach.

And to be clear, we will be using Ada 2012. And going forward, unless specifically an earlier release is stated (Ada 95 or Ada 2005), in this book, the word Ada always refers to Ada 2012. If you try to run this code on earlier compilers and encounter issues, you will be on your own.

2) The other reason is to – and this is a long shot – improve the quality of software that is created. So much of it is in such a broken state (especially when you add layers of broken code on top of other broken code). The goal is to get people more interested in writing Ada code and get others to start thinking about how to improve the reliability of applications.

3) And lastly, the author is a fan of Ada and figured that the best way to contribute to the community is to make it easier for new individuals learn more about how to develop in this wonderful language. Also, numerous myths and falsehoods need to be dispelled. An honest assessment of the pros and cons of Ada is needed.

Myths About Ada

As any language that has been around for a long enough time, Ada has acquired a reputation. While much of it is quite excellent, there are some points that continue to stick without merit. Here are some of them in no particular order and why they are wrong:

1) The first release of Ada was financed by the Department of Defense and the US Federal Government, and therefore the United States influences how this language can evolve. This is patently untrue. Yes, the first standard was indeed paid for by the

Department of Defense. However, for future releases there are independent committees, which are not tied to any government organization, that develop the standard. Furthermore, all subsequent standards (Ada 95, 2005, and 2012) were created by AdaCore and other independent entities. New compiler and language features are always added on if they appear to be useful. While the original requirements from Ada 83 were inherited, new features and developments were added to Ada as they became available in other languages.

2) Ada is "slow." Ada does perform constraint checks when it runs, which does incur a certain performance penalty when compared to C. So, assuming you write the same code for C and Ada and the only difference between the generated assembly is that Ada has constraint checks, the Ada application will run *slightly* slower.

However, this is a very gray area. There are a number of assumptions that one needs to make in order to make a very good comparison of the performance of the binaries that are generated from either the Ada or C compiler. One would have to ensure that the hardware executing the two applications is the same, the runtime environment is very similar, and the compiler flags used to generate the code (and this requires very careful reading of the documentation about what each flag does) produce very similar binaries (this is not something that you can easily compare and contrast). Often, if performance seems lacking in the Ada application that you have written, then the problem is usually the need to optimize the slowest algorithm or locate a resource leak that might be slowing things down. You can also add more RAM or simply start an independent task (an Ada version of a thread, which we will cover in later chapters) to speed things up.

The concrete and existing benefits of reducing programming errors down the road, which means fewer patches and updates, are far greater than many theoretical performance hits that are

often talked about. With the cost of very fast RAM can be $150–
$300 per module, but the cost of a programmer that is paid $30+
an hour might spend 50 hours debugging faulty code, which cost
would you rather have?

3)   Ada is difficult to learn. False. This myth has been mentioned by
a number of C/C++ developers that were set in their ways and
did not want to learn a new programming language. When the
Department of Defense came out with the Ada mandate that
required new projects be written in Ada unless an exception
was granted (which happened far too often), many software
engineers came up with this myth since they did not want to
switch to the new standard or give up their existing competitive
advantage of knowing their current language. The only true way
to compare the ease of learning a brand new language is to do
a study of individuals that are new to programming and teach
them how to write code in Ada and a different programming
language that is comparable; for example, Perl would not be a
good comparison.

If anything, Ada is actually fairly easy to learn. The syntax is so
explicit, that it is much more difficult to misunderstand what the
code is doing than in C/C++. The number of assumptions that
need to be made is less.

4)   Ada is old, is not used very often, or is "dead." This one is the most
puzzling one. Since Ada 83, this language has been constantly
updated. In fact, there is talk of Ada 2020 as the next version. It
has been used and continues to be used in aerospace, defense
industry, and other applications that are simply seldom discussed.
Ada is here; it will continue to be here and is a proven quantity
that other languages are unlikely to replace. Ada's cousin,
SPARK, is used in the medical industry to make reliable medical
equipment; do you foresee a time when X-ray machines are no
longer needed?

Layout of This Book

The first six chapters comprise the introductory part of the book that provides you the absolute bare minimum to get you going. You will learn how to use the default primitives, values, functions vs. procedures, arrays and records, as well as some basic things about object-oriented programming. After this, you will know how to write simple code and the basics of how to organize basic applications.

Chapters 7–9 are where you pick up some of the more intermediate topics. This is where storing data in files is covered, along with how to handle exceptions (also, when not to use them) and how to better work with strings. After this, you will be able to create slightly more mature programs. At this stage, your applications will have the look and feel of something that you might actually deploy in the field, if only for very small and straightforward tasks.

Chapters 10–17 are where genuinely complex topics are covered. This is where multiprocessing is covered so that your programs will take advantage of multi-core processors. Advanced topics such as custom types and inheritance are discussed at length so that you will know how to make the best use of such programming methodologies. Data containers will be displayed, showing how to organize information inside your program. Access types are also covered, which will give you more power to create custom data containers. Then, contracts (an Ada 2012 feature) are covered, giving you a peace of mind that your code works each and every time (even in production). In Chapter 15, we will cover network connections. As your projects become more complex, with more than one binary files generated and custom compilation rules, you will need a way to organize all of this in a logical manner. Lastly, the topic of libraries will be covered, giving you the ability to create binaries of your code to be included elsewhere. After all of this, you will feel comfortable creating complex applications that seemed out of reach initially.

The appendixes are there to help you along, such as installing the Ada compiler for your OS and knowing which words you can and cannot use for variables, functions, procedures, and packages. Topics that could not be fit into the rest of the flow of the book are also covered here. One topic of particular interest is how to debug your Ada applications. Debugging can become indispensable when you are designing a custom algorithm and working out various kinks in its execution and performance.

If any content is difficult to understand, go over it as often as you feel necessary in order to understand it. Do not memorize the syntax (for that, use this book or the ARM as a reference), but focus on understanding the underlying concept. And you are free to

CHAPTER 1   INTRODUCTION

experiment with the code in this book as you see fit. Try breaking things, making your own changes, and so on. If everything that you have done has never broken, then most likely you have not tried anything truly daring.

Standards in This Book

In order to make the learning process as smooth as possible, keep in mind that code is displayed like so:

```
procedure HelloWorld(ToPrint : String);
```

Getting Started

Let's take care of a few items before progressing further. If you have not done so already, go to the appendices at the end of this book and install the compiler for the operating system that you plan to use. There are many compilers that can be used, but in this book, we will stick to the one provided by AdaCore; you are welcome to use others as you see fit. Follow the directions carefully in order to make the install go smoothly.

Pick out a text editor that you are planning on using for your OS:

1) For Windows, a very popular option is Notepad++ (`https://notepad-plus-plus.org/`).

   Using Notepad (the default Windows text editor) is not encouraged. It lacks many of the features that are conducive toward becoming a productive Ada developer, such as syntax highlighting and being able to efficiently work with line endings from different operating systems. WordPad is also discouraged for the same reasons.

2) For Linux and Unix operating systems, there is Vi/Vim, Emacs, Kate, and Gedit. Check your distribution's package manager and install whichever is easiest for you.

3) Atom (`https://atom.io`) is also an excellent editor. It runs on all of the major operating systems. Make sure to install language-ada and linger-ada packages. You will get syntax highlighting and other benefits.

Please keep in mind that you can use just about any text editor that you would like. It is highly recommended that whichever text editor you choose, it should be able to handle file line endings from different operating systems; the default text editor Notepad in Windows does not display Linux line endings correctly. The preceding options are suggestions. However, installing any of these editors is beyond the scope of the book.

Once you have both of the preceding features completed, proceed to the next section.

The Obligatory "Hello World" Example

Most books about programming languages have a similar example, so here is one in Ada:

```
-- hello_world.adb

with Ada.Text_IO;

procedure hello_world is
begin
  Ada.Text_IO.Put_Line("Hello world!");
  Ada.Text_IO.Put("It's a wonderful day!");
  Ada.Text_IO.New_Line;
end hello_world;
```

Now, it needs to be compiled. Copy (or type in) the preceding code into your favorite text editor and save it. Then, open up a terminal (or a command prompt in Windows) and go to the location of that file. Now, compile it like so:

```
> gnatmake -g hello_world.adb
```

The output of the compiler will be the following:

```
gcc -c -I.\ -g -I- .\hello_world.adb
gnatbind -x hello_world.ali
gnatlink hello_world.ali -g
```

Pay attention to the "-g". This tells the compiler to include debug information in the executable. This will make it possible to debug your code and more informative exceptions will be thrown.

During the compilation process, the following files will be generated:

1) `hello_world` – This is our binary and what we will execute.

2) `hello_world.ali` – This file is the result of the linker running during the compilation process in order to combine binary object files into an executable. When our applications become more complex, the role of this utility will grow.

3) `hello_world.o` – This is the binary object file that is generated after compiling our source code.

4) The following files are created as a result of the "-g" flag. It is used in order to include the debug information in the executable:

   a. `b~hello_world.adb`

   b. `b~hello_world.ads`

   c. `b~hello_world.ali`

   d. `b~hello_world.o`

The *.adb file is consumed by the compiler, which generates the *.o and *.ali files. Afterward, the binder and linker take over; they consume the *.ali and *.o files to generate an executable that you can run. After this, you will have a binary called hello_world (or hello_world.exe in Windows) and you will need to run it, like so:

```
> ./hello_world
Hello world!
It's a wonderful day!
```

In the end, the most important files are your source code and the resulting binary.

What Do the File Endings Mean?

Programming languages come with their own file endings that better differentiate it from other text files. Python has *.py and Java *.java.

Ada has two file formats for its source code. They are ∗.adb and ∗.ads. There is no standard or required file ending. However, generally the "b" in ∗.adb indicates the body, or the code will be executed. The "s" in ∗.ads is for files that hold the specification or the code that will describe the functions, procedures, and packages that are inside.

Now, let's go through the source code of the preceding "hello world" example line by line:

1) `hello_world.adb` – Anything that shows up after the two minus signs is considered to be a comment and is ignored by the compiler. Ada does not have multi-line comments, but many IDEs (as well as Emacs) give you the ability to comment out whole blocks of code with just a few key presses. Read the documentation of your IDE on how to do this.

2) `with Ada.Text_IO;` – This is how you can import system libraries to do things such as print to console by using the "with" keyword. In this case, we are importing the library that will permit us to print data to the command line.

3) Semicolons are used to terminate statements. They are included inside of blocks of code, after methods and packages. Their purpose is to tell the compiler where a piece of code ends.

4) `procedure hello_world is` – The declaration of the function from where the code will start executing when the application is started. Keep in mind that when you give a file a particular name, inside of that file there must be a procedure that has same name to serve as an entry for the code to start executing; otherwise, the compiler will give you an error; when you start object-oriented programming, a similar rule is observed when working with packages and classes.

   When the body of a method or a package is implemented, the "is" keyword becomes a requirement. This is done in order to indicate the beginning of the body of this block of code. In later chapters, when you will begin working with packages, the declaration portion of the code will not have an "is" right after it.

   Right after the declaration of a method, you can describe your variables that will be used in your code. At the moment, this is blank.

5) `begin` – This keyword indicates the beginning of the section where your code starts executing. After this line, you can implement your algorithms and output text for the user to see.

6) `Ada.Text_IO.Put_Line("Hello world!");` – This function call does several things at the same time. First, it takes a String type and prints it out to the screen. Second, it puts a new line after that output (hence, the "_Line" in the function name).

7) `Ada.Text_IO.Put("It's a wonderful day!");` – This one does even less than the preceding one. All it does is print a value to the screen and that is it. A new line is not created.

8) `Ada.Text_IO.New_Line;` – By running this, a newline character is printed to command line.

9) `end hello_world;` – At the end of every function, procedure, or package body, there is an explicit ending for the compiler.

Run the preceding code and see what you get. Then re-read and understand what is actually going on. This is a simple example, but it is best if you fully understand this example before reading further.

What else can we learn about Ada?

1) Ada is a case-insensitive language. "Procedure," "procedure," and "pRoCeDuRe" are all the same to the compiler. Most programming languages are case-sensitive.

2) There are no brackets or parentheses for bodies of code. A function and a block of code after an if statement all need an accompanying "begin" and "end" keyword.

3) Many statements end with a semicolon. Although when you declared the start of the procedure you did not have a semicolon, at the end of it you needed one. The same holds true for loops, if statements, packages, and so on. Try to insert or delete the semicolon at specific places to see what happens; the compiler will let you know if you did something wrong.

If you purchased the print version of this book, you will notice that the code has different shades of gray. The original manuscript had the code colorized so that it will appear to how it should is a modern text editor.

Contacting the Author and Source Code

Contacting the author is best done by writing to the following e-mail address: introductory.ada@gmail.com. Please note, responses might be delayed due to various and unforeseen circumstances.

The source code for this book can be found in this online repository:

```
https://github.com/apress/beginning-ada-programming
```

Feel free to go there and download the code as you see fit. One way to do this is to just grab all of it in the form of a compressed file.

Lab

Create a small application that prints out the following:

```
##################################################################
##################################################################
##                                                              ##
##      00000000000    0000000000    00000000000                ##
##      00        00   00        00   00        00              ##
##      00        00   00        00   00        00              ##
##      00000000000    00        00   00000000000              ##
##      00        00   00        00   00        00              ##
##      00        00   00        00   00        00              ##
##      00        00   0000000000     00        00              ##
##                                                              ##
##################################################################
##################################################################
```

Feel free to experiment with trying to break it or cause some other calamity. Breaking things and putting them back together is the best way to learn.

CHAPTER 2

Basic Types

What You Will Get Out of This Chapter

The purpose of this chapter is to introduce some basic types, also called primitive types. You will use these types most frequently, and having a big picture understanding how they work is a big plus. How to manipulate these types is also discussed to some degree. Strings are covered in greater detail – and there is plenty to cover – later on in the book; for now the basics are discussed. The goal is not to overwhelm you from the beginning.

The Basics of Variable Creation and Assignment

Let's get the basics of making a new variable out of the way.

Whenever you want to declare a new variable of any sort in Ada, you can only do this in the declarative area of the procedure, function, or package, like so:

```
procedure ThisIsATest is
  -- only here
begin
...
```

It can only be done before the begin keyword. This is done in order to make your code more organized. The benefit is that it relieves you from the burden of having to hunt down a particular variable that you declared in a very long function and do not remember where.

Now that you know where, how do you declare a new variable? Like so:

```
SomeInt : Integer := 44;
```

© Andrew T. Shvets 2020
A. T. Shvets, *Beginning Ada Programming*, https://doi.org/10.1007/978-1-4842-5428-8_2

Unlike in other programming languages where the equals "=" denotes assignment, Ada actually uses the mathematically correct approach of ":=" and reserves the equals sign for comparison (to check if two values are the same). This approach makes it impossible for you to make the mistake of assigning a value to a variable inside the if statement – as many have done a few times in C/C++ – and having to hunt down a particularly annoying bug. A semicolon is required at the end of each assignment statement.

The colon after "SomeInt" does not need to have spaces on both sides of it. You can omit them. However, it is recommended that you do use spaces in order make your code more readable.

As mentioned before, it is important to keep in mind that Ada is a case-insensitive language and all of the following refer to the same variable:

- SomeVar

- SOMEVAR

- somevar

- SoMeVaR

Furthermore, when selecting a name for a variable (or procedure or function or package name or custom type), you are free to use any letter, number, or underline "_". All other characters cannot be used. The starting character must be a letter and not an underline or a number.

Numbers – Integers

The basics of Ada numbers can be described as either integers or floats. Now, there are other types of integers that can be used, and they all have different ranges. Let's start by looking at the following example:

```
-- basic_types_ranges.adb:

with Ada.Text_IO;

procedure basic_types_ranges is
begin
  Ada.Text_IO.Put_Line("The min range of an integer [" &
    Integer'Image(Integer'First) & "] and the max range of an integer [" &
    Integer'Image(Integer'Last) & "].");
```

```
Ada.Text_IO.Put_Line("The min range of a positive [" &
    Positive'Image(Positive'First) & "] and the max range of a positive [" &
    Positive'Image(Positive'Last) & "].");
Ada.Text_IO.Put_Line("The min range of a natural [" &
    Natural'Image(Natural'First) & "] and the max range of a natural [" &
    Natural'Image(Natural'Last) & "].");
end basic_types_ranges;
```

Since you already know the basic structure of a procedure, where it begins and ends, the explanation will not be repeated. What the preceding example illustrates is which values can be assigned to a given type. It is easily done with the 'First and 'Last attributes. This is very important, because Ada is a strictly typed language and assigning a value that is either too large or too small will not result in undefined behavior, but a runtime error (or a compile-time error if you assign an initial incorrect value to a type). The preceding example will print out the min and max of the Integer, Positive, and Natural.

These are the three that we will be looking at. One is just a plain signed integer. Signed means that you can have negative values as well as positive values. The range of this integer is specified by the attributes 'First and 'Last. It is declared simply as "Integer," as shown in the preceding example.

What Are Attributes?

Think of attributes as parts of the whole Integer object that can be called, read, and set (depending on how they are created). They are very useful when it comes to understanding any sort of underlying assumptions that you have about types. The 'Image attribute turns an input integer into a string when it comes to writing it to the console or using it with other strings.

The second one is the positive integer. This one is similar to the regular integer, but its minimum is 1 and not –2147483648 (the max is the same as it is for the Integer). This value can be used to keep track of an iteration in an array. If you were to try to set a value of 0 to a positive integer, you will get a compilation error (or a runtime limit violation if this happened during program execution). This is similar to an unsigned value in other programming languages, in that you can only assign positive numbers to it. The difference is that in this case you cannot assign a 0 to a variable of this subtype.

The third is the natural. The natural is a genuine unsigned variable from the perspective of other programming languages such as C/C++. You can assign any number of 0 to 2147483647 to it. This is great for keeping track of values that cannot be negative (e.g., the number of liters in a pool, negative volume just does not make any sense).

Three Types of Integers?

Not quite, there is actually just one type and that is "Integer." The rest are derived from this type, but we will worry about this later in the book.

Some readers who have some programming experience might point out that in other programming languages they can have unsigned numbers ranging from 0 to 4294967296. This is true. The reason why the same does not hold for Positive and Natural is due to Ada types not being bound to the underlying computer architecture (usually x86, 32-bit, or 64-bit). This has the advantage of making your code more portable across different machines while retaining the performance benefits of a compiled language. And we will see later some of the ways that you can increase or decrease these ranges at will, something that is very difficult (if not impossible) in C/C++ or Java.

For now, let's review this example on how to modify these integers:

```
-- basic_operations.adb:

with Ada.Text_IO;

procedure basic_operations is
  TestInteger : Integer  := 7;
  TestNatural : Natural  := 0;
  TestPositive : Positive := 1;
begin
  -- do some basic operations on the Integer.
  TestInteger := TestInteger - 14;
  Ada.Text_IO.Put_Line("This is the integer: " &
    Integer'Image(TestInteger));

  -- do some basic operations on the Natural.
  TestNatural := TestNatural + 25;
  Ada.Text_IO.Put_Line("This is the natural: " &
    Natural'Image(TestNatural));
```

```
  -- do some basic operations on the Positive.
  TestPositive := TestPositive + 8;
  Ada.Text_IO.Put_Line("This is the positive: " &
    Positive'Image(TestPositive));
end basic_operations;
```

Here we have an Integer, a Positive, and a Natural. You can easily add a value to each and then have them be displayed to the console. How about a small experiment? Change the preceding operations so that you subtract the numbers that were added. What do you see? Any errors? Can you run the generated executable? If so, what do you see?

The next topic of our Integer discussion is Long_Long_Integer. This is the number when you need to work with exceptionally large numbers. This is when you know full well that you need to count something that is more than two billion (the upper maximum of an Integer). Usually a number of this size is an index in a database table or a keeping track of a multitude of records. Admittedly, this is not something that you will need to resort to often. Most of the time, iterating within far smaller ranges is far more common.

It is worthwhile to note that Long_Long_Integer also has the attributes of 'Image, 'First, and 'Last.

There Are No Long_Long_Naturals or Long_Long_ Positives!

Unlike the Integer object, there are no Long or Long_Long alternatives for Natural and Positive. Do keep in mind that this option does not exist and you will get a fully unsigned (very large) integer. Depending on how many of these values you allocate (such as a very large array), this can consume quite a bit of RAM. We will talk about how to specify these limits later when custom types are created.

There Is Also a Long_Integer...

This type also exists, but it has the same range as Integer. There is little point in covering this value if the only difference is having one "Long_" in front of the type name.

Now, let's get down to looking at some code that works with this new integer:

```
-- longer_integers.adb:

with Ada.Text_IO;
```

```
procedure longer_integers is
  TestLI : Long_Long_Integer := 4;
begin
  Ada.Text_IO.Put_Line(" Long_Long_Integer:      " &
    Long_Long_Integer'Image(TestLI));
  Ada.Text_IO.Put_Line(" Long_Long_Integer min: [ " &
   Long_Long_Integer'Image(Long_Long_Integer'First) &
   " ] and max: [ " &
   Long_Long_Integer'Image(Long_Long_Integer'Last) & " ]");
end longer_integers;
```

And this is the output that you will see:

```
 Long_Long_Integer:      4
 Long_Long_Integer min: [ -9223372036854775808 ] and max:
 [   9223372036854775807 ]
```

It is obvious that the range has increased dramatically over that of an Integer type. Hopefully, you will find this type to be useful in certain cases where such large ranges are a must.

Numbers – Floats

Now let's talk about Floats. Floats give you the ability to represent numerical data with decimal values. This becomes important when whole numbers are insufficient to show portions or subdivisions. For example, if you are making an accounting application that and you need to add $53.98 to $94.22. An integer is useless in this situation. For this, you will need a float. Let's have a look at this example:

```
-- floats_ranges.adb:

with Ada.Text_IO;
with Ada.Float_Text_IO;

procedure floats_ranges is
  Sum1Float : Float := 53.98;
  Sum2Float : Float := 94.22;
  Total : Float     := 0.0;
```

```
begin
  Ada.Text_IO.Put_Line("The min range of a float [" &
    Float'Image(Float'First)
    & "] and the max range of a float [" &
    Float'Image(Float'Last) & "].");

  Total := Sum1Float + Sum2Float;

  Ada.Text_IO.Put_Line("The total of the two sums: " &
    Float'Image(Total));
  Ada.Float_Text_IO.Put(Total, Exp => 0);
end floats_ranges;
```

This is the output of the preceding code:

```
The min range of a float [-3.40282E+38] and the max range of a float
[ 3.40282E+38].
The total of the two sums:   1.48200E+02
148.20000
```

Let's digest the new syntax that makes up this example:

1) with Ada.Float_Text_IO; – This is a specific package that can be used to have a finer level of control over how floats are printed. For example, it can permit you to set the numbers that should appear after the decimal value.

2) Sum1Float : Float := 53.98; – This is just a standard assignment to a variable.

3) The code right after begin (which is split up across multiple lines) prints out the limits of the Float type.

4) Total := Sum1Float + Sum2Float; – A pretty simple arithmetic example.

5) Float'Image(Total) – Will convert the float to a string for printing out. There is an interesting situation though; when you see the output, it will be something like this: 1.48200E+02.

   This is called scientific notation. It is a way to represent large float values in a more compact way.

25

6) `Ada.Float_Text_IO.Put(Total, Exp => 0);` – This is an example of how to print out the float in non-scientific notation so that you can view the number as a decimal. It will print out 148.20000.

7) One thing to keep in mind about Floats, you cannot assign an integer to a variable and expect the compiler to just like it. You will receive a compilation error.

   At this point, you might be thinking of how to add floats and integers or convert between the two.

8) To convert from an integer to a float is straightforward:

   `SomeFloatVal := Float(SomeInt);`

   You can even do some operations on the resulting Float like so:

   `SomeFloatVal := Float(SomeInt) / 3;`

9) Going from a float to an integer can also be done, but there is a catch. Double-precision values contain decimal values that cannot be represented in an integer and as a result will be lost in the conversion process. Let's look at this example:

   `IntTotal := 44 + Integer(23.2);`

   The result of the preceding operation will be 67. However, it is important to know what really happens. The Integer cast actually rounds up/down the inputted float value. If the input had been instead 23.5 (or higher), the sum of this operation would be 68. The inputted value is either rounded up or down based on whether the decimal value is less than 0.5 (down) or equal/greater than 0.5 (up).

10) Casting to and from a Long_Integer is as easy as the preceding Float example. You can try to cast to a Long_Integer using either a Float or a plain Integer (as well as a Natural and Positive). However, keep in mind that going from a Long_Integer to an Integer (or Float) potentially can land you in some hot water. If you have a very large number in the Long_Integer (larger than you can fit into the max value of an Integer) and you cast it to an

Integer, you could encounter a loss of information. This is hardly ideal and make sure that you check that the source Long_Integer does not exceed the limits of the destination data container that you are trying to use for storage.

It needs to be noted that a Float is not the best possible way to implement an accounting application. Floats have a problem called a rounding error. This means that whenever you use these types to do arithmetic, the result can be incorrect. The reason for this is due to the CPU doing its best to perform the operation, and if it's too specific, then that will result in the CPU trying to approximate the most accurate result possible. Due to the IEEE standard that is implemented in the processor, the result can be incorrect. In later chapters, we will see how to specify your own types and avoid this problem entirely.

Boolean Type

These values are fairly straightforward. They can have either one value or the other. They are either true or false. Ambiguity about the limits of this data type does not exist; there are only two possible options. Boolean types are the results of boolean operations that execute in your code. They are useful for control flow in Ada code (which is covered in the next chapter). The goal is to familiarize you with Boolean types and explain some of the operations that can be done.

Let's look at this example:

```
-- bool.adb:

with Ada.Text_IO;

procedure bool is
  BoolVal1 : Boolean := True;
  BoolVal2 : Boolean := True;
  BoolVal3 : Boolean := False;
begin
  Ada.Text_IO.Put_Line(" Bool1: " &
    Boolean'Image(BoolVal1 and BoolVal2));
  Ada.Text_IO.Put_Line(" Bool2: " &
    Boolean'Image(BoolVal2 and BoolVal3));
```

```
  Ada.Text_IO.Put_Line(" Bool3: " &
    Boolean'Image(BoolVal1 or BoolVal2));
  Ada.Text_IO.Put_Line(" Bool4: " &
    Boolean'Image(BoolVal1 or BoolVal3));
  Ada.Text_IO.Put_Line(" Bool5: " &
    Boolean'Image(not BoolVal1));
  Ada.Text_IO.Put_Line(" Bool6: " &
    Boolean'Image(not BoolVal3));
  Ada.Text_IO.Put_Line(" Bool7: " &
    Boolean'Image(BoolVal1 xor BoolVal2));
  Ada.Text_IO.Put_Line(" Bool8: " &
    Boolean'Image(BoolVal1 xor BoolVal3));
end bool;
```

This is how a Boolean is declared. You can give it a default value – in this case true – or not and assign one later.

```
BoolVal1 : Boolean := True;
```

Default Values

Giving a variable a default value from the outset is good programming practice and strongly encouraged. There is less of a chance of a variable causing a problem later on simply because it was not initialized. This is a good rule of thumb, no matter the language that you are using.

Let's go through the previous example line by line and gain an understanding of the boolean operations that took place:

1) `Boolean'Image(BoolVal1 and BoolVal2)` – In this line, there are two things going on. First, the BoolVal1 and BoolVal2 take both inputs and compute the logical "and" (&) operation of both values. The result is true. Second, the `Boolean'Image` converts the result of the boolean operation (which is a Boolean type) to a string so that we can print it out.

Let's have a look at the table of boolean operations and what outputs we can expect with the given operations:

AND operator

Input 1	Input 2	Result
True	True	True
True	False	False
False	True	False
False	False	False

2) `BoolVal2 and BoolVal3` – Let's consult the preceding AND operation table. BoolVal3 is false, so no matter what the state of BoolVal2 is, the result is always false.

3) `BoolVal1 or BoolVal2` – This is a logical "or" operation. It works a little bit different than a logical "and" operation. Unlike in a logical "and" operation, where just one of the inputs that is false can render the output to be false, in this case, just one of the inputs can be true in order to render the output to be true. Here is a table that describes all of the inputs and operations:

OR operator

Input 1	Input 2	Result
True	True	True
True	False	True
False	True	True
False	False	False

4) `BoolVal1 or BoolVal3` – Again, since only one of the inputs is true, the result is guaranteed to be true no matter what. This is described in the previously mentioned OR operation table.

5) `not BoolVal1` – This is the "not" operation. All it does is simply flip the resulting boolean value from true to false and vice versa. This comes in very handy in if statements and loops that will be discussed in the next chapter. The result of "not" is false. This is the table of operations:

NOT operator

Input	Result
True	False
False	True

6) `not BoolVal3` – This operation flips the value of the BoolVal3. Since BoolVal3 is False, the result of this is that the output is True.

7) `BoolVal1 xor BoolVal2` – "xor" is the exclusive or. Exclusive or is written as "xor" even when not inside of a source file. What this does is return true only when the two inputs are different; otherwise, the result is false. Please look at the following table:

XOR operator

Input 1	Input 2	Result
True	True	False
True	False	True
False	True	True
False	False	False

In this instance, the result of this operation is true.

For now, this is the end of the boolean section. If it is difficult to understand how you might actually use this, it will be explained when discussing control structures in the next chapter.

Strings

Strings are absolutely essential if you want to display sensible information to the user. A number 223 means little without the correct context. Ada has three types of strings; the reasons for each one of them and the benefits that they bring will be discussed:

1) Fixed length string – These strings are of fixed length, which is defined at runtime or compile-time. This is the standard string type that is usually defined by Ada when working text. It is fairly straightforward to understand, but a little bit difficult to manipulate. It is the type of choice for many functions that are part of Ada because of this hard limit.

   One caveat of this type is simply assigning a shorter string to a string variable that is of longer length will yield a runtime error and the program will stop running. However, you can use a Move procedure to do this.

2) Bounded length string – In order to properly use this type, the maximum length of what this string can be must be specified (just like its cousin the fixed string).

   This type will not be discussed, so as to give more attention to the types that programmers from other languages are used to.

3) Unbounded length string – For all other things, especially where strings can be manipulated as necessary, this is the type that should be used. Using this type, you can append, insert, and delete and other changes that you might want (you can do this with other strings, but it is simply easier to work this way with an unbounded string). This works best in a runtime environment such as a desktop or when resources are plentiful and exceeding your character buffer will not result in a catastrophic crash of the application. In embedded systems, this string type should never be used.

At this point, you might think why not have just one type. The reason for this design is to take into account instances where you might be writing embedded or system-level code and there are very strict runtime conditions. At this level, you have to account for just about every byte that you allocate and ensure that you use your RAM as efficiently as possible.

The fixed string is the most basic string type. It can be initialized with a string in the declaration section or later on. However, once initialized, you cannot write to it a string that is of greater length than the maximum allowed. But, you can move a shorter (or equal) in length string to a longer one. Let's look at the following example:

```ada
-- strings_example.adb:

with Ada.Text_IO;
with Ada.Strings;
with Ada.Strings.Fixed;

procedure strings_example is
  someVal : String := "Hello there!";
  someVal2 : String := "Hallo Kevin!";
  longString : String(1 .. 250);
  longText : String := "Hello there back!";
  -- NOTE!! this will not compile!!
  unAssigned : String;
begin
  -- the following lines will work just fine.
  Ada.Strings.Fixed.Move(someVal, longString);
  Ada.Text_IO.Put_Line(someVal);
  Ada.Text_IO.Put_Line(longString);

  -- NOTE!! this will cause a run-time error!!
  longString := someVal;

  -- this will work just as well.
  Ada.Strings.Fixed.Move(someVal, longText);
  Ada.Text_IO.Put_Line(longText);
  Ada.Text_IO.Put_Line(Natural'Image(longText'Length));
```

```
-- this will work exactly as you would expect it to.
someVal := someVal2;
Ada.Text_IO.Put_Line(someVal);

Ada.Strings.Fixed.Move(longString, someVal);
Ada.Text_IO.Put_Line(someVal);

longText := "Hello there back!";
Ada.Text_IO.Put_Line(longText);
end strings_example;
```

If you would like to see how this code works without the errors intentionally inserted, simply comment out the offending lines or delete them outright.

Now, let's break this code down line by line (the output statements will not be mentioned, since they are self-explanatory):

1) Between the procedure declaration and the begin keyword, a number of fixed size strings are being declared. This is to be used later on. The one problem that is listed previously is the variable unAssigned. This string variable is uninitialized and the compiler will give you an error at compile time.

2) `Ada.Strings.Fixed.Move(someVal, longString);` – This copies the shorter string (someVal) into the longer string (longString). This is important, because making a simple assignment will get you a compile-time warning and a runtime constraint error that will stop your application.

3) `longString := someVal;` – By executing this line of code, the application attempts to assign a string that is of shorter length to that of a longer length. This is not possible and will give you an error when your code is executing (but it will compile). Ada erects these barriers so that developers are more thoughtful about their assignments and so that variables have data assigned to them more thoughtfully.

4) `Ada.Strings.Fixed.Move(someVal, longText);` – What will happen here is that the longer text will simply be erased by the shorter text. Keep in mind that you can still assign a much longer

piece of text in longText later, just as long as it does not exceed the limit that has been assigned to it when the variable was created. The longer text has been assigned to longText (but not longer than its max) on the 2nd and 3rd last lines of the source code.

5) `someVal := someVal2;` – An assignment of this nature will execute flawlessly. You see, both are strings and both have text that is of the exact same length. As a result, someVal will now have a greeting toward someone named Kevin.

6) `Ada.Strings.Fixed.Move(longString, someVal);` – This is a tricky piece of code. Instead of a regular assignment, you are using the move method. This will succeed since longString's contents can fit into someVal, since longString was not changed because a value was not assigned to it.

    However, if longString's contents were more than what could fit into someVal, then an error would be thrown and the program would stop executing.

7) `longText := "Hello there back!";` – A simple assignment to longText's original contents and it works flawlessly.

Regular fixed strings are somewhat tricky, but you can definitely work with them. Go into the preceding example and make changes, and see what you can break and the errors that are displayed.

Unbounded strings are much better suited when it comes time to modify the underlying strings. Being able to expand and shrink our strings as we see fit is a must.

Wordy Class Paths

You might have noticed strings such as `Ada.Text_IO.Put_Line(...)`, the text that is right before Put_Line can be shortened to just the function call by including `use Ada.Text_IO;` right after `with Ada.Text_IO;`

However, in this book, the longer version will be used. The reason is that there are many packages that have a function with the same name, and unless made explicit, this can be quite confusing. Since this is an introductory book, the more verbose notation will be used; when you feel you are more confident working with Ada, use the less verbose option.

Let's look at this example:

```
-- unbounded_strings.adb:

with Ada.Text_IO;
with Ada.Strings.Unbounded;

procedure unbounded_strings is
  Temp1 : Ada.Strings.Unbounded.Unbounded_String :=
    Ada.Strings.Unbounded.To_Unbounded_String("Hello, ");
  Temp2 : Ada.Strings.Unbounded.Unbounded_String :=
    Ada.Strings.Unbounded.To_Unbounded_String("world!");
begin
  Ada.Text_IO.Put_Line(Ada.Strings.Unbounded.To_String(Temp1));

  Ada.Strings.Unbounded.Append(Temp1, Temp2);
  Ada.Text_IO.Put_Line(Ada.Strings.Unbounded.To_String(Temp1));

  Ada.Strings.Unbounded.Append(Temp1, "  From Ada!");
  Ada.Text_IO.Put_Line(Ada.Strings.Unbounded.To_String(Temp1));

  Ada.Text_IO.Put_Line("Temp1 length: " &
    Natural'Image(Ada.Strings.Unbounded.Length(Temp1)));
  Ada.Text_IO.Put_Line("Temp2 length: " &
    Natural'Image(Ada.Strings.Unbounded.Length(Temp2)));
end unbounded_strings;
```

Let's take this example apart:

1) `Temp1 : Ada.Strings.Unbounded.Unbounded_String := Ada.Strings.Unbounded.To_Unbounded_String("Hello, ");` – This is how assignment to the unbounded string works. Any string in Ada that is "" is a String of fixed length and cannot be simply assigned to an unbounded string variable. This is due to the strict typing of the language.

2) `Ada.Text_IO.Put_Line(Ada.Strings.Unbounded.To_String (Temp1));` – The same goes for printing text to command line. The function Put_Line takes a fixed string, and in order to get this out of the unbounded string, the To_String function is needed.

3) `Ada.Strings.Unbounded.Append(Temp1, Temp2);` – This one is a bit tricky. The goal is to append two unbounded strings together and then store the result in some specific location. In this case, the procedure Append takes the reference of the first variable (Temp1) and appends the contents of Temp2. Taking the reference means that this variable can be modified in the procedure, and those modifications will remain after procedure has finished executing and is out of scope.

4) `Ada.Strings.Unbounded.Append(Temp1, " From Ada!");` – Not very different from point 3. The only difference is that any string between "" is a fixed size string. In this case, there is a different function Append that can take different types of variables (this is called polymorphism and is covered in greater detail later in the book) and then store the results in the first variable Temp1.

5) `Ada.Text_IO.Put_Line("Temp1 length: " & Natural'Image(Ada.Strings.Unbounded.Length(Temp1)));` – Unbounded strings do not have the 'Length attribute like fixed strings do. In order to find their length, a special Length function is used. This method returns a natural number that can then be converted and printed out.

In order to find the length of an unbounded length string, attributes cannot be used. Strings will be covered in greater detail in a later chapter. The purpose of this section is to introduce you to certain basics so that you can continue with this book.

Characters

This topic is quite the character! The best possible way to look at characters is to think of them as the individual building blocks of strings. Characters can be appended to strings using the operator &. A full-blown example will not be provided, since this is a very minor topic.

What differentiates a character from a string is that a character can only be a single letter enclosed by single quotes, like so: 'a'; whereas a string can be several letters enclosed in double quotes, like so: "hello". Now, you can have a single letter inside of double quotes – "e" – but that is not a character, it is a string with a length of 1.

However, here is how one would create a character and assign a value to it:

```
Char1 : Character := 'a';
...
Ada.Text_IO.Put(Char1);
```

And this is how a character can be concatenated with a string:

```
Char1 : Character := 'z';
...
Ada.Text_IO.Put("A character is created: " & Char1);
```

In the next chapter, we will see how we can use loops and if statement to give our applications the ability to make different paths based on the inputs received. The loops will be especially helpful since they will give us the ability to repeat whatever we want as often as necessary.

Lab

1) You work at an accounting office for a trucking company. One day you receive the following six invoices for things that need to be paid. Some of the numbers are integers and some are floats. Create a small report where all of these values will be listed as well as the sum.

440	Oil change
98.40	Washing fluid
23	Air filter
900.40	Fuel
71.49	Company pizza luncheon
90.01	Fuel

2) Build an exclusive or using only the "and," "or," and "not" boolean operators. Basically, get a true and a false input and then simulate the entire table of "xor" listed previously.

3) In Chapter 1, you created a simple application that printed out ADA in large letters using ASCII text. This time do the same thing, but first build a string that contains the entire message and print it all out at once.

## CHAPTER 3

Basic Control Structures

What You Will Get Out of This Chapter

Thus far, your applications were pretty linear. You would do something and it was fairly straightforward. If there were steps that needed to be repeated, then it would be necessary to copy and paste as often as necessary. This not only makes our code fairly unintelligent, but copying and pasting code all over your application is poor programming form.

The purpose of this chapter is to give you the ability to write code that can do all of this as often as necessary and take different execution paths as needed. This is necessary if we are to make genuinely intelligent applications. After all, having one massive print and doing most of the thinking yourself make just about any programming language pointless. You are better off just typing the end results in a text file and are done with it.

One control structure that will not be covered is the goto. 99.9999% of the time the goto is, at best, unnecessary and, at worst, a potential problem. This control structure has been directly responsible for all sorts of vague and bizarre logic errors that break the flow of the application that you are working on. Just say no to goto.

Edsger W. Dijkstra

Edsger Dijkstra was the one that wrote about the issues surrounding the goto statement. Its presence was considered to an indicator of poor application design. Furthermore, relying on goto (even just a little bit) can create confusing and impossible to understand code, "spaghetti code."

© Andrew T. Shvets 2020
A. T. Shvets, *Beginning Ada Programming*, https://doi.org/10.1007/978-1-4842-5428-8_3

If Statement

Any if statement starts with an `if ... then` and must end with `end if;` the text following the word "if" must evaluate to a boolean (or the boolean could be a return value from a function call). The boolean can be created as a result of certain operations, which were covered in the previous chapter. However, there are comparison values that can be used in order to create the same values. Here is a description of these values:

1) = a standard comparison of equality. This can be used to compare fixed strings as well as numbers of the same type. The only way to generate a true boolean is if both values compared are the same.

2) > a greater than comparison. The left value has to be greater than the right to obtain a true boolean. Having exact same values or the left value being smaller gives you a false boolean.

3) < a less than comparison. The left value has to be less than the right to obtain a true boolean. Having exact same values or the right value being larger gives you a false boolean.

4) >= equal or greater than comparison. The left value has to be greater or the same as the right to obtain a true boolean. Having a left value that is smaller than the right yields a false.

5) <= equal or less than comparison. The left value has to be less than or equal to the right in order to obtain a true boolean. Having a left value that is larger than the right yields a false.

6) /= not equal. The same as =, but not equal. If two variables of the same type are different from another, then you will get a true boolean; otherwise, you will get a false.

If is the most basic control structure that you will use and quite often. It is very simple and yet very powerful. Let's have a look:

```
-- if_statement.adb:

with Ada.Text_IO;
```

```ada
procedure if_statement is
  Int1 : Integer := 45;
  Int2 : Integer := -23;
  Int3 : Integer := 45;
begin
  if Int1 = Int2 or Int1 > Int2
  then
    Ada.Text_IO.Put_Line("Int1 is the same as Int2 or greater.");
  elsif Int1 = Int3 and Int2 <= Int1
  then
    Ada.Text_IO.Put_Line("Int1 and Int3 are the same.");
  else
    Ada.Text_IO.Put_Line("In the else part of if-statement.");
  end if;

  if Int3 in 4 .. 200
  then
    Ada.Text_IO.Put_Line("Int3 is between 4 and 200.");
  else
    Ada.Text_IO.Put_Line("Int3 is not between 4 and 200.");
  end if;

  if Int3 in 90 .. 100
  then
    Ada.Text_IO.Put_Line("Int3 is between 90 and 100.");
  else
    Ada.Text_IO.Put_Line("Int3 is not between 90 and 100.");
  end if;
end if_statement;
```

1. if Int1 = Int2 or Int1 > Int2 – This is the start of the if
    statement. Whatever the result of the operation, it must evaluate
    to a boolean type (if it does not, the compiler will let you know).

    "then" can be on the same line as the if statement or on the one
    below it. Where it is located is a question of personal taste and
    does not affect the logic that is being executed.

2. `elsif Int1 = Int3 and Int2 <= Int1` – The keyword "elsif" is optional and depends on what is needed to be done. If you need to check for other options, then it is necessary. As before, a "then" keyword is needed in order for things to flow smoothly.

3. `else` – This is the last statement that is executed assuming all of the previous ones are false. It is good practice to have this default value in case the previous logic comparison fails for some reason.

4. `if Int3 in 4 .. 200` and `if Int3 in 90 .. 100` – These two lines of code show you how to check whether a value falls within a specific range of numbers. In the former, it will evaluate to true, and in the latter, it will evaluate to false.

Parentheses and If Statements

Notice the parentheses around the latter two comparisons in the first if statement:

`if Int1 = Int2 or (Int1 > Int3 and Int1 /= Int2)`

If you remove the parentheses, this will give you a compile-time error of "mixed logical operators in expression." This is due to the fact that you need to have a product of your boolean operations generated for the "or" operator and this is the only way to do this.

The if statement is the cornerstone of our control structures. However, there are instances when this can be optimized in a way that would require less typing and would be more readable.

Case Statement

This one is a continuation of the if statement. Using a case statement, you can specify ranges over which you can execute certain instructions. For example, if you have a temperature range and if it is within 0 to 15 C, the heating system turns on in order to warm your home up. Unlike the if statement, you cannot put strings or floats to check if it matches a particular value; the compiler needs discrete types (meaning that the data needs to take only specific values and not decimals that are difficult to specify exactly). Values such as integers, enumerated types, and positive and natural types work well, but floats and strings do not work.

Let's have a look:

```ada
-- switch_statement.adb:

with Ada.Text_IO;

procedure switch_statement is
  SomeVal : Integer := 3;

  type Days is (Monday, Tuesday, Wednesday, Thursday,
    Friday, Saturday, Sunday);
  Today : Days := Wednesday;
begin
  case SomeVal is
    when 0 =>
      Ada.Text_IO.Put_Line("The value is 0.");
    when 1 =>
      Ada.Text_IO.Put_Line("The value is 1.");
    when 2 .. 4 =>
      Ada.Text_IO.Put_Line("The value is from 2 to 4.");
    when 5 | 6 =>
      Ada.Text_IO.Put_Line("The value is either 5 or 6.");
    when 7 .. 9 | 11 | 13 =>
      Ada.Text_IO.Put_Line(
        "The value is between 7 and 9 or can be 11 or 13.");
    when others =>
      Ada.Text_IO.Put_Line("I don't know what the value is.");
  end case;

  Ada.Text_IO.New_Line(2);

  case Today is
    when Monday =>
      Ada.Text_IO.Put_Line("Today is Monday.");
    when Tuesday =>
      Ada.Text_IO.Put_Line("Today is Tuesday.");
    when Wednesday | Thursday | Friday =>
      Ada.Text_IO.Put_Line(
        "Today is either Wednesday, Thursday or Friday.");
```

```
    when Saturday | Sunday =>
      Ada.Text_IO.Put_Line(
        "Today is either Saturday or Sunday.");
    when others =>
      Ada.Text_IO.Put_Line("I don't know what today is.");
  end case;

  Ada.Text_IO.New_Line(2);
end switch_statement;
```

At first, the length of this code might intimidate you into thinking that this example is much more difficult. But this is not so; let's have a look:

1) `type Days is (Monday, Tuesday, Wednesday, Thursday, Friday, Saturday, Sunday);`

   `Today : Days := Wednesday;` – This is a little more advanced and is covered later on in the book. The point was to illustrate how to use a discrete type. All that those lines of code do is create a custom type that represents the day today by specifying an atom and then from that type creates a variable with a day assigned to it. Its use will be more apparent in the upcoming example.

2) `case SomeVal is` – This is the start of the case statement. You need to specify the variable or source that we will need to check.

3) `when 0 =>` – In this line of code, the variable SomeVal is being checked to see if it is equal to 0. Notice how little actual code was written in order to make this check possible and now think about how much code you would need to write for an if statement.

4) `Ada.Text_IO.Put_Line("The value is 0.");` – Here are the instructions that will be executed when this particular option is selected. The minute that these steps stop executing, then that will signify the end of the case selection and the case statement structure will be exited.

5) `when 2 .. 4 =>` – This is how you can specify a range of values. When there is a need for running code over a set of values, this is how you would do this.

6) `when 5 | 6 =>` – But what if certain instructions should be run only when certain values are found and not just a single number or a range? The "|" is used to make this distinction.

7) `when 7 .. 9 | 11 | 13 =>` – What if you want to combine ranges and specific values? This is how you would do it.

8) `when others =>` – If no other value is found in the case statement, then this option is triggered. Here you can run cleanup code or print out an error message that an unusual condition was encountered.

   Like the "else," having this declared as a backup is good programming practice and you are encouraged to use it.

If you want to have ranges of floats, then your best option is to specify one using an if statement, like so:

```
if 0.0 <= Val and Val < 10.0
then
  -- execute code...
end if;
```

Let's have a look at how we can do the preceding code, but not just once, but as often as necessary while the condition is true.

While Loop

Now that you can run through code once and check to see if it meets certain conditions, what if you want to run through the same code as often as necessary while the condition is met? This functionality is essential when it comes to waiting for certain task to complete or a particular state to arise. For example, if you have a sensor that measures the height of the water in a local river. If the water rises past a certain height, then someone should be notified of this. So your small sensor is hooked up to a Raspberry Pi processor that checks every 5 minutes and keeps going until the required height is reached.

Let's have a look at this a little closer:

```
-- while_loop.adb:

with Ada.Text_IO;

procedure while_loop is
  River_Height : Natural := 0;
  Keep_Going   : Boolean := True;
begin
  while Keep_Going loop
    Ada.Text_IO.Put_Line(" The current value that is within range: " &
      Natural'Image(River_Height));

    if River_Height >= 20
    then
      Keep_Going := False;

      exit;
    end if;

    River_Height := River_Height + 2;
  end loop;

  Keep_Going := True;
  River_Height := 0;

  While_Loop2 :
  while Keep_Going loop
    Ada.Text_IO.Put_Line(" The current value that is within range: " &
      Natural'Image(River_Height));

    if River_Height >= 40
    then
      Keep_Going := False;

      exit While_Loop2;
    end if;

    River_Height := River_Height + 3;
  end loop While_Loop2;
```

```
Ada.Text_IO.Put_Line("The current value that is out of range: " &
  Natural'Image(River_Height));
end while_loop;
```

Let's have a closer look as to what is going on:

1) `while Keep_Going loop` – This is the start of a basic while loop. So long as the Keep_Going boolean variable holds true, this loop will keep going.

   Within the body of this loop, if the River_Height variable exceeds 20, then the boolean value is set to false, halting the iteration. And as long as the loop keeps executing, the River_Height is being incremented.

2) On line 16, the exit keyword is used. This is used to break out of the loop entirely. It comes in handy when you know that the iteration should finish without continuing. A plain exit will stop executing the loop that is currently in.

Note   Be careful how you use this. Without diligent planning, your software can become more difficult to read and debug. Always look into ways of terminating the loop in a way that will not leave your application in an undefined state.

---

3) `while_Loop2 :`
   `while Keep_Going loop`

   `...`

   `end loop While_Loop2;` – This loop is slightly different. In this case, the loop is assigned a name. A name can be quite useful when taking into account what you see on line 33. Here, you are exiting according to an identifier. This is handy when there are multiple nested loops in the same method and you want to terminate the one that is outside the current loop.

   And heed the warning about being careful how you exit your loops. In haste it is very easy to write spaghetti code that is difficult to read and then debug.

And now you know how to run a loop while a certain condition remains true (or false, if you use a not keyword). However, how would you make a simple loop that has to run just 20 times? Well, you could use a while loop, and when it reaches a certain count, it will terminate. However, there is a better way and one that will prove to be much more useful later on when we have to work with data containers such as linked lists.

For Loop

Ostensibly, you could use the for loop and the while loop as interchangeably and massage each to do what the other does. But it is not sensible to ram a round peg into a square hole and vice versa.

The purpose of the for loop is to iterate a set number of times to do a specific task, not less and not more. For example, if you have an array, a linked list, or a set number of files over which, you would like to perform a certain action.

This example describes how to run 400 times and make the iterator available for the user:

```ada
-- for_loop.adb:

with Ada.Text_IO;

procedure for_loop is
begin
  Ada.Text_IO.Put("|");

  for iter in 1 .. 400 loop
    Ada.Text_IO.Put(Integer'Image(iter) & " |");
  end loop;

  Ada.Text_IO.New_Line;
end for_loop;
```

This example is very easy; let's have a quick look at the new things shown:

1) `for iter in 1 .. 400 loop` – This is the start of our loop. The "iter" is a variable that is generated on the fly within the context of this for loop. If you try to reference iter outside of this loop, then you will get an error saying that the variable is undefined. Furthermore, iter is an instance of the dataset that is being iterated over. In this case this is a signed integer, but when we start dealing with linked lists and built-in data structures, you will see that can be a single object in the list.

2) `end loop;` – This indicates the end of the loop.

Very handy and very easy. The next topic is helpful if you need something to run non-stop. Most of the times that you encounter such a state, it is usually a bug in your code, but there are rare instances when this is a must have (such as a loop in a game that processes player inputs and then has to decide what the output ought to be).

Going Back

With a for loop, you can easily iterate over a specific range. But what if you wanted to reverse the order over the range that you just traversed? Sure, you can easily just flip the limits of that range and be done with it, but there is a better way. You would only need to insert the keyword "reverse" in the loop and you are done. Please have a look at this snippet: `for iter in reverse 1 .. 10 loop`.

Infinite Loop

Most of the time infinite loops occur due to logic errors where a counter was not increased in a for loop or changed the condition which would affect the state of the while loop. Despite these mistakes, which you will make as well in your programming career, there are instances when this might be necessary. For the moment, do not worry too much about this topic; it is here for the sake of completeness. If you are short on time, feel free to skip it entirely.

Let's have a look:

```
-- infinite_loop.adb:

with Ada.Text_IO;

procedure infinite_loop is
begin
  loop
    Ada.Text_IO.Put_Line("Inside of the infinite loop!");
    delay 0.5;
  end loop;
end infinite_loop;
```

This is the breakdown of the preceding code:

1) `loop` – This simply runs the loop non-stop. You have a loop that will run until you explicitly kill this process.

2) `delay 0.5;` – Pause for half a second so that you are not swamped with output to the screen. Feel free to change this value as needed.

3) `end loop;` – And here is the end of the loop.

A Simple Loop and an Infinite Loop

Sometimes these loops are called "simple loops" because they are very simple to create. And if you want to exit out of one, you would need to use the exit keyword. These loops have no default exit condition (for a while loop, the condition in the loop needs to turn to false; in a for loop, this is after the iterator has reached the end of the specified range), and you need to be more explicit in when you want to stop. Here is an example:

```
loop
  Ada.Text_IO.Put("Iterator = ");
  Ada.Text_IO.Put(Natural'Image(iter));
  iter := iter + 1;
  exit when iter = 5;
end loop;
```

You now have a basic understanding of the Ada control structures at hand. This is what you will mostly use going forward.

Do Not GOTO!

There is one keyword that is strongly disliked by most developers and you should never use: goto. It has few legitimate uses and can be easily abused. The potential for you to create spaghetti code is immense and render your application unreadable (and unmaintainable).

Lab

1) Create an application that will generate a random value that the user then has to guess. Note, the following example shows you how to take inputs from the console and generate random integers:

```ada
-- this is how you would make an integer input to the
--   command line.
with Ada.Text_IO;
...
TempString : String(1 .. 3);
Last : Natural   := 0;
Value : Integer := 0;
...
Ada.Text_IO.Get_Line(TempString, Last);
Value := Integer'Value(TempString(1 .. Last));

-- this is how you would generate a random integer within a
--   specific range.
with Ada.Numerics.Discrete_Random;
...
subtype Vals is Positive range 1 .. 10;
package Random100 is new
  Ada.Numerics.Discrete_Random(Result_Subtype => Vals);
...
```

```
Gen : Random100.Generator;
GeneratedNum : Vals := 1;
...
Random100.Reset(Gen => Gen);
GeneratedNum := Random100.Random(Gen => Gen);
```

In the preceding example on entering a number into the command line, make sure to only enter an integer; otherwise, you will receive an exception. Exception handling will be covered in a later chapter.

In the example of generating random integers, you can either adjust the Vals type's range or enter another type such as Integer, Positive, or Natural (just be aware that the latter strategy will generate numbers in the range of billions and this might not be what you want).

2) Make an application that generates a random integer from 1 to 100 and then prints out whether it is within ranges of tens. For example, for the value of 5, the range within it should be from 1 to 10; for the value of 21, the range within it should be from 21 to 30; and so on. Do this until the user enters a value to stop the application.

3) Write an application that will iterate from 1 to 10,000. Then, print out only the values that are divisible by 3, 13, and 23.

Tip   Use the "rem" operator in order to get the remainder of a value in an arithmetic operation, like so:

```
20 rem 5 -- is equal to 0
```

## CHAPTER 4

Procedures and Functions

What You Will Get Out of This Chapter

This chapter will introduce the basic concepts of encapsulating your code into containers that can be used later. Think about it; if you wrote a sorting algorithm that would be able to organize a bunch of values from largest to smallest, you would need to repeat the entire algorithm elsewhere if you wanted to use it in other parts of the application. This does not make any sense. Furthermore, if you have a bug in your algorithm, you would need to go over every single copy of it and fix it. What a waste of time!

There is a better way. That way is using either a function or a procedure. They are very similar, but there is a slight difference between the two that will be discussed. Furthermore, the different ways of passing in information to and from procedures and functions will be covered. The topics of declare block and recursion are touched on as well.

Difference Between a Procedure and a Function

The only major difference is that in a function, you can return a value; procedures cannot do this. A function can be useful for instances when you have reached a point where it does not make any sense to continue executing and you have your result, so returning with the result to the top will do. Now, a procedure can stop executing also and then simply assign a value to a passed in by reference variable. This distinction is important when it comes to designing your code.

For example, if you have method (in this context, a method can mean either a procedure or a function) that you would like to return to you true or false based on whether the inputted record is in an array, a function will do quite well. With this approach, you can easily include this function in an if statement or a while loop.

© Andrew T. Shvets 2020
A. T. Shvets, *Beginning Ada Programming*, https://doi.org/10.1007/978-1-4842-5428-8_4

However, if you need to return a value from a method that is rather large (if it is an array of very large records or a very long string), using a return value is sub-optimal. Why? Because every time you return from function, you make a copy of this very large variable and this can be a slow and memory-hungry operation (repeat this often enough and in a parallel executing instance and your application will quickly turn into a memory hog).

At this point you might be wondering, if using a return is a bad idea for bringing back large pieces of information, then what is the alternative? That is what the next section is for.

Getting Information In and Out of Procedures and Functions

Ada has three different ways of passing in variables into a procedure and a function. Each has its own quality that makes it useful. Let's look at the first one:

1) in – This is the default, meaning, if you do not specify an operator, "in" is assumed. When you put it near the passed in type in a procedure/function, the method will make a copy of the value from the caller function and passes it to the copy for called method. This is useful when you really do not want the original value to be modified. However, the flip side of this is that if the passed in variable is very large, then the copy will be very time- and memory consuming. At first this performance penalty might not be very obvious, but if called often enough or done in another task very often, performance will be impacted.

One thing to keep in mind is that you cannot assign a value to a variable passed to a function/procedure by value. This will get you a compile-time error:

```
procedure foo(var1 : in Integer) is
begin
  var1 := 25;
end foo;
```

2) `in out` – The benefit of this is that you can now pass in values based on reference. With pass by reference, what is being passed in is the reference value, not the whole variable. Unlike "in," there is no performance hit. The downside is that you do have to worry about modifying the passed in value, unless this is what you really wanted to happen.

This approach is highly recommended over the return if you are working with very large strings or very large data types. When using in out, you must pass in a variable – from the caller – as opposed to a static value (passing in a static value will get you a compile-time error).

3) `out` – This is an interesting one. In this case, the actual value of the passed in variable going in does not matter. You will need to assign a value to this variable once inside of the function/parameter (not doing this will make the compiler complain). Think of it this way, "out" acts as if you have a new variable created for you in the method, except when you assign a value to it, it returns the value assigned to the caller.

When using `out`, you must pass in a variable – from the caller – as opposed to a static value, passing in a static value will get you a compile-time error.

Choosing one over the other will depend exclusively on what you are trying to achieve. If one approach does not seem to be working too well, try another approach instead.

Explicitly mentioning the different ways you are inputting values into a method is highly recommended. At first it might seem tedious or unnecessary, but it only reinforces the readability of your code.

How to Declare and Implement Procedures and Functions

Now that we have covered some theory, it is time to dig through some code. After all, without any sorts of examples, what is the point of bothering with nebulous concepts in the first place?

```ada
-- functions_procedures.adb:

with Ada.Text_IO;

procedure functions_procedures is
  procedure test_proc(
    Val1 : in Integer;
    Val2 : in out Integer;
    Val3 : out Integer) is

  begin
    -- this will cause a compilation error.
    --Val1 := 4;
    Ada.Text_IO.Put_Line(" Input1 before assignment: " &
      Integer'Image(Val2));
    Val2 := 6;
    -- this value does not get set and instead you get some
    --  nonsense.
    Ada.Text_IO.Put_Line(" Input2 before assignment: " &
      Integer'Image(Val3));
    Val3 := 8;
    Ada.Text_IO.Put_Line(" Input2 after assignment: " &
      Integer'Image(Val3));

    return;
  end test_proc;

  function test_func(
    Val1 : in Integer;
    Val2 : out Integer)
      return Boolean is

  begin
    -- this will cause a compilation error.
    --Val1 := 22;
    Val2 := 44;
```

```
    return True;
  end test_func;

  Input1 : Integer := 23;
  Input2 : Integer := 92;
begin
  Ada.Text_IO.Put_Line(" Input1 before test_proc: " &
    Integer'Image(Input1));
  Ada.Text_IO.Put_Line(" Input2 before test_proc: " &
    Integer'Image(Input2));
  Ada.Text_IO.New_Line;

  test_proc(25, Input1, Input2);

  Ada.Text_IO.New_Line;
  Ada.Text_IO.Put_Line(" Input1 after test_proc: " &
    Integer'Image(Input1));
  Ada.Text_IO.Put_Line(" Input2 after test_proc: " &
    Integer'Image(Input2));
  Ada.Text_IO.New_Line;

  Ada.Text_IO.Put_Line(" test_func return value: " &
    Boolean'Image(test_func(54, Input2)));
  Ada.Text_IO.New_Line;

  Ada.Text_IO.Put_Line(" Input2 after test_proc: " &
    Integer'Image(Input2));
end functions_procedures;
```

And this is the output of the preceding example:

```
Input1 before test_proc:  23
Input2 before test_proc:  92

Input1 before assignment:  23
Input2 before assignment:  38599564
Input2 after assignment:  8
```

```
Input1 after test_proc:   6
Input2 after test_proc:   8

test_func return value: TRUE

Input2 after test_proc:   44
```

The preceding example covers all of the possible ways that can be used to input information into a function (or procedure) and then retrieve the very same information. Some of the ideas that were described earlier in this chapter will be demonstrated in practice:

1) `--Val1 := 4;` – In this case, the instance that you try to modify the passed in value, the compiler will prevent you by stopping the compilation process and giving you an error (which is why it is commented out). Whenever you pass a variable using the "in" keyword, the compiler will forbid you from modifying it.

2) `Val2 := 6;` – Here, on the other hand, you can easily modify the variable. After all, you passed it in using in out. As a result of this change, when test_proc is done executing, this will be transferred to the caller of this method (functions_procedures).

3) `Ada.Text_IO.Put_Line(" Input2 before assignment: " & Integer'Image(Val3));`

   `Val3 := 8;` – This case is much different. What do you think will be printed out for Val3? Hard to say! This is undefined behavior and what is stored in Val3 is nonsensical data. You give this variable a sensible state when you assign the value 8 to it. Furthermore, this change is transferred over when test_proc finishes executing. In fact, if you look above at the output of the application after it has run, you will see the number "38599564"; this is the application doing its best to interpret whatever data was held inside of the variable before something sensible was assigned to it.

   On the next line, you can easily print out Val3 and it will have the value 8 in it.

4) `return;` – Now, it is true that you cannot return a value from a procedure, but that does not mean that you cannot return from one without a value. What this does is that it simply goes back to the caller. You do not need an explicit call of this nature at the end of the procedure, but if you have several if statements and want to return after a specific condition is met, then this is how you would do it.

5) If you look at the function test_func, you will see that it is virtually the same as a procedure except that it has the keyword "function" before it and a type is specified that is supposed to be the return value. Then, on the last line of that procedure, the boolean – information – value of "True" is returned. In the following line, the result of this computation is printed out:

```
Ada.Text_IO.Put_Line(" test_func return value: " &
Boolean'Image(test_func(54, Input2)));
```

At this point, you might be wondering if a procedure can return from the middle of executing and then go back to the top, then why bother with functions? After all, you are simulating the exact same functionality and do not need to keep track of one more type of method. The advantage that the function has is that if you have a very small value to return to the caller (a Boolean, Integer, Float), then simply returning that value is preferred in terms of making your code more readable.

Whether you choose to use a procedure or a function boils down to the problem that needs to be solved and some personal taste. Try different options and make mistakes in order to make a better application. After all, what do you stand to lose? A compilation error?

Lastly, you might notice that you make your functions and procedures in the declare portion of the main procedure. In a future chapter, you will learn how to separate this code into a block so that you can better include it in your code.

Uninitialized Values Are Risky

Let's revisit the preceding example where you got the absurd number of "38599564." Uninitialized values can easily put your application in an unpredictable state. If you wanted to check if your number is larger than 50 – for example – and you assumed that it would not be greater than 100 typically, well your number easily surpassed your earlier thinking.

Let's say that you are writing software that is supposed to control a pump where pumping speed is regulated from the integer 1 to 1000. However, the pump cannot run greater than 500 for extended periods of time. If you assume that your pump speed control variable will never be greater than 500 at any given moment, but do not initialize this variable correctly, you could easily break hardware.

In future chapters we will see how to create your own custom types where such a scenario will be impossible.

The Declare Block

This one is very interesting and very useful. When you first create a function/procedure, there is a declaration section (its end is marked with the begin keyword, ironically enough) where you must declare all of your variables. This makes perfect sense. You want an application that works and there are no surprises during runtime (something Ada is quite good at), so you declare all of your variables well ahead of time (when you compile) and the compiler has a chance to run extra checks in order to make your code more stable. So why have a block that allows you to create more variables during runtime? Here are some of the ways that this can be answered:

1) Let's say you might need a very large object to work with. For example, you have an array of 1000 records that themselves have quite a bit of information stuffed inside of them. Declaring all of this beforehand would result in a waste of RAM, especially if you might not need this object at all (combine this with the fact that Ada could be used in an embedded environment, and where RAM is in even higher demand, this could create an unworkable application). This is where the declare block might come in handy. This can be wrapped in an if statement and will not be declared unless a certain condition is met.

2) You do not need to bother with something as complex as a procedure. If you need to execute a handful of easily understood instructions (and the code does not need to be used in other parts of the application), a declare block will be perfect. There is no headache about whether to pass in variables and which ones; you can just as easily make use of what you have in your procedure.

And yes, it will have to be a procedure. A function must return
a value of some sort and is functionally different from what a
procedure does.

One disadvantage of the declare block is that you cannot easily move it to be called
elsewhere (unless you turn it into a separate method entirely). If, at a later date, you need
to move the functionality of this declare block down to the bottom of the caller method,
this can be done much more easily with a procedure.

Let's have a look at one such example:

```ada
-- declare_block.adb:

with Ada.Text_IO;

procedure declare_block is
  Counter : Natural := 0;
begin
  Ada.Text_IO.Put_Line("Right before the declare: " &
    Natural'Image(Counter));

  declare
    Bool : Boolean := True;
  begin
    Counter := 3;
    Ada.Text_IO.Put_Line(" Inside the declare: " &
      Natural'Image(Counter));
    Ada.Text_IO.Put_Line(" The boolean:        " &
      Boolean'Image(Bool));
  end;

  --Ada.Text_IO.Put_Line("The boolean after declare: " &
  --  Natural'Image(Bool));
  Ada.Text_IO.Put_Line("Right after the declare: " &
    Natural'Image(Counter));
end declare_block;
```

1) Creating a declare block is very simple. It has three parts to it, the "declare," the "begin," and the "end."

2)  ```
    Ada.Text_IO.Put_Line(" Inside the declare: " &
        Natural'Image(Counter));
    Ada.Text_IO.Put_Line(" The boolean: " &
    ```

    `Boolean'Image(Bool));` – Inside of the declare block, you have easy access to the Counter variable declared at the start of the procedure declare_block. Also, you can declare a Boolean and easily access it as well.

3) `--Ada.Text_IO.Put_Line("The boolean after declare: " & Natural'Image(Bool));` – This code will not compile; you will get a compilation error. The variable Bool exists only within the scope of the declare block.

4) `Ada.Text_IO.Put_Line("Right after the declare: " & Natural'Image(Counter));` – This will print out the value of 3. While the Bool value exists within the scope of the declare block, if you modify any of the variables declared within the parent method, those changes will be carried over to the rest of the procedure.

If you see yourself making a declare block, keep an eye out for instances where you are repeating yourself. If you do see such instances, consider making a procedure to do the job.

Recursion

Recursion is when a function (or procedure) keeps calling itself over and over until a specific condition has been met to stop it. It is similar to that of a loop.

So, how does recursion compare to a loop and why would you use it:

1) **Q:** Is recursion faster?

    A: No. The added overhead of maintaining a stack and working with it takes up more processing and is generally slower.
    ```

2) **Q:** Okay, does it take up less RAM when it is running?

   A: No, that is not the case. Again, the overhead takes up more
   memory since you need to keep track of multiple instances of
   the same function as it goes through the various instances of the
   function.

   In fact, if you ever get infinite recursion, you will overflow your
   entire allocated stack and your application will crash (or be killed
   by the operating system).

3) **Q:** What the heck! Then what is the point of recursion?!

   A: There are many instances of algorithms that look more
   elegant or are easier to implement and understand when
   recursion is used.

Recursion: Functions or Procedures?

Okay, you decided to use a recursion in order to create an algorithm to solve a particular
problem. The question remains, should you use a function or a procedure? That
depends. If the goal is to build a large data structure and then return it, passing it in using
"in out" is a superior choice (and therefore using a procedure). If the goal is to come to
a particular conclusion for an answer (such as whether a certain condition is met or a
count of actions performed), then a function would work well.

Let's have a look at an application that keeps going down its own stack until a
random number is generated that is greater than the one specified by the caller:

```
-- max_recursion.adb:

with Ada.Task_Identification;
with Ada.Numerics.Discrete_Random;
with Ada.Numerics;
with Ada.Text_IO;

procedure max_recursion is
  Minimum_Val : Integer := 1;
  Maximum_Val : Integer := 100;
```

```ada
function generate_random_int(
  Min : in Integer;
  Max : in Integer)
    return Integer is

begin
  -- if the min is not less than the max, then terminate this process.
  if (Min >= Max)
  then
    Ada.Task_Identification.Abort_Task(
      Ada.Task_Identification.Current_Task);
  end if;

  -- now that it is certain that the correct limits are observed,
  --  proceed to generate a random value within those limits.
  declare
    subtype Vals is Integer range Min .. Max;
    package CustomRandom is new Ada.Numerics.Discrete_Random(
      Result_Subtype => Vals);

    Gen : CustomRandom.Generator;
    GeneratedNum : Vals := Min;
  begin
    CustomRandom.Reset(Gen => Gen);
    GeneratedNum := CustomRandom.Random(Gen => Gen);

    return Integer(GeneratedNum);
  end;
end generate_random_int;

-- count the number of times that it took to get a number that is
--  larger than the guess that is passed in.
function count_tries(
  Largest : in Integer;
  Index : in Integer)
    return Integer is
```

```
    Random_Val : Integer := generate_random_int(Minimum_Val, Maximum_Val);
  begin
    -- check if the randomly generated value is less or more than the
    --  passed in number.
    if (Largest > Random_Val)
    then
      return count_tries(Largest, Index + 1);
    else
      return Index;
    end if;
  end count_tries;
begin
  -- find the number of times that are necessary in order to exceed
  --  the maximum value that we passed in.
  Ada.Text_IO.Put_Line(" Maximum number of tries: " &
    Integer'Image(count_tries(90, 1)));
end max_recursion;
```

Recursion is actually a fun mental exercise; let's get to it:

1) function generate_random_int(– This function's job is to return
   an integer that it randomly generated that is within a specific
   range. The function first ensures that the min is indeed smaller
   than the max.

2) subtype Vals is Integer range Min .. Max; – This code is
   a little advanced, but the gist of it means that you are creating a
   new type from an Integer that will have newly defined limits for a
   minimum value that can be assigned to it and a maximum value
   as well.

3) package CustomRandom is new

   Ada.Numerics.Discrete_Random(Result_Subtype => Vals); –
   CustomRandom is a custom package that is created to generate
   random values that fall only within the range of the Vals subtype.

This code is a little bit more advanced for this chapter. However, it is the only way to show how to generate a random integer within a specific range.

4) `Gen : CustomRandom.Generator;` – A custom random number generator also needs to be created. This will actually return random numbers to the caller.

5) `CustomRandom.Reset(Gen => Gen);` – This ensures that the numbers will be generated randomly each and every time that the next line is executed.

6) `GeneratedNum := CustomRandom.Random(Gen => Gen);` – This is where the random number is produced. In the line following this one, the Vals type is cast to an Integer – which is trivial given that Vals is a subtype of Integer – and returned to the caller.

7) `Random_Val : Integer := generate_random_int(Minimum_Val, Maximum_Val);` – Now we call our random number generator function.

8) The body of the count_tries function shows the gist of this application is supposed to do. It keeps going down its own stack until a number that is larger than the passed is generated. Afterward, a simple logic if statement determines whether to keep going or return to the caller with the total number of function calls made.

Keep in mind, when dealing with recursion, this is something that you would use when you not use in an embedded environment.

The preceding example perfectly illustrates the utility of a function. Look at the amount of code that you need to write just to generate a single random integer. It is more than one or two lines. By wrapping all of that complexity in a single package, you do two things:

1) The code can be more easily reused. Say you want to use the same function in a different part of the project. If you were to write the instructions to create random values in each location, then you would create unnecessarily complex code and fail to better reuse what you have built in other areas.

2) Functions make it easier to break down the complexity of your application into components that you can better understand. Think about how you would write the preceding example as one continuous project. Now, what would make it easier to understand the code? One monolithic chunk or the same functionality split up among smaller components?

Whenever you can, think about whether a chunk of code can be used elsewhere. If it can, then create either a function or a procedure.

Lab

1) Look at the very first example, where you printed out "Hello world" in ASCII. Many of those lines that you used there are repeated. Put the repeated lines into their own procedures and call the procedures to simulate the same functionality.

2) Create a function that can calculate if a passed in string is a palindrome or not. The input should be an unbounded string, and the returned value is a boolean value indicating if this is true or not.

   A palindrome is a word which reads the same thing forward and backward, for example, racecar, bob, and kayak.

   For more information, visit

   `https://en.wikipedia.org/wiki/Palindrome`

3) Make the previously mentioned palindrome detecting function recursive.

4) Look at the declare block listed previously and figure out a way to have it replaced with a procedure.

CHAPTER 5

Arrays, Records, and Access Types

What You Will Get Out of This Chapter

In this chapter, more sophisticated types will be covered. Arrays, records, and access types are discussed. All are very basic data containers, and while they are different from one another, they play important roles in Ada.

Let's say you have 500 different numbers of the same type (an Integer). You would like to either search through them in order to find the largest/smallest or find the average and so on. If you had to allocate 500 different variables for each number, you would waste time creating unwieldy code that is very difficult to expand later on. Honestly, the very idea is so absurd that it is not even worth trying to visualize it. In order to make this easier for you, Ada has arrays. Arrays permit you to create a single variable that can be iterated over in order to actually store these variables and manipulate them as you would like. This basic container is crucial if you want your applications to grow into something even remotely more complex than a simple hello world example.

Great, now you know how to create many variables of the same type. However, what if you wanted to create a data container that holds some strings, an integer, and a float? What if you could create your own little boxes to represent the problem as accurately as possible? For that Ada has records. A record is wonderful in terms of being able to represent an item, a quantity about the real world that would be very cumbersome and difficult otherwise. This ability to encapsulate data complexity is a must. Other languages call records structs or structures.

© Andrew T. Shvets 2020
A. T. Shvets, *Beginning Ada Programming*, https://doi.org/10.1007/978-1-4842-5428-8_5

Lastly, access types are mentioned. An access type is a special variable that is used to point to a space in your RAM that is used to store the actual data that you care about; it's called a pointer in other programming languages. The best real-world analogy is a dog on a leash. The leash is not the dog, but it does point to your pet. Reasons for using this type are covered.

A Very Simple Array

An array of integers or floats is very easy to understand. This concept is best illustrated in the following example:

```
-- simple_array.adb:

with Ada.Float_Text_IO;
with Ada.Text_IO;

procedure simple_array is
  ArrayFloat : array (1 .. 20) of Float;
  ArrayInteger : array (-5 .. 35) of Integer;
begin
  -- make default assignments to the entire array.
  ArrayFloat := (others => 0.0);
  -- make default assignments to the entire array, but
  --   give certain instances a specific value.
  ArrayInteger := (-5 => 1, -4 => 2, -3 => 3, -2 => 4, -1 => 5, 0 => 6,
    others => 0);

  -- another way to do assignment, in a for-loop.
  for iter in ArrayFloat'Range loop
    ArrayFloat(iter) := 5.13;
  end loop;

  -- this is for printing values to the console.
  for iter in ArrayInteger'Range loop
    Ada.Text_IO.Put(" " & Integer'Image(ArrayInteger(iter)) & " ");
  end loop;

  Ada.Text_IO.New_Line(3);
```

```
  for iter in ArrayFloat'Range loop
    Ada.Text_IO.Put(" ");
    Ada.Float_Text_IO.Put(ArrayFloat(iter), Aft => 2, Exp => 0);
    Ada.Text_IO.Put(" ");
  end loop;

  Ada.Text_IO.New_Line;
end simple_array;
```

This is a very simple example, very easy to digest and make sense of. Now I will breakdown the most the new portions of the code:

1) `ArrayFloat : array (1 .. 20) of Float;` – In this case, you are creating an array that has 20 items in it. The unique thing about this array declaration – when compared to C/C++ and Java – is that the arrays do not have to have the starting index be 0.

2) `ArrayInteger : array (-5 .. 35) of Integer;` – This is even more interesting. In this example, the array is that of Integers, but the starting index is –5 and not 1. Ada lets you specify your index as you like.

3) `ArrayFloat := (others => 0.0);` – After instantiating the array, it is now time to assign some values to the elements. In this case, all of the values are assigned a default value of 0.0.

4) `ArrayInteger := (-5 => 1, -4 => 2, ... , others => 0);` – ArrayInteger has instances –5, –4, –3, –2, –1, and 0 set for them to a number other than zero. All of the other values are set to zero.

5) `for iter in ArrayFloat'Range loop` – This gives you an instance over the entire array with the range property. The `ArrayFloat'Range` gives you the range of that particular array (the same can be done like so: `ArrayFloat'First .. ArrayFloat'Last`). In this loop, you see that you can also use a loop to initialize an array.

At this point you might think: Why use a loop to instantiate the contents of an array when the "others" keyword will work just as well? The reason for this is when you need to execute an algorithm and use the results of that in order to populate an array.

6) `Ada.Float_Text_IO.Put(ArrayFloat(iter), Aft => 2,`
    `Exp => 0);` – This is not array related, but if you want to print out
    a float and not do so in scientific notation, the best way to do this
    is to specify that the exponent (Exp) is 0 and that you would like
    only two decimal points shown after the float (Aft). This can turn
    out to be quite handy when working with the Float type.

Now that we have gotten our feet wet just a bit, let's go out into the pool a little bit
deeper by working with two-dimensional arrays (and we can extend the array to be more
than two dimensions). Here is how:

```
-- complex_array.adb:

with Ada.Integer_Text_IO;
with Ada.Float_Text_IO;
with Ada.Text_IO;

procedure complex_array is
  ArrayInteger : array(1 .. 6, 1 .. 10) of Integer;
  ArrayFloat : array(-5 .. 20, 1 .. 15) of Float;
begin
  -- make some default initializations.
  ArrayInteger := (others => (others => 0));
  ArrayFloat := (others => (others => 0.0));

  for iterA in ArrayInteger'Range(1) loop
    for iterB in ArrayInteger'Range(2) loop
      Ada.Integer_Text_IO.Put(ArrayInteger(iterA, iterB));
    end loop;

    Ada.Text_IO.New_Line;
  end loop;

  for iterA in ArrayFloat'Range(1) loop
    for iterB in ArrayFloat'Range(2) loop
      Ada.Float_Text_IO.Put(ArrayFloat(iterA, iterB), Exp => 0);
    end loop;
```

```
    Ada.Text_IO.New_Line;
  end loop;
end complex_array;
```

Let's take a closer look at the preceding code:

1) `ArrayInteger : array (1 .. 10, 1 .. 10) of Integer;` – This is just a simple declaration. Note that if you want to add a dimension to your array, then you would insert a comma and then enter a new range for the array. Keep in mind that this example explores two dimensions, but nothing is stopping you from having 35 dimensions or more, although this would be rather difficult to track in your head as you continue to write code.

2) `ArrayInteger := (others => (others => 0));` – Make all values in the two-dimensional array set to 0 by default. Notice that unlike in a one-dimensional array where a single "others" would suffice, a second "others" keyword is needed in a two-dimensional array.

3) `for iterA in ArrayInteger'Range(1) loop` – This is the standard for loop that iterates over a range. The difference is that when you specify 'Range, the number 1 is passed in. This tells the compiler that you want to iterate over the first range that is specified in a multi-dimensional array (the `1 .. 6` range of the declared ArrayInteger). By passing in a 2, you would get the second range. However, if you pass in any number greater and your array does not have that dimension, the compiler will produce a compilation error stating that the dimension is wrong.

An Array of Strings

There will be times when you will need to store strings in an array. The best way to do this is to use the Unbounded_String type for this task. The reason for this is that if you were to use a String (which by default means that it is a string of fixed length), every single entry in the array will have to have the exact same length. This is not practical for most real-world applications.

Here is an example using unbounded strings:

```ada
-- string_array.adb:

with Ada.Strings.Unbounded; use Ada.Strings.Unbounded;
with Ada.Text_IO;

procedure string_array is
  StringArray : array (1 .. 2, 1 .. 6) of
    Ada.Strings.Unbounded.Unbounded_String;
begin
  StringArray := ((To_Unbounded_String("John"),
    To_Unbounded_String("Michael"),
    To_Unbounded_String("Mathew"), To_Unbounded_String("Bob"),
    To_Unbounded_String("Jacob"), To_Unbounded_String("Heiko")),
   (To_Unbounded_String("Big"), To_Unbounded_String("Mighty"),
    To_Unbounded_String("Artistic"),
    To_Unbounded_String("Bright"), To_Unbounded_String("Quick"),
    To_Unbounded_String("Brilliant")));

  for iterA in StringArray'Range(1) loop
    for iterB in StringArray'Range(2) loop
      Ada.Text_IO.Put(To_String(StringArray(iterA, IterB)) & " ");
    end loop;

    Ada.Text_IO.New_Line;
  end loop;
end string_array;
```

1) use Ada.Strings.Unbounded; – You might remember in Chapter 1 that it was said the "use" keyword will not be applied in order to improve the readability of the code since you will know which package is used, when, and which method is called. So why is the "use" keyword here? Without it – in this instance only – the preceding example would be less readable. First of all, the page has only a certain amount of width. And second of all, even if you had plenty of space, the extra text – again, in this example only – would drown out the interesting points of the code with a block of text that does nothing other than create a bunch of unbounded strings.

2) `StringArray := (...);` – When assigning a default (all at once) value to this array, it can be done by placing all of the default values in parentheses. And since this is a two-dimensional array, there are two sets of parentheses within the first set.

One thing that you need to remember when working with strings and unbounded strings is that whenever you include characters between double quotes, that makes it into a fixed size string. In order to use it as an unbounded string, a call to the To_Unbounded_String function is needed so that these strings can be assigned to the StringArray. Skipping this step will cause the compiler to throw an error and state that you are assigning a plain string to where an unbounded string is supposed to be.

3) `Ada.Text_IO.Put(To_String(StringArray(...)));` – And once again, convert the unbounded string into a regular string before printing it to the console.

Making an array of strings is very useful. You could use it to create an impromptu database to store the names of a number of individuals. There is one problem with all of the examples shown earlier. Everything so far has made you specify the exact number of items in an array. What if you wanted to be able to alter the number of instances? What if one day you are dealing with 10 people and the next 10,000? Changing your source code and then re-compiling is impractical. Let's look into how you can dynamically allocate elements in an array.

Runtime Allocation of Arrays

This is how you can dynamically allocate the size of a two-dimensional array. Feel free to modify this example to your needs to add more dimensions:

```
-- dynamic_alloc_array.adb:

with Ada.Numerics.Discrete_Random;
with Ada.Integer_Text_IO;
with Ada.Text_IO;
```

```
procedure dynamic_alloc_array is
  Dim_1 : Positive := 1;
  Dim_2 : Positive := 1;

  type Matrix_Int_Type is array (Positive range <>,
    Positive range <>) of Integer;

  package RandomInt is new Ada.Numerics.Discrete_Random(
    Result_Subtype => Integer);
  Gen : RandomInt.Generator;
begin
  Ada.Integer_Text_IO.Get(Item => Dim_1);
  Ada.Integer_Text_IO.Get(Item => Dim_2);

  RandomInt.Reset(Gen => Gen);

  declare
    Matrix_Int : Matrix_Int_Type(1 .. Dim_1, 1 .. Dim_2)
      := (others => (others => 0));
  begin
    for IterA in Matrix_Int'Range(1) loop
      for IterB in Matrix_Int'Range(2) loop
        Matrix_Int(IterA, IterB) := RandomInt.Random(
          Gen => Gen);
      end loop;
    end loop;

    for IterA in Matrix_Int'Range(1) loop
      for IterB in Matrix_Int'Range(2) loop
        Ada.Integer_Text_IO.Put(Matrix_Int(IterA, IterB));
      end loop;

      Ada.Text_IO.New_Line;
    end loop;
  end;
end dynamic_alloc_array;
```

Let's have a look at what is going on in the preceding example:

1) `type Matrix_Int_Type is array (Positive range <>,`
   `Positive range <>) of Integer;` – In order to dynamically
   allocate the size of an array in Ada, you need to create a specific
   type without pre-defined sizes. The language (and the compiler
   as well) will not permit you to create an instance of an array type
   without specifying its size.

2) `package RandomInt is new Ada.Numerics.Discrete_`
   `Random(Result_Subtype => Integer);` – Create a custom
   package that we will instruct it to generate custom discrete values.
   In this case, this package will generate random values that are
   within the range of an integer.

3) `Ada.Integer_Text_IO.Get(Item => Dim_1);` – Using the Get
   procedure, have the user input a value that will be used to create
   the dimensions of the array. Just make sure to input an integer and
   nothing else (otherwise the application will give you an error).

4) `Matrix_Int : Matrix_Int_Type(1 .. Dim_1, 1 .. Dim_2) :=`
   `(others => (others => 0));` – From the preceding custom type
   that was created, this makes an instance of the type in the form of
   a two-dimensional array variable. After the instance of the type is
   created, give the two variable default values by assigning zeroes to
   them.

   You can iterate over this two-dimensional array just like you did in
   the example preceding this one.

In the next section, we will switch gears a little. We will be creating records and using
them. Unlike arrays that store many instances of the same type, records are useful for
storing many different types all in one entity.

Creating and Populating Records

It helps if we can turn this into a real-world example. Individual numbers and strings are
great for describing names, accounts, and quantities, but putting them together under
the same roof will make it even easier to create relationships among these different

components. For example, what if you wanted to keep track of the maintenance done on your car. You could have the car be the entire record and then different maintenance tasks or problems encountered with it could be the individual entries in a record. An array of any sort – or individual variables – is not useful in this context.

Many times, it makes perfect sense to pass in a record into a function. Let's say you need to pass in 50 different pieces of information into a function; the best way to do this is with a record. Having a function that has 50 input variables makes it difficult to document, difficult to maintain, and unwieldy when to call:

```
-- records_example.adb:

with Ada.Float_Text_IO;
with Ada.Strings;
with Ada.Text_IO;

procedure records_example is
   type CarRecords is record
     NumOilChanges : Natural        := 0;
     NumCollisions : Natural        := 0;
     YearsOwned : Natural           := 0;
     Kilometers : Natural           := 0;
     MoneySpentMaintenance : Float := 0.0;
     MoneySpentRepairs : Float      := 0.0;
     TopSpeed : Float               := 0.0;
     CarLoanPrincipal : Float       := 0.0;
     Model : String(1 .. 11)        := "Porsche 911";
   end record;

   YourCar : CarRecords;
begin
   -- initialize some of the values to defaults.
   YourCar.NumOilChanges          := 23;
   YourCar.NumCollisions          := 1;
   YourCar.YearsOwned             := 3;
   YourCar.Kilometers             := 65923;
   YourCar.MoneySpentMaintenance := 6981.45;
   YourCar.MoneySpentRepairs      := 7200.00;
   YourCar.TopSpeed               := 215.0;
```

```
YourCar.CarLoanPrincipal       := 1948.97;

Ada.Text_IO.Put_Line(" Name of car:              " &
  YourCar.Model);
Ada.Text_IO.Put_Line(" Number of oil changes: " &
  Natural'Image(YourCar.NumOilChanges));
Ada.Text_IO.Put_Line(" Number of collisions:  " &
  Natural'Image(YourCar.NumCollisions));
Ada.Text_IO.Put_Line(" Number years owned:    " &
  Natural'Image(YourCar.YearsOwned));
Ada.Text_IO.Put_Line(" Number of kilometers:  " &
  Natural'Image(YourCar.Kilometers));
Ada.Text_IO.Put(" Spent on maintenance:    ");
Ada.Float_Text_IO.Put(YourCar.MoneySpentMaintenance,
  Aft => 2, Exp => 0);
Ada.Text_IO.New_Line;
Ada.Text_IO.Put(" Spent on repairs:         ");
Ada.Float_Text_IO.Put(YourCar.MoneySpentRepairs,
  Aft => 2, Exp => 0);
Ada.Text_IO.New_Line;
Ada.Text_IO.Put(" Top speed:                ");
Ada.Float_Text_IO.Put(YourCar.TopSpeed, Aft => 2, Exp => 0);
Ada.Text_IO.New_Line;
Ada.Text_IO.Put(" Car loan principal:      ");
Ada.Float_Text_IO.Put(YourCar.CarLoanPrincipal,
  Aft => 2, Exp => 0);
Ada.Text_IO.New_Line;
end records_example;
```

The preceding example is very easy to comprehend. You can just about stuff any value that you would like into a record (even existing record types), which in turn can be used to represent the object that you are trying to model in the real world. In this case, a car is represented using a record type. We will look into this even more when it comes to understanding the concepts behind object-oriented programming. Here are the only points that need to be covered:

1) `type CarRecords is record` – It is how a record is created. It
    needs to be ended with `end record;`. What this code does is
    create a container, a type, that has a series of different values in
    them. That is all.

    Anything inside of it are the parts that make this entity what it is.

2) `YourCar.NumOilChanges := 23;` – By using a period, you can
    specify the internal values of the record and assign or read values
    from them.

Creating records is easy. However, it would be nice to have many of the same data
structures to better model different types of items that are very similar.

Creating Array of Records

An array of records is the best of both worlds. You can create a record in order to better
represent something, but if you have more than one such item, then you would need
an array of such records. For example, you sell and fix cars and you need an easy way to
keep track of when cars were bought, sold, and for how much, as well as the year and
make of the car, mileage, and so on:

```
-- records_array.adb:

with Ada.Strings.Unbounded;
with Ada.Float_Text_IO;
with Ada.Text_IO;

procedure records_array is
  type Bird is record
    BirdName : Ada.Strings.Unbounded.Unbounded_String :=
      Ada.Strings.Unbounded.Null_Unbounded_String;
    AverageWeight : Float    := 0.0;
    AverageWingSpan : Float := 0.0;
    Migrating : Boolean      := False;
  end record;
```

```ada
   Birds : array (1 .. 3) of Bird;
begin
   -- instantiate some values.
   Birds(1).BirdName        :=
     Ada.Strings.Unbounded.To_Unbounded_String("Canadian Goose");
   Birds(1).AverageWeight   := 7.5;
   Birds(1).AverageWingspan := 160.0;
   Birds(1).Migrating       := True;
   Birds(2).BirdName        :=
     Ada.Strings.Unbounded.To_Unbounded_String("Sparrow");
   Birds(2).AverageWeight   := 0.03;
   Birds(2).AverageWingspan := 0.15;
   Birds(3).BirdName        :=
     Ada.Strings.Unbounded.To_Unbounded_String("Finch");
   Birds(3).AverageWeight   := 0.047;
   Birds(3).AverageWingspan := 0.17;

   for iter in Birds'Range loop
     Ada.Text_IO.Put_Line(" Bird name: " &
       Ada.Strings.Unbounded.To_String(Birds(iter).BirdName));
     Ada.Text_IO.Put("  Average weight:   ");
     Ada.Float_Text_IO.Put(Birds(iter).AverageWeight,
       Aft => 3, Exp => 0);
     Ada.Text_IO.New_Line;
     Ada.Text_IO.Put("  Average wingspan: ");
     Ada.Float_Text_IO.Put(Birds(iter).AverageWingspan,
       Aft => 2, Exp => 0);
     Ada.Text_IO.New_Line;
     Ada.Text_IO.Put_Line("  Migrating bird:    " &
       Boolean'Image(Birds(iter).Migrating));

     Ada.Text_IO.New_Line;
   end loop;
end records_array;
```

In this example, the concepts of arrays and records are combined. This is a very simple example, and these two points cover the only two unclear concepts:

1) `Migrating : Boolean := False;` – Inside of your record (where it is declared), you can assign default values as needed. This way, all of your variables will have a starting value that can be used.

2) `Birds : array(1 .. 3) of Bird;` – With the custom type Bird, you now have an array of records.

Now that we are done with these two concepts, they will serve us very well when our applications grow in complexity and functionality. In the next section, the topic of access types will be discussed and how they can be used.

Access Types

Just like the example in the introduction, access types are not something that you can use in the same way as you would a regular Integer or Unbounded_String. These types are merely pointers to a piece of memory in your computer. These pointers can be used to point to a variable that is a limited type or an object that is dynamically allocated on the heap, assuming that the object is very large and making multiple copies of it either cannot be done or is not recommended.

A note to all C/C++ developers, unlike in those languages, you cannot do pointer arithmetic in Ada. This means you cannot iterate over an array by simply adding to the pointer. The removal of such functionality is to eliminate the possibility of iterating over a data type and then gaining access to the stack or heap. Such functionality often enabled attackers to compromise and harm applications written in these programming languages.

This is how access types can be used:

```
-- access_type_example.adb:

with Ada.Unchecked_Deallocation;
with Ada.Text_IO;

procedure Access_Type_Example is
  type Int_Access is access all Integer;
  type Flo_Access is access all Float;
  type Str_Access is access all String;
```

```ada
type Test_Rec is record
  Int_Point : Int_Access;
  Flo_Point : Flo_Access;
  Str_Point : Str_Access;
end record;

type Rec_Access is access Test_Rec;
Rec_Point : Rec_Access;
Backup_Ac : Rec_Access;

Test_Int : aliased Integer := 94;

-- functions for deallocation.
procedure Deallocate is new Ada.Unchecked_Deallocation(
  Test_Rec, Rec_Access);
procedure Deallocate is new Ada.Unchecked_Deallocation(
  String, Str_Access);
procedure Deallocate is new Ada.Unchecked_Deallocation(
  Float, Flo_Access);
procedure Deallocate is new Ada.Unchecked_Deallocation(
  Integer, Int_Access);
begin
  -- allocate memory of the pointers.
  Rec_Point := new Test_Rec;
  Rec_Point.Int_Point := Test_Int'Access;
  Rec_Point.Flo_Point := new Float'(0.0);
  Rec_Point.Str_Point := new String'("Hello world!");

  Backup_Ac := Rec_Point;

  -- print out the contents of the allocated memory.
  Ada.Text_IO.Put_Line(
    " The contents of our dynamically allocate structure:");
  Ada.Text_IO.Put_Line(
    "    Integer: " & Integer'Image(Backup_Ac.Int_Point.all));
  Ada.Text_IO.Put_Line(
    "    Float:   " & Float'Image(Backup_Ac.Flo_Point.all));
```

```ada
Ada.Text_IO.Put_Line(
   "     String:  " & Backup_Ac.Str_Point.all);

-- give the allocated some assigned values for illustrative purposes.
Backup_Ac.Int_Point.all := 299;
Backup_Ac.Flo_Point.all := 3.14;
Rec_Point.Str_Point.all := "Hello Ada!!!";

-- print out the contents of the allocated memory.
Ada.Text_IO.Put_Line(
   "  The contents of our dynamically allocate structure:");
Ada.Text_IO.Put_Line(
   "     Integer: " & Integer'Image(Backup_Ac.Int_Point.all));
Ada.Text_IO.Put_Line(
   "     Float:   " & Float'Image(Backup_Ac.Flo_Point.all));
Ada.Text_IO.Put_Line(
   "     String:  " & Backup_Ac.Str_Point.all);

-- deallocate memory of the pointers.
--Deallocate(Rec_Point.Int_Point);
Deallocate(Rec_Point.Flo_Point);
Deallocate(Rec_Point.Str_Point);
Deallocate(Rec_Point);

Ada.Text_IO.Put_Line(
   "  The contents of our dynamically allocate structure:");
Ada.Text_IO.Put_Line(
   "     Integer: " & Integer'Image(Backup_Ac.Int_Point.all));
end Access_Type_Example;
```

This example shows a very powerful feature of Ada; let's take this example apart piece by piece:

1) with Ada.Unchecked_Deallocation; – Include the package that will give this application the ability to free up allocated memory. This is the memory that you can claim for yourself, and even when you go from function to procedure, you can easily pass the access type to this RAM and it will not be forgotten even if it is out of scope.

2) `type Int_Access is access all Integer;` – Pay attention as to how this was written. Notice how the type Int_Access is created. First, the compiler is made aware that this is an access type (hence "access").

Next, the "all" keyword is included. With this, the type Int_Access is understood to be able to take any other integer's memory (within certain limits). Basically, if you have a variable that was not allocated dynamically, you can grab its address and assign it to this integer access type. Without this keyword, Int_Access can only have dynamically allocated pieces of memory assigned to it (this can be a desired feature if you want the access type to be very limited in scope).

It is not recommended that you use "all." It's far better to allocate the memory and then copy into it a value. The reason is if you assign the address of a variable that is within the scope of a method, when the scope of the said method is finished, that piece of memory will be deallocated and you will have an access type pointing to an unknown piece of virtual memory. Let's just say, if your application enters an uncertain state down the road, this could be why.

3) In lines 11–15, we have the dummy record created. Notice how the three internal variables are all access types' instances.

4) `type Rec_Access is access Test_Rec;` – Now, create an access type for our record. This way, you will have a pointer to a record that itself has a bunch of pointers.

5) `Rec_Point : Rec_Access;` and `Backup_Ac : Rec_Access;` – These are the two instances of the access type for the record. This will be used for illustrative purposes of how two access types can point to the same piece of memory.

6) `Test_Int : aliased Integer := 94;` – Test_Int variable is
aliased. Making a variable aliased tells the compiler that this
value needs to be in RAM because later on you would like to get a
pointer aimed at its value. In effect, this will prevent the variable
from being assigned to a register in your CPU since its access type
is what we are after.

Note   If you make an array aliased, you will only ensure that the entire array will
be pointed at, but its individual elements will not be (remember, you cannot do
pointer arithmetic in order to iterate over its parts).

Lastly, you cannot deallocate this piece of memory. As a result,
on line 55, if you try to deallocate that memory, you will get an
exception.

7) `procedure Deallocate is new Ada.Unchecked_`
`Deallocation(Test_Rec, Rec_Access);` – The Deallocate
procedure is unique in that it gives you the ability to free up
memory that you have piled on the heap. This is crucial in order
to free up consumed RAM; otherwise, your program (after some
time) will simply run out of free memory and crash.

In order to create one, the type of the variable is needed as well as
the derived access type.

Note   The name Deallocate is not a standard. You have to choose a different
name, such as "Free," "LetGo," or "Whatever." Deallocate was simply chosen for
this example.

---

8) `Rec_Point := new Test_Rec;` – The new operation is what grabs
a piece of RAM on the heap and assigns its access to this access
type variable.

Keep in mind the order of how RAM is allocated. First, the record
pointer is assigned a piece of memory. Second, all of the internal
access types are allocated some storage.

If you were to do things out of order, a runtime exception would be thrown stating that attempting to manipulate the memory location of an unallocated piece of RAM is not possible.

9) `Rec_Point.Int_Point := Test_Int'Access;` – And now, we can easily grab the address of our statically created variable and assign it to the integer access type inside of the structure.

10) `Rec_Point.Flo_Point := new Float'(0.0);` – In this instance, the float access type has a piece of memory assigned to it that is a float type and the value 0.0 is assigned to it.

11) `Backup_Ac := Rec_Point;` – As there are two instances of the access type, the access that Rec_Point has assigned to it will also be assigned to Backup_Ac. It will be used for illustrative purposes.

12) `Backup_Ac.Int_Point.all := 299;` – By putting the "all" keyword at the end of the access type, we are "dereferencing" the access type. Dereferencing means that we are grabbing the memory where the access is pointing. After this, one can simply copy a value to that location by using a plain ":=".

13) `Ada.Text_IO.Put_Line(" Float: " & Float'Image(Backup_Ac.Flo_Point.all));Ada.Text_IO.Put_Line(" String: " & Backup_Ac.Str_Point.all);` – Now, it is time to print out what was stored. This is done very simply by recalling everything that was stored. If a variable needs to be converted to a string, it is done by passing it through the Float'Image(...) procedure.

14) After making changes to the contents of the record (lines 44–46), we print this out again. This is shown in lines 48–52. Notice that the changes are made successfully when they are output.

15) `Deallocate(Rec_Point.Str_Point); Deallocate(Rec_Point);` – Deallocate(...) is the dynamically created procedure that was created at the start of this procedure. Now, we can call it to deallocate the occupied RAM.

But as before, keep in mind the order of deallocation. At the start of this procedure, the record was the first that had a value assigned to it. Now, it is the last. The reason for this is simple. If the record were to be deallocated first, the pointers that point to the allocated integer, float, and string will be lost and can no longer be retrieved. Your application will now have a memory leak. As a result, the record is deallocated last.

16) `Ada.Text_IO.Put_Line(" Integer: " &` `Integer'Image(Backup_Ac.Int_Point.all));` – This is the last line in the application. It is an intentional mistake. The purpose is to illustrate that when you deallocate memory and then try to reuse it somehow, you will receive an exception thrown at you.

Please keep in mind that when you deallocate memory, you will no longer be able to retrieve the information that it was pointing to.

This is the output of the preceding example:

```
> .\access_type_example.exe
  The contents of our dynamically allocate structure:
    Integer:  94
    Float:    0.00000E+00
    String:  Hello world!
  The contents of our dynamically allocate structure:
    Integer:  299
    Float:    3.14000E+00
    String:  Hello Ada!!!
  The contents of our dynamically allocate structure:

raised CONSTRAINT_ERROR : access_type_example.adb:61 access check failed
```

Later on in this book, we will talk about data containers (such as linked lists). Keep in mind that you can create your own linked lists using access types, but you are discouraged from doing so for production code. The reason for this is you already have a package that has tested code and will work as intended. However, feel free to use access types to create data containers that have not been implemented or for custom solutions.

Lab

Make an application that will represent a small company of ten people. Each individual should have a first and last name, a title, a salary, number of vacation hours per year as well as hours off for sick time, and the number of years with the company. Have all of the numeric values be randomly generated each time that the application runs.

Hint   This is how you would create a random value that is an integer.

```
subtype Vals is Natural range 40 .. 600;
package Random_Val is new Ada.Numerics.Discrete_Random(Result_
Subtype => Vals);

Gen : Random_Val.Generator;
begin
  Random_Val.Reset(Gen => Gen);

  return Positive(Random_Val.Random(Gen => Gen));
```

And now an explanation of the preceding sample.

The subtype is a keyword that permits you to make your own custom type. Do not think about this too much right now as it will be covered later in the book. Using the type Vals, a new package is created called Random_Val, and from this package, an instance is created called Gen which will be used to generate the new types.

When the generator is instantiated, you need to reset it so that when you generate values they will be truly random, meaning that new values will be generated each time that Random_Val.Random(Gen => Gen) is called.

The type Vals can then be turned into a Positive, Natural, or Integer, like so: Positive(Vals);.

Hint   This is how you would create a random value that is a float.

```
   Seed : Ada.Numerics.Float_Random.Generator;
begin
  Ada.Numerics.Float_Random.Reset(Seed);

  return 400.0 + (Ada.Numerics.Float_Random.Random(Seed) * 5000.0);
```

Here is how the preceding code works.

You create an instance of the float random number generator. You also seed this. However, when you call Float_Random.Random(Seed), if you need a value within the range of 400.0 to 5400.0 (and this goes for just about any other random value that is generated within that range), then first add 400.0 and then multiply the result of the random generator method by 5000.0. You can do this for just about any range.

Basics of Object-Oriented Programming (OOP)

What You Will Get Out of This Chapter

So far just about every topic about the basics has been covered. There is one more topic that is quite worthwhile and will help you to better understand how to make your code more modular. This is the topic of packages. Packages are just as they are described, containers where you can insert things such as methods as well as custom types that you can create instances of in order to use as you please. If you are coming from another object-oriented programming language, the benefits of classes and objects will become self-evident.

This is a very simple introduction to packages and what they can do. More complex topics (such as inheritance) are discussed in greater detail later on in the book. If you have a C++ or Java background, please read carefully since packages are conceptually slightly different from classes. If you have no experience with object-oriented programming, then pay even more attention (and you are strongly encouraged to re-read parts of this chapter) since this is somewhat of a difficult idea to master for some.

Packages and Objects in a Nutshell

What are the advantages of putting your code into packages? You can very easily make your code more flexible, compartmentalized, and easier to reuse. By having defined functions and procedures, creating a standardized interface for a given set of functionality is very easy. This topic has been shown and alluded to in other examples, but has not been formally introduced. Now you will be able to take your functions, put them in a different container, and reuse them in other code very easily.

© Andrew T. Shvets 2020
A. T. Shvets, *Beginning Ada Programming*, https://doi.org/10.1007/978-1-4842-5428-8_6

One topic that needs a brief introduction is called polymorphism. The simplest explanation that can be offered is that this is when you have the same function name, but different input values. Also in Ada, even if you have the same function, with the same inputs, but different return values, this will also be acceptable. The function that gets called depends on what type of variable is waiting for its return. The Ada compiler is very thorough in this regard. In C++, if the only difference is the return type, you will receive an error saying that you have re-defined an existing method.

How this works is very simple. Behind the scenes, the compiler creates different names for the various methods, and at every point one is called, it inserts the name of that function. Let's say that you have two functions called Total and one lets you input an array of integers and the other an array of floats. However, when either of the functions are called, the compiler will be able to figure out which one needs to be invoked for the call to happen correctly (whether it is the function that takes the input of a float or an integer). If the appropriate function is missing entirely, you will get a syntax error.

Do not concern yourself too much about the internal specifics of how Ada's compiler does this. Just remember that each function (or procedure) that has the same name needs to have different inputs (or return type) in order to be valid. If it does not, then the compiler will gladly inform you of your error (there are three certainties in life: death, taxes, and your Ada compiler not being afraid to tell you where you messed up).

The key difference between packages in Ada and classes in other languages is that packages – when imported – are static by default and cannot be instantiated in their entirety; this means that you can call them by just specifying the package where they are located and not from an instance of an object. However, individual records inside of packages can be instantiated and can have specific methods that will proceed to manipulate them as needed. In C++ or Java, both of these concepts are combined together, and if you want a static method, you do that with the "static" keyword in front of a function.

The advantage of the Ada approach of doing this is that the functionality of the package and the state of an object are inherently separate. This enables you to pass the record around even to different packages entirely, so long as those packages are aware of the type of the record.

Not Every Problem Is a Nail and OOP Is Not a Universal Hammer

OOP is fantastic and brings quite a bit to the table. However, do not view object-oriented programming as the silver bullet to each and every problem. Sometimes having a less encapsulated solution will be more optimal.

Experiment with how you create software and do not be afraid to throw out previous code if there is a better option. The author of this book has done did just that many times in his life.

The Guts of a Package

In its most basic form, a package is composed of two files. There is the file that offers declaration of the package (the interface) and the one with the actual code that does the real work (also known as the body or implementation). The interface file needs to have the same name as the package declared inside of it and has the file ending of "ads". The body file also needs to have the same name as the package declared inside of it and has a file ending of "adb". If you wanted to include any other packages, you would do so inside the file that is using it; if it is used in both, then it should be included in the *.ads file.

Now that we have those basics out of the way, let's create a simple static calculator package:

```
-- calculator.ads:

with Ada.Text_IO;

package Calculator is
  -- this is for addition.
  function Addition(
    Input1 : in Integer;
    Input2 : in Integer)
      return Integer;

  -- this is for subtraction.
  function Subtraction(
    Input1 : in Integer;
    Input2 : in Integer)
      return Integer;
```

```ada
  -- this is for multiplication.
  function Multiplication(
    Input1 : in Integer;
    Input2 : in Integer)
      return Integer;

  -- this is for division.
  function Division(
    Input1 : in Integer;
    Input2 : in Integer)
      return Integer;

  -- this is for addition.
  function Addition(
    Input1 : in Float;
    Input2 : in Float)
      return Float;

  -- this is for subtraction.
  function Subtraction(
    Input1 : in Float;
    Input2 : in Float)
      return Float;

  -- this is for multiplication.
  function Multiplication(
    Input1 : in Float;
    Input2 : in Float)
      return Float;

  -- this is for division.
  function Division(
    Input1 : in Float;
    Input2 : in Float)
      return Float;
end Calculator;

-- calculator.adb:
```

```ada
package body Calculator is
  function Addition(
    Input1 : in Integer;
    Input2 : in Integer)
      return Integer is
begin
  return Input1 + Input2;
end Addition;

  function Subtraction(
    Input1 : in Integer;
    Input2 : in Integer)
      return Integer is
begin
  return Input1 - Input2;
end Subtraction;

  function Multiplication(
    Input1 : in Integer;
    Input2 : in Integer)
      return Integer is
begin
  return Input1 * Input2;
end Multiplication;

  function Division(
    Input1 : in Integer;
    Input2 : in Integer)
      return Integer is
begin
  return Input1 / Input2;
end Division;

  function Addition(
    Input1 : in Float;
    Input2 : in Float)
      return Float is
```

```
  begin
    return Input1 + Input2;
  end Addition;

  function Subtraction(
    Input1 : in Float;
    Input2 : in Float)
      return Float is
  begin
    return Input1 - Input2;
  end Subtraction;

  function Multiplication(
    Input1 : in Float;
    Input2 : in Float)
      return Float is
  begin
    return Input1 * Input2;
  end Multiplication;

  function Division(
    Input1 : in Float;
    Input2 : in Float)
      return Float is
  begin
    return Input1 / Input2;
  end Division;
end Calculator;
```

This package is simple and is nothing more than a pretty wrapper on actual operators that are available in Ada automatically. The point is to illustrate a concept.

Keep in mind that all of the functions are defined first in the interface file. And if you look at the body of the package – in the ∗.adb file – there are two noteworthy points:

1) `package Calculator is` – This starts the actual package definition. This is where all of the interfaces are specified.

2) `package body Calculator is` – The keyword "body" is included. This clearly indicates that it contains the body of our package and will have the implementation code.

3) Notice that there are two of each function, one for integers and the other for floats. This is the polymorphism that was mentioned previously in the chapter. The compiler will realize that despite having the same name, there are two different sets of functions. Later on, when you call the Addition function and pass in two integers, the compiler will know exactly which division function to use.

How to Use a Package

Using a package is pleasantly simple. First off, ensure that it is in the same directory as the code that is trying to use the package. Then, simply using the "with" keyword, import its functionality. And then, you are free to call whichever function you want:

```
-- main.adb:
-- This is how you compile this file along with the
--   Calculator package.
--   $ gnatmake -g main.adb

with Ada.Text_IO;

with Calculator;

procedure Main is
begin
  Ada.Text_IO.Put_Line(" Addition:       " &
    Integer'Image(Calculator.Addition(44, 29)));
  Ada.Text_IO.New_Line;
  Ada.Text_IO.Put_Line(" Subtraction:    " &
    Integer'Image(Calculator.Subtraction(34, 56)));
  Ada.Text_IO.New_Line;
  Ada.Text_IO.Put_Line(" Multiplication: " &
    Integer'Image(Calculator.Multiplication(13,  71)));
```

```
  Ada.Text_IO.New_Line;
  Ada.Text_IO.Put_Line(" Division:        " &
    Integer'Image(Calculator.Division(59, 13)));
  Ada.Text_IO.New_Line;

  Ada.Text_IO.Put_Line(" Addition float:       " &
    Float'Image(Calculator.Addition(12.0, 3.2)));
  Ada.Text_IO.New_Line;
  Ada.Text_IO.Put_Line(" Subtraction float:    " &
    Float'Image(Calculator.Subtraction(65.9, 63.1)));
  Ada.Text_IO.New_Line;
  Ada.Text_IO.Put_Line(" Multiplication float: " &
    Float'Image(Calculator.Multiplication(2.3,  7.88)));
  Ada.Text_IO.New_Line;
  Ada.Text_IO.Put_Line(" Division float:       " &
    Float'Image(Calculator.Division(130.9, 13.4)));
  Ada.Text_IO.New_Line;
end Main;
```

Let's break it down:

1) `$ gnatmake -g main.adb` – Compilation is very easy. You just specify the main file. The compiler is smart enough to figure out where the package's files are located and include them in the entire build process.

2) `with Calculator;` – Do this and your package is included. Now you can access all of the addition, multiplication, subtraction, and division functions.

3) `Calculator.Addition(44, 29)` – This is how to call a function from a package. You have the name of the package and the name of the function/procedure inside of the package.

4) Furthermore, you will notice that the arithmetic functions for floats are also called in the same main.adb. Notice how the compiler was smart enough to figure out which function to use based on the inputs.

At its simplest form, working with a package is remarkably straightforward. This will be discussed in even more detail in the next section.

State, Information Hiding, Constructors, and Destructors

Now that you have an introduction into object-oriented programming as well as packages, it is time to talk about some of the basic features that are crucial in order to develop more serious applications:

1) State – This is represented in the form of an instance of a record (you can call it an object). You can use a record to represent various states while using the same functions on the object in question.

2) Information hiding – Ada has the keyword private. This will give you the opportunity to hide methods and types that you do not want users to freely call. How to modify these items in a more safe and consistent manner will be demonstrated. Being able to control the modification of information becomes crucial when you are working with systems that need protection from incorrect input.

3) Constructors – Now that you have your record, you need instantiate it. Constructors are functions (these can only be functions, procedures would not work) that will return to you an object that has been instantiated (you can set the individual items inside of the record as you see fit). There is no limit on the number of constructors that you can have. A constructor provides a consistent way of initializing an object each and every time.

4) Destructors – Wut what if the record goes out of scope? For example, you instantiate an object for the duration of a function that is being run. After the function finishes running and goes back to the caller, it makes sense that the object is deallocated in a sensible manner; since not going through this step, will not free up a specific resource and will cause problems later in the

application. You could simply remember to call this function when necessary. But then, you are running the risk of forgetting or calling it in the wrong order. This is where the destructor comes into play. It will be run every time that an object goes out of scope (or is destroyed in some other fashion), and there you can easily do some cleanup.

This is especially useful when memory needs to be freed up or a piece of hardware needs to be used by other applications. You can have only one destructor, because there can only be one set of steps that need to be run in a consistent fashion after the object goes out of scope.

Let's have a look at the following example that will demonstrate the preceding concepts:

```
-- animal.ads:

with Ada.Strings.Unbounded;
with Ada.Finalization;
with Ada.Text_IO;

package Animal is
  type Creature is new Ada.Finalization.Controlled with private;

  -- this is the constructor where one can specify all of
  --    the inputs.
  function Init(
    Name          : in String;
    Legs          : in Natural;
    WeightInGrams : in Positive;
    HeightInCm    : in Positive)
      return Creature;

  -- this is the constructor where all of the inputs are
  --    defaults.  Also known as the default constructor.
  function Init return Creature;

  -- print out the entire record.
  procedure Print_Record(Creat : in out Creature);
```

```
  -- setter and getter methods.
  procedure Set_Legs(
    Creat : in out Creature;
    Legs : in Natural);
  procedure Set_Weight(
    Creat : in out Creature;
    WeightInGrams : in Positive);
  procedure Set_Height(
    Creat : in out Creature;
    HeightInCm : in Positive);
  function Get_Legs(
    Creat : in out Creature)
      return Natural;
  function Get_Weight(
    Creat : in out Creature)
      return Positive;
  function Get_Height(
    Creat : in out Creature)
      return Positive;
private
  type Creature is new Ada.Finalization.Controlled with record
    Name          : Ada.Strings.Unbounded.Unbounded_String :=
      Ada.Strings.Unbounded.Null_Unbounded_String;
    Legs          : Natural  := 0;
    WeightInGrams : Positive := 1;
    HeightInCm    : Positive := 1;
  end record;

  -- a private version of the procedure that will do the
  --   actual printing.
  procedure Private_Print_Record(Creat : in out Creature);

  overriding procedure Finalize(
    Creat : in out Creature);
end Animal;
```

1. `type Creature is new Ada.Finalization.Controlled with private;` – In this line of code, we are saying that the record Creature is private and needs to be cleaned up after it is no longer needed. The task of cleaning up is done by the Finalize procedure. The Finalize procedure is the one that will do the task since it has been specified. This is the destructor.

2. `function Init(` – This is the constructor. In essence, the constructor declares an object of the record type in question and then returns it to the caller. Being able to input values and assign them to the state of the package is a plus. The reason for this is the fact that the Creature record is private and cannot be modified directly.

3. `function Init return Creature;` – This is called the default constructor. It would be called when a very plain object is needed, and there is little concern for the record's internal values, at least initially.

4. `procedure Print_Record(...)` and `procedure Private_Print_Record(...)` – These are interesting ones. The former is a public method, allowing anyone to call it. The latter is a private method, meaning that only functions and procedures inside the package can call it. How they work together is illustrated in the body of the package. This is useful when there is functionality that you do not want to be so easily exposed.

5. `type Creature is new .. with record` – This is the actual record itself. Notice how the code here is not much different from how this record was made visible in the first point of this list. However, instead of specifying that this type is private, it explicitly states that the type is a record.

6. `overriding procedure Finalize(Creat : in out Creature);` – This procedure is interesting and it needs to be named "Finalize" and take in an instance of the Creature record (and only the instance of this record). If you call this procedure "Last" or "Stuff5000," the compiler will reject this with an error message. Also, unlike a constructor where you can have many of them, there can be only one destructor.

At this point, you might be wondering, how does this work? Every time an instance of an object goes out of scope, this procedure fires off. Even if you make a copy of a record and that goes out of scope, this procedure runs.

7. procedure Set_Legs(and function Get_Legs(– These are setter and getter methods. Their sole purpose is to modify the private data in the instantiated record. You might be wondering why you would need something like this. Why not just modify the object directly? The reason is to ensure the integrity of the data inside. For example, if you are inputting a Positive type variable that is supposed to subtract a value from another Positive type, it makes sense to ensure that the value that is being subtracted from is greater than the value that is being used to subtract. To do such logic, you would use the setter procedure.

    The getter function can be used to convert the underlying record type to something else entirely. If you have a long array of characters that is used to represent a DNA sequence, then it would make sense to give the user not the array but a complete string representing this sequence. This way the user will actually understand the values contained inside the record.

```
-- animal.adb:

package body Animal is
   function Init(
      Name          : in String;
      Legs          : in Natural;
      WeightInGrams : in Positive;
      HeightInCm    : in Positive)
        return Creature;

   TempCreature : Creature;
begin
   TempCreature.Name         :=
     Ada.Strings.Unbounded.To_Unbounded_String(Name);
```

```ada
    TempCreature.Legs              := Legs;
    TempCreature.WeightInGrams := WeightInGrams;
    TempCreature.HeightInCm    := HeightInCm;

    return TempCreature;
  end Init;

  function Init return Creature is
    TempCreature : Creature;
  begin
    TempCreature.Name             :=
      Ada.Strings.Unbounded.To_Unbounded_String("dog");
    TempCreature.Legs             := 4;
    TempCreature.WeightInGrams := 3000;
    TempCreature.HeightInCm    := 40;

    return TempCreature;
  end Init;

  procedure Set_Legs(
    Creat : in out Creature;
    Legs : in Natural) is

  begin
    Creat.Legs := Legs;
  end Set_Legs;

  procedure Set_Weight(
    Creat : in out Creature;
    WeightInGrams : in Positive) is

  begin
    Creat.WeightInGrams := WeightInGrams;
  end Set_Weight;

  procedure Set_Height(
    Creat : in out Creature;
    HeightInCm : in Positive) is
```

```
begin
  Creat.HeightInCm := HeightInCm;
end Set_Height;

function Get_Legs(
  Creat : in out Creature)
    return Natural is

begin
  return Creat.Legs;
end Get_Legs;

function Get_Weight(
  Creat : in out Creature)
    return Positive is

begin
  return Creat.WeightInGrams;
end Get_Weight;

function Get_Height(
  Creat : in out Creature)
    return Positive is

begin
  return Creat.HeightInCm;
end Get_Height;

overriding procedure Finalize(
  Creat : in out Creature) is
begin
  Ada.Text_IO.Put_Line(
    "Resetting values of Creat to defaults.");

  Creat.Name          :=
    Ada.Strings.Unbounded.Null_Unbounded_String;
  Creat.Legs          := 0;
  Creat.WeightInGrams := 1;
  Creat.HeightInCm    := 1;
end Finalize;
```

105

```
procedure Print_Record(Creat : in out Creature) is
begin
  Private_Print_Record(Creat);
end Print_Record;

procedure Private_Print_Record(Creat : in out Creature) is
begin
  Ada.Text_IO.Put_Line(" The animal:");
  Ada.Text_IO.Put_Line("  The name:          " &
    Ada.Strings.Unbounded.To_String(Creat.Name));
  Ada.Text_IO.Put_Line("  Number of legs:  " &
    Natural'Image(Creat.Legs));
  Ada.Text_IO.Put_Line("  Weight in grams: " &
    Positive'Image(Creat.WeightInGrams));
  Ada.Text_IO.Put_Line("  Height in cm:    " &
    Positive'Image(Creat.HeightInCm));
  end Private_Print_Record;
end Animal;
```

1) This is where the actual guts of the declarations made in animal. ads are implemented. Here you will find the two constructors that were previously declared. One thing to note is that each of those constructors creates its own declarations of records before returning them; this fact is important when it comes to dealing with the destructor described next.

2) overriding procedure Finalize – This is the destructor. Finalize is actually a procedure inside of the Ada.Finalization package and the keyword overriding forces the creation of a Finalize procedure inside of the Animal package. Now, it is called every time that a declared record goes out of scope. Remember how in the constructor we have our own local declarations of records? When those constructors finish executing and TempCreature is out of scope, the destructor is called.

Keep in mind, when the record is returned, a copy of it is created and then that copy promptly goes out of scope after it is copied to the contents of the caller. This may or may not be what you want to happen. Usually, this functionality is harmless. However, if you cannot afford to have this happen (such as deallocating a resource, but only after it has been allocated), the best option would be to use an access type that is pointing to the resource in question and it (not the resource) is copied. That way you will call the destructor more than once, but the unnecessary replication will not occur.

In this specific example, after the records have been initialized, there will be two printouts from the destructor (and the entire application has not finished executing yet!) How? Simple! You first create an instance in the constructor (that's one object), then you create another instance by returning it (the original is copied and returned to the caller). When the application finishes executing, the destructor will be called again.

3) Lastly, you will notice Print_Record (a public procedure) calling Private_Print_Record (a private procedure). This is on purpose in order to better show how private methods can be used. In the next example, you will see that only public functions and procedures can be used on declared records:

```
-- main_animal.adb:

with Ada.Text_IO;

with Animal;

procedure main_animal is
  Var1 : Animal.Creature := Animal.Init;
  Var2 : Animal.Creature := Animal.Init("Elephant", 4,
    4000000, 500);
begin
  Animal.Print_Record(Var1);
  Animal.Print_Record(Var2);
  --Animal.Private_Print_Record(Var2); ERROR
end main_animal;
```

1) `with Animal;` – The entire package can be imported into our main method by using the with keyword (and make sure that the ads and adb files are located in the same directory as the main_animal.adb file).

2) `Animal.Private_Print_Record(Var2);` – This code will never compile. Private_Print_Record is a private procedure, and when you attempt to call it, an error about this function not being visible will be thrown at you. This is on purpose, since this procedure is supposed to be hidden.

3) Running the preceding code, you will see six printouts from the destructor. The first four happened when you called Animal.Init, the last two happen after the Print_Record. This has been covered in the preceding text; if you find it confusing, please re-read the previous page.

Thus far, this has been a fairly straightforward example. In a future chapter on OOP, even more interesting topics will be covered.

Lab

Look at the Animal package and create functions and procedures that will give you the ability to modify existing declarations of records and return individual values of the record. In short, make getter and setter methods.

PART II

Intermediate Topics

Exception Handling

What You Will Get Out of This Chapter

In this chapter, the concept of exceptions is introduced. Exceptions are software interruptions for anomalous things that might occur when your application is running. For example, if you are working on controller software and it is monitoring sensors on a drone, it would be wise to execute some code to land the vehicle safely if a motor is overheating.

The three topics that will be covered are

1) How to catch existing exceptions, which you will trigger on purpose.

2) How to throw exceptions so that specific actions can be triggered.

3) How to make your own exception, throw, and catch them.

Lastly, we will talk about when it is appropriate to throw exceptions. This functionality does exist and that does not mean that it should be used carelessly.

Description of Exceptions

As said before, exceptions are interruptions that can be caused from your application. These interruptions are for errors (most of the time due to something very wrong occurring) that can severely impact the operations of your application. They are sent from the method where this error occurred up the calling stack. An exception keeps going until it finds a matching catch statement where it can be processed; if it does not find a catch statement, then it will halt the execution of your program.

© Andrew T. Shvets 2020
A. T. Shvets, *Beginning Ada Programming*, https://doi.org/10.1007/978-1-4842-5428-8_7

For example, you call a function (let's call it "file_counter") that is supposed to return the count of files in a directory tree and takes the input as the path from where it needs to start out. In a situation like this, you will most likely have to make many calls to different functions. Let's say that as this code is executing, it encounters a serious error condition and throws an exception, like someone has deleted part of the directory tree and your application is in an undefined state. The exception will keep going up the stack of functions/procedures that were called until it finds something that will handle this exception. Let's say that the function that does handle it is "file_counter". As a result, when the exception does get to it, there will be an "exception" keyword right before the "end file_counter;" to take care of it.

If at this point you are wondering whether this might be a fairly disruptive and computationally expensive operation, read on to the next section.

When to Use Exceptions

Exceptions are great for passing an immediate error condition upward that might take much more time to accomplish, if you were using plain return statements or passing in values by reference, especially if wasting time doing other processing might cause damage to hardware or hurt someone. They should be used in this context all the time. The last thing that you want to do is to create a problem that is very difficult (or impossible) to recover from by simply wasting time doing irrelevant processing. One other instance where this should be used is if something changes in the application's runtime environment that is fairly substantial (loss of a key directory/file, loss of network connectivity, a USB cable getting unplugged that the program depended on, etc.), and it will need to do processing that is done usually in an emergency.

However, there are instances where using exceptions is a terrible idea. You might create a package that parses XML files. Let's say that the user passes in the path to an XML file that is incorrectly structured. This would be an error condition. The file is wrong, throw an exception, right? Not quite. In this instance, it would be more sensible to return an integer (or some other small value) that indicates that there has been an error, or print a message to standard error indicating this. Or what if there is a typo in the path of the file? Returning a sensible error code is preferable. An error in an XML file is a problem, but it is not something critical that needs to be fixed within seconds of finding this problem, usually.

The reason for this is when an exception bubbles up the call stack (until it is finally trapped and appropriate action taken), it is very disruptive to the process of the application and can be a major performance hit. There are times when such a performance penalty is warranted, but it is to be used seldom and wisely. If your code is run many times and over several processes (or tasks) and they are all throwing/catching exceptions, do not be surprised if your application does its job inefficiently; that would be in the best case, and in the worst case, be prepared to have to deal with unnecessarily complex debug situations when something does go wrong.

Catching Exceptions

Now that we have a decent understanding of what we are dealing with, it's time to simulate catching some errors. In the following example, division by zero is performed and an exception will be thrown:

```
-- exceptions_catching.adb:

with Ada.Text_IO;

procedure Exceptions_Catching is
  Val1 : Integer := 45;
  Val2 : Integer := 0;
begin
  Ada.Text_IO.Put_Line("Before division by 0.");

  Val1 := Val1 / Val2;

  Ada.Text_IO.Put_Line("After division by 0.");
exception
  when Constraint_Error =>
    Ada.Text_IO.Put_Line("ERROR: Division by 0.");
  when others =>
    Ada.Text_IO.Put_Line("ERROR: I don't know what it is though...");
end Exceptions_Catching;
```

This is the result of the operation:

```
ch07> .\exceptions_catching.exe
Before division by 0.
ERROR: Division by 0.
```

Let's take a moment and digest the preceding code:

1) Everything that you see from begin to exception is what would normally be in any given function. This is the type of thing that you would expect from any given block of code, except the difference is that the end keyword is a little later.

2) Right after that, you will see the "exception" keyword. This is where you specify where to catch the exception that you have specified. In this case, the program needs to catch the Constraint_Error, which is thrown whenever there is division by zero. Then, you can specify what action should be taken (in this case, an error is printed to the command line).

3) After the first block of when Constraint_Error, you can include other exceptions that you might need. For the last exception that is caught, when others, this catches all of the exceptions that might come up. Be careful with when others, because you will catch all exceptions, but it does not permit you to differentiate among the different types and is best used at the very end of the list if something unexpected happens.

The Ever-Helpful Compiler

When you compile this code, you will get a warning from the compiler saying that there will be a division by zero. This is a good thing, since it makes your life easier by detecting silly mistakes that you make. However, in this case, we will ignore this warning:

```
declare_exceptions_catching.adb:15:18: warning: division by zero
declare_exceptions_catching.adb:15:18: warning: "Constraint_Error" will
be raised
    at run time
```

You might be wondering at this point: This is great, but after the exception has been processed, what if I want to do some other things? What if I want my application to keep working and run other functionality as necessary?

There are two ways you can do this:

1) Create a wrapper function/procedure around the one that catches the exception that will continue executing other tasks as needed. You already know how to do this from Chapter 4.

2) Create a declare block that will produce the exception while having the parent function continue to work on other things.

In the following example, we will do the latter:

```ada
-- declare_exceptions_catching.adb:

with Ada.Text_IO;

procedure Declare_Exceptions_Catching is
  Val1 : Integer := 45;
  Val2 : Integer := 0;
begin
  Ada.Text_IO.Put_Line("Getting started with cathing exceptions!");

  declare
  begin
    Ada.Text_IO.Put_Line("Before division by 0.");

    Val1 := Val1 / Val2;

    Ada.Text_IO.Put_Line("After division by 0.");
  exception
    when Constraint_Error =>
      Ada.Text_IO.Put_Line("ERROR: Division by 0.");
    when others =>
      Ada.Text_IO.Put_Line("ERROR: I don't know what it is though...");
  end;

  Ada.Text_IO.Put_Line("Continuation and such!");
end Declare_Exceptions_Catching;
```

CHAPTER 7   EXCEPTION HANDLING

This can be a much better way to solve your exception handling problems. If the exception handling code is not length, then using this convention can be an easier way to organize your source code. Lastly, it mitigates the need to create a new function. Use your judgment and feel free to switch from one to another as you see fit.

Throwing Existing Exceptions

You now know how to catch exceptions, but what about throwing them? It can be useful to throw a Constraint exception in a particular algorithm if an error condition is met. Let's look at the following example when it comes to converting Celsius to Fahrenheit:

```
-- temp_exception.adb:

with Ada.Text_IO;

procedure Temp_Exception is
  function Convert_F_To_C(
    Fahren : in Float)
      return Float is

  begin
    if Fahren < -459.67 then
      raise Constraint_Error;
    else
      return (Fahren - 32.0) * (5.0 / 9.0);
    end if;
  end Convert_F_To_C;
begin
  Ada.Text_IO.Put_Line(" - Convert 100 Fahrenheit to Celsius: " &
    Float'Image(Convert_F_To_C(100.0)));
  Ada.Text_IO.Put_Line(" - Convert 100 Fahrenheit to Celsius: " &
    Float'Image(Convert_F_To_C(0.0)));
  Ada.Text_IO.Put_Line(" - Convert 100 Fahrenheit to Celsius: " &
    Float'Image(Convert_F_To_C(-100.0)));
  Ada.Text_IO.Put_Line(" - Convert 100 Fahrenheit to Celsius: " &
    Float'Image(Convert_F_To_C(-459.68)));
```

```
exception
  when Constraint_Error =>
    Ada.Text_IO.Put_Line("ERROR: Minimum value exceeded.");
  when Others =>
    Ada.Text_IO.Put_Line("ERROR: I don't know what this error is though...");
end Temp_Exception;
```

Let's jump right into the most relevant part of this example:

1) `raise Constraint_Error;` – On line 12, we can just as easily throw an exception that is already inside of Ada. This is all of the code that is needed to throw this exception, just the keyword "raise".

2) `when Constraint_Error =>` – And on line 23 is where this thrown error is caught. Not much different from the previous example.

Throwing exceptions is easy and you can do it with just the "raise" keyword.

Throwing and Making Your Own Exceptions

Catching existing exceptions is helpful. It can make your application more robust and better able to withstand unpredictable situations. However, this can be very limiting. What if you know of a particular error condition that is raised in your application that is not described within the existing set of exceptions that you MUST handle? If there were no way to create your own exceptions, you would be out of luck.

Let's look at this example on how to raise custom exceptions:

```
-- throwing_exceptions.adb:

with Ada.Text_IO;

procedure Throwing_Exceptions is
  Custom_Exception_Just_For_Fun : exception;

  procedure Throw_Exception is
  begin
    Ada.Text_IO.Put_Line("Right about to throw an exception.");
    Ada.Text_IO.New_Line;

    raise Custom_Exception_Just_For_Fun;
```

```
  --Ada.Text_IO.Put_Line("This will never be printed to command line.");
 end Throw_Exception;

 procedure Catch_Exception is
 begin
   Ada.Text_IO.Put_Line("Right before receiving an exception!");

   Throw_Exception;

   Ada.Text_IO.Put_Line("Right after catching the exception.");
 exception
   when Custom_Exception_Just_For_Fun =>
     Ada.Text_IO.Put_Line("!!! The custom exception was received!!!");
 end Catch_Exception;
begin
 Ada.Text_IO.Put_Line(" ==> Beginning the experiment!");

 Catch_Exception;

 Ada.Text_IO.Put_Line(" ==> Ending the experiment!");
end Throwing_Exceptions;
```

This is the output of running the preceding code, which will be more important in the following explanation:

```
> throwing_exceptions.exe
 ==> Beginning the experiment!
Right before receiving an exception!
Right about to throw an exception.

!!! The custom exception was received!!!
 ==> Ending the experiment!
```

This is will be a more complex example. So let's go through the explanation carefully.

1) First off, the compiler does not know anything about a custom exception that you have created. In the preceding example, in the Throwing_Exceptions procedure, it is necessary to declare the exception right away. You do not need to instantiate it, since this is done when the exception is raised.

2) The procedure Throw_Exception is the one that raises an
exception and lets the caller (in this case, Catch_Exception)
process it as needed. Notice that the code right after the `raise`
`Custom_Exception_Just_For_Fun` is commented out. This is on
purpose, the reason being that the Ada compiler will give you
an error stating that anything after the raise keyword will not
be executed and it should be removed (since the scope of this
procedure will be exited).

3) Catch_Exception is a procedure that actually catches the raised
exception. Notice how after calling the Throw_Exception
procedure, the compiler permitted the placement of the `Ada.`
`Text_IO.Put_Line(…)`. Why did it allow this? Simple, the
compiler has no way of knowing if that procedure will raise an
exception or not. Granted, when you run that snippet of code,
you will not see "Right after catching the exception." displayed,
but that is because Catch_Procedure caught and processed
an exception (which is why you can see "!!! The custom
exception..." printed out).

4) Lastly, the Throwing_Exception procedure, the text "Beginning
the experiment" and "Ending the experiment" printed out just
fine. This worked correctly. After all, the exceptions in question
were taken care of in the method Catch_Exception.

This should give you a good grasp of how exceptions work in Ada. If something
is unclear, feel free to modify the preceding code and experiment with it. In the
next chapter, we will be dealing with output to files, the lessons learned here can
be put in effect.

Lab

Building on the Animal package that was done in the previous chapter, make at least two exceptions for instances that are considered errors, for example, if the number of legs of an animal turns out to be larger than 1000 or the height exceeds 2000 centimeters.

Note   This is poor design on purpose. The described error conditions are indeed minor and should not be attempted in real life. The point is to give you hands-on experience on how this is done.

The Basics of I/O and Interacting with the Operating System

What You Will Get Out of This Chapter

Having an application crunch numbers and catch exceptions is nice. However, it is very limiting. Without being able to interact with the outside world, you might as well have something that exists only in a bubble and is of limited use at best. In this chapter the goal is to explain how your application will work outside the scope of its running process.

Here is what we will cover:

1) How to read and write text files. You will find out how to import the contents of a file and work with it in a way that is useful for you.

2) Being able to ask the operating system to run commands is also useful. After all, talking with other services is key when your application increases in complexity.

3) Thus far, if you wanted to feed information into your program, you would modify the source, compile, and re-run the program. How repetitive! Command-line arguments will be introduced.

The goal is to demonstrate how you can make your application talk to the operating system that it is running on.

© Andrew T. Shvets 2020
A. T. Shvets, *Beginning Ada Programming*, https://doi.org/10.1007/978-1-4842-5428-8_8

Reading from a Text File

Being able to work with text files is the most basic requirement of any programming language. This is the next step above the "Hello world!" example. For the following example, extensive use was made from the following RosettaCode snippet, located here:

http://rosettacode.org/wiki/Count_occurrences_of_a_substring#Ada

The one difference from that code is that as this application reads a text file (its own source code), it prints out only the lines that have the string "Ada" in it:

```
-- line_by_line.adb:

with Ada.Strings.Fixed;
with Ada.Text_IO;

procedure Line_By_Line is
  Filename   : String := "line_by_line.adb";
  File       : Ada.Text_IO.File_Type;
  Line_Count : Natural := 0;
begin
  Ada.Text_IO.Open(File => File,
                   Mode => Ada.Text_IO.In_File,
                   Name => Filename);

  while not Ada.Text_IO.End_Of_File(File) loop
    declare
      Line : String := Ada.Text_IO.Get_Line(File);
    begin
      if Ada.Strings.Fixed.Count(Line, "Ada") > 0
      then
        Line_Count := Line_Count + 1;
        Ada.Text_IO.Put_Line(Natural'Image(Line_Count) & ": " & Line);
      end if;
    end;
  end loop;

  Ada.Text_IO.Close(File);
end Line_By_Line;
```

This is a cool little example that is very straightforward. This is what is going on:

1) Right after the begin keyword, the file is opened in order for it to be read. In this case, the application opens its own source code (sort of like how people look at a picture of where a person's organs are located). There is one thing that you need to keep in mind and that is the file needs to exist, or else you will get an exception raised. The exception can be caught and handled, so feel free to adjust the preceding example in order to catch this exception.

2) `while not Ada.Text_IO.End_Of_File(File) loop` – This basically creates a loop which iterates over all of the lines – one by one – until the end of the file.

3) `if Ada.Strings.Fixed.Count(Line, "Ada") > 0` – Here the number of "Ada" sub-strings are counted. If it is greater than 0, then we have met the condition to keep going in the if statement and print out the line in question.

4) `Ada.Text_IO.Close(File);` – This will close the file that we opened. This is sometimes done automatically by default when the application finishes running by the operating system, but it makes sense to get into habit of doing this, even more so if you have many files open and do not want to create a condition where resources are not being deallocated.

Now that we have an example of reading from a file, let's look at how to write into one.

Writing to a Text File

Let's make things a little bit more complicated. Let's write the contents of a record into a file. Here are the things that need to be accomplished in this example:

1) Create a record that we can work with.

2) Instantiate the record.

3) Populate the record with default values.

4) Create a procedure that will take the record and write its contents to a file of our choice.

```
-- write_record_to_file.adb:

with Ada.Strings.Unbounded;
with Ada.Text_IO;

procedure Write_Record_To_File is
  type Person_Rec is record
    Age        : Natural;
    First_Name : Ada.Strings.Unbounded.Unbounded_String;
    Last_Name  : Ada.Strings.Unbounded.Unbounded_String;
    -- True is for male and False is for female.
    Sex        : Boolean;
  end record;

  procedure Write_Person(
    Individual : in Person_Rec;
    Filename : in String) is

    F_Type : Ada.Text_IO.File_Type;
  begin
    -- open the file that I want, if it does not exist, create it.
    declare
    begin
      Ada.Text_IO.Open(
        File => F_Type,
        Mode => Ada.Text_IO.Out_File,
        Name => Filename);
    exception
      when Ada.Text_IO.Name_Error =>
        Ada.Text_IO.Create(
          File => F_Type,
          Mode => Ada.Text_IO.Out_File,
          Name => Filename);
    end;
```

```ada
      -- write to the file.
      Ada.Text_IO.Put(
        File => F_Type,
        Item => Ada.Strings.Unbounded.To_String(Individual.First_Name));
      Ada.Text_IO.Put(
        File => F_Type,
        Item => "  ");
      Ada.Text_IO.Put_Line(
        File => F_Type,
        Item => Ada.Strings.Unbounded.To_String(Individual.Last_Name));
      Ada.Text_IO.Put_Line(
        File => F_Type,
        Item => Natural'Image(Individual.Age));

      if Individual.Sex = True
      then
        Ada.Text_IO.Put_Line(File => F_Type, Item => "Man");
      else
        Ada.Text_IO.Put_Line(File => F_Type, Item => "Woman");
      end if;

      -- close the file.
      Ada.Text_IO.Close(File => F_Type);
   end Write_Person;

   Jim_T  : Person_Rec;
   Mary_Y : Person_Rec;
begin
   -- assign values to the Jim_T instance.
   Jim_T.Age         := 43;
   Jim_T.First_Name := Ada.Strings.Unbounded.To_Unbounded_String("Jim");
   Jim_T.Last_Name  := Ada.Strings.Unbounded.To_Unbounded_
String("Thompson");
   Jim_T.Sex         := True;

   -- assign values to the Mary_Y instance.
   Mary_Y.Age        := 25;
   Mary_Y.First_Name := Ada.Strings.Unbounded.To_Unbounded_String("Mary");
```

```
Mary_Y.Last_Name   := Ada.Strings.Unbounded.To_Unbounded_String("Yannis");
Mary_Y.Sex         := False;

Write_Person(Jim_T, "jim_file.txt");
Write_Person(Mary_Y, "mary_file.txt");
end Write_Record_To_File;
```

Here is what this example does:

1) At the very start of the declaration portion of Write_Record_To_
    File procedure, a record specification is created.

2) Next is the procedure – Write_Person – that is responsible for
    printing out the record to file. This is a somewhat verbose method,
    so let's take it apart piece by piece:

    a) The procedure takes a copy of the instance of a record and the name of the
        file that will be created for storage.

    b) Right before the begin keyword, the File_Type object is created; this is
        important later on in the method.

    c) This is where things get interesting. All of the concepts described here have
        been covered already in this book. The declare block is where a separate
        scope level is created, perfect for working with our file. If the file that we
        need is not created, then an exception is thrown. Without an exception,
        we could end up halting our application in an inconvenient way. With this
        declare block, an unforeseen situation can be easily handled (in this case,
        a new output file will be created and assigned the file pointer to the F_Type
        variable).

    d) This next chunk of code is where we output the record to a text file.
        Basically, you are taking the contents of the record and then turning all of
        them into the string type before writing to file. On the first line, you will
        see the first and last name. On the second line, there will be the age of the
        person. On the last line, you will see whether the person in question is a
        man or woman.

        In this case, the inputs to the Put_Line procedure were
        explicitly specified for instructive purposes.

    e) The last thing that we do is close the file.

3) If you look at the body of Write_Record_To_File, things are pretty simple. You instantiate the individual records and write each to file.

The preceding example can be fairly confusing. If things do not make much sense, you are encouraged to place Put_Line statements and see how the logic of the application flows.

This might be a little bit challenging, but make a small application that will read in the files that were generated line by line and store the contents of it as a series of strings. Try it. You will have a much better grasp of what is going on.

Executing Commands

Okay, you have learned how to have your application "communicate" using files. This is a good start, but we can do better. How about sending actual commands to the operating system itself? What if you would like to display the contents of the directory where your application is running? Let's see how this can be done:

```ada
-- talk_to_os.adb:

with Ada.Text_IO;

with GNAT.OS_Lib;

procedure Talk_To_OS is
  function OS_Command(
    Command   : in String;
    Arguments : in String)
      return Integer is

    Return_Value : Integer := 0;

    Arguments_List : GNAT.OS_Lib.Argument_List :=
        (1 => new String'(Command),
          2 => new String'(Arguments));

    use type GNAT.OS_Lib.File_Descriptor;
    File_Descriptor : GNAT.OS_Lib.File_Descriptor := GNAT.OS_Lib.Standout;
  begin
```

```
    GNAT.OS_Lib.Spawn(
      Program_Name              => Command,
      Args                      => Arguments_List,
      Output_File_Descriptor => File_Descriptor,
      Return_Code               => Return_Value);

    return Return_Value;
  end OS_Command;

  Return_Int : Integer := 0;
begin
  Return_Int := OS_Command(
    Command   => "cmd.exe",
    Arguments => "/C dir C:\introductory_ada_book\source_code\ch08\*.adb");
  --Return_Int := OS_Command(
  --  Command   => "ls",
  --  Arguments => "-l *.adb");
end Talk_To_OS;
```

This is a very short and powerful little application. It was adapted from a Rosetta Code example. Let's start from the top:

1) `with GNAT.OS_Lib;` – This is not a standard Ada compiler library, but it has a number of things that we really need for this small application. For one, we can spawn processes that can run specific tasks in the operating system itself. We will use this as needed in order to implement some very useful functionality.

2) On line 8, a function is created to run commands. In it, a command with its parameters will be passed in. This is done purely for convenience.

3) `Arguments_List : GNAT.OS_Lib.Argument_List :=` `(1 => new String'(Command), 2 => new String'(Arguments));` – The command and the arguments now need to be turned into a specific format for the function that we need. The function Spawn (on line 22) will take only this input.

4) `GNAT.OS_Lib.Spawn` – After preparing all of the inputs in a particular order, the spawn function is called. This will actually run our command.

   One thing that is worth paying attention to is the fact that Output_File_Descriptor is set to File_Descriptor which is set to standard output. If you want to save the output somewhere, then you can open a file and redirect the output there.

5) Now, have a look at the code after the begin keyword in the Talk_To_OS procedure. The preceding example will run in Windows and a Unix operating system. You just need to comment out the initial call to OS_Command and remove the comments for the second call to the same function.

   Also, you will need to alter the structure of the arguments list to be like so:

   ```
   Arguments_List : GNAT.OS_Lib.Argument_List :=
   (--1 => new String'(Command),
   1 => new String'(Arguments));
   ```

If you are feeling adventurous, make an improvement to the preceding example where you check to see if the command in question does exist on your system before you actually execute it.

Command-Line Arguments

There will be times when you will want to start up your application and put in certain variables at startup. Basically, these are settings that you set once when the program starts and continue (unless changed internally) to be set. We call these variables command-line arguments. You would set them when you first start up the program at the command line. Here is an example that illustrates this:

```
-- command_line_arguments.adb:

with Ada.Command_Line;
with Ada.Text_IO;
```

```
procedure Command_Line_Arguments is
begin
  -- this will print out the name of the application.
  Ada.Text_IO.Put_Line("Application name and path: " &
    Ada.Command_Line.Command_Name);

  for Arg in 1 .. Ada.Command_Line.Argument_Count loop
    Ada.Text_IO.Put_Line(Ada.Command_Line.Argument(Arg) & " ");
  end loop;
end Command_Line_Arguments;
```

Here is what is going on in the preceding snippet:

1) `with Ada.Command_Line;` – This is the package that is necessary in order to work with command-line arguments.

2) On line 9, this is what will show the name of the application as well as the directory of the application:
   `Ada.Command_Line.Command_Name`

   This is useful for debug purposes also. The preceding function will print out the name of your application and its location in the file system; the author will confess that he has wasted many hours trying to figure out why his application does not have the latest feature only to find out that he was running the wrong binary.

3) `for Arg in 1 .. Ada.Command_Line.Argument_Count loop` – In this loop an artificial range is created from the value of 1 to Argument_Count. When your application starts, the Argument_Count includes the total number of passed in arguments that were passed into it. This is useful for when you want to put things into a for loop and iterate over the arguments one by one.

4) `Ada.Text_IO.Put_Line(Ada.Command_Line.Argument(Arg) & " ");` – Building on top of the preceding example, you make use of a generated array that gives you the passed in command-line arguments, which is what happens when the Arg variable goes into it (from the previous line in the for loop).

Entering Runtime Text

Okay, you know how to get your application to talk to the operating system, read/write files, and set certain configuration settings at the command line. This is all great, but we are missing something very crucial. The question now is: how can you enter text into your application while it is running? In order to cover this case, you will see how to create a small program that can safely handle a string of any length:

```ada
-- name_entry.adb:

with Ada.Text_IO.Unbounded_IO;
with Ada.Strings.Unbounded;
with Ada.Text_IO;

procedure Name_Entry is
  First_Name : Ada.Strings.Unbounded.Unbounded_String :=
    Ada.Strings.Unbounded.Null_Unbounded_String;
  Last_Name  : Ada.Strings.Unbounded.Unbounded_String :=
    Ada.Strings.Unbounded.Null_Unbounded_String;
begin
  Ada.Text_IO.Put("Hello.  What is your first name => ");
  Ada.Text_IO.Unbounded_IO.Get_Line(First_Name);
  Ada.Text_IO.Put("What is your last name => ");
  Ada.Text_IO.Unbounded_IO.Get_Line(Last_Name);

  Ada.Text_IO.Put("Nice to meet you ");
  Ada.Text_IO.Unbounded_IO.Put(First_Name);
  Ada.Text_IO.Put(" ");
  Ada.Text_IO.Unbounded_IO.Put(Last_Name);
  Ada.Text_IO.Put_Line(".");
end Name_Entry;
```

The preceding example is very simple, but let's go through the more difficult parts:

1) `with Ada.Text_IO.Unbounded_IO;` – This is a new one. This package is similar to Text_IO, but permits working with unbounded strings directly, without having to convert an unbounded string into a fixed – regular – string.

You will learn more about unbounded strings in the next chapter.

2) In the declaration portion of Name_Entry, create two variables for an unbounded string.

3) `Ada.Text_IO.Unbounded_IO.Get_Line(First_Name);` – This is where input from the user is obtained. As you can see, with an unbounded string, you can have an input as long as you want, so long as you do not hit the Enter key on your keyboard. When the user hits Enter, the program assumes that it got all of the input that it could ever want and proceeds further.

4) In the remainder of the application, you are seeing the output of your inputs.

Lab

Create an application that does the following:

1) It should use a command-line argument in order to specify a file that needs to be read in entirely.

2) Modify the read-in data from the text file. However you want. Append text, replace text, delete text, and so on.

3) While the application is running, ask the user to enter the name of a new file that will store the newly modified contents. After all that is done, exit the application.

Note   If you are doing this in Windows, when you write the file to disk, you can get an extra carriage return before the Linux new line character LF. This is due to writing to a file in Windows.

CHAPTER 9

String Operations

What You Will Get Out of This Chapter

Some of the topics that we will discuss here were already taken care of in previous chapters, but here we will delve in much deeper and provide far more complicated examples. Primarily, the focus will be on unbounded strings. The reason is that unbounded strings are the only ones that you can manipulate as you would in other programming languages and it can be done easily; fixed strings can also be manipulated the same way, but some of those approaches can be counterintuitive. This is important because you will need to work with strings in a flexible manner, such as concatenating names together, looking if an address is from a particular town or not, and so on.

Here is what will be covered in this chapter:

1) How to concatenate and split apart strings. There will be times when you want just the first three characters of a string, or you will need to combine different strings.

2) How to search inside a string to find a sub-string. For example, let's say you want to find if an address has the name of a particular street. It is one thing to find out if the street exists, but it is another if you want to find the index where the name of the street actually starts.

3) How to insert text into a string at a specific point or replace the existing text with something else entirely. This will become more important as you develop ever more complex applications.

4) How to execute regular expressions. The preceding approaches are very useful. However, there will be times when you will absolutely need to execute at least some basic regular expressions. Writing custom string processing code for each case is a terrible idea and is an invitation to vague bugs.

© Andrew T. Shvets 2020
A. T. Shvets, *Beginning Ada Programming*, https://doi.org/10.1007/978-1-4842-5428-8_9

How to Concatenate and Split Apart Strings

Concatenation means that you are adding words together. Let's say you have first name and last name and you want to create complete strings of these items. So, you take the first name and then attach the last name to it. This can be done with addresses as well as anything else imaginable.

Splitting strings apart means that you have one index that indicates where exactly you would like to divide the original. One thing that must be kept in mind is the fact that the index must not be less than zero and not greater than the length of the entire string. Let's get started:

```
-- concat_string.adb:

with Ada.Text_IO.Unbounded_IO;
with Ada.Strings.Unbounded;
with Ada.Text_IO;

procedure Concat_String is
  First_Name : Ada.Strings.Unbounded.Unbounded_String :=
    Ada.Strings.Unbounded.To_Unbounded_String("John");
  Last_Name : Ada.Strings.Unbounded.Unbounded_String :=
    Ada.Strings.Unbounded.To_Unbounded_String("Campbell");
  Result : Ada.Strings.Unbounded.Unbounded_String :=
    Ada.Strings.Unbounded.Null_Unbounded_String;
begin
  -- first concatenate the string in question.
  Result := First_Name;
  Ada.Strings.Unbounded.Append(Result, " ");
  Ada.Strings.Unbounded.Append(Result, Last_Name);

  Ada.Text_IO.Unbounded_IO.Put_Line(Result);
```

```
-- now, we want to print out only "John C."
Result := Ada.Strings.Unbounded.Unbounded_Slice(Result, 1, 6);
Ada.Strings.Unbounded.Append(Result, ".");
Ada.Text_IO.Unbounded_IO.Put_Line(Result);
end Concat_String;
```

Here is the output:

```
> .\concat_string.exe
John Campbell
John C.
```

The example is pretty simple, but let's take you through the logic just to be sure that you are on the same page:

1) On lines 8–10, we create a bunch of variables to have some material to work with.

2) `Ada.Strings.Unbounded.Append(Result, " ");` – This might strike some people odd. Why bother with an empty space? Because, you do not want the words "John" and "Campbell" to be stuck together. Keep this fact in mind when working with more complex string operations.

3) `Result := Ada.Strings.Unbounded.Unbounded_Slice(Result, 1, 6);` – On this line of code, the splitting of strings happens. You need to remember that strings and arrays in Ada start with the index of 1 and keep going. When you know this, you can specify the starting position of the slice and the ending position.

   If you want to grab the remainder of the string from a particular position, then you will need to specify the index of the starting position (the 2nd parameter) and then the length of the string as the 3rd parameter.

You are encouraged to make an even more complex example out of the preceding ones. For example, try to string together an address.

How to Search Inside Strings

Fantastic! You can now concatenate strings. However, there is still the matter of knowing how to find the sub-string of a string and its location. Knowing the character positions in advance does not happen often when your code runs in the real world. That is the purpose of this section. With the following example, you will be able to do just that:

```
-- search_string.adb:

with Ada.Strings.Unbounded;
with Ada.Text_IO;

procedure Search_String is
  Example : Ada.Strings.Unbounded.Unbounded_String :=
    Ada.Strings.Unbounded.To_Unbounded_String(
      "Hello there!  We're having very nice weather today!");
  Position_Holder : Positive := 1;
begin
  Ada.Text_IO.Put_Line("Location of 'v': "
    & Natural'Image(Ada.Strings.Unbounded.Index(Example, "v")));
  Ada.Text_IO.Put_Line("Location of apostrophe: "
    & Natural'Image(Ada.Strings.Unbounded.Index(Example, "'")));
  Ada.Text_IO.Put_Line("Location of 'i': "
    & Natural'Image(Ada.Strings.Unbounded.Index(Example, "i")));
  Ada.Text_IO.Put_Line("Location of '!': "
    & Natural'Image(Ada.Strings.Unbounded.Index(Example, "!")));
  Ada.Text_IO.Put_Line("Location of 'x': "
    & Natural'Image(Ada.Strings.Unbounded.Index(Example, "x")));

  Position_Holder := Positive(Ada.Strings.Unbounded.Index(Example, "!")) + 1;
  Ada.Text_IO.Put_Line("Location of second '!': "
    & Natural'Image(Ada.Strings.Unbounded.Index(
      Example, "!", Position_Holder)));
end Search_String;
```

Here is the output:

```
> .\search_string.exe
Location of 'v':  23
Location of apostrophe:   17
Location of 'i':  24
Location of '!':  12
Location of 'x':  0
Location of second '!':  51
```

This is yet another feather in your cap. Not only do you know how to split up strings and recombine, but you can also search through them and locate specific strings. Let's see how this works:

1) `Ada.Strings.Unbounded.Index(Example, "v")` – This is the heart of the preceding example. All that you are doing is passing in the string that you would like to search and the string that you would like to search for. The return value is a Natural type, which is an Integer value that's equal or greater than 0.

   The passed in values are the unbounded and fixed strings as first and second arguments, respectively. In this case, the passed in search string is just one character long. If something is found, a positive and non-zero value is returned.

2) The one fault of the Index(...) – The function is that it only finds the first occurrence of the sub-string and then immediately returns. You might be wondering, how can I keep going and find all of the other occurrences? That is easy. A Positive type was created – Position_Holder – that will serve as a marker of the first instance of the sub-string in question. Then, increment Position_Holder to skip over the first instance of the sub-string, and run the search again while specifying the position from where to start the search in the second call to the Index(...) function.

   At this point you might be thinking: Very well, you have found the second instance of a sub-string – in this case, it is "!" – but what if there are hundreds of them? Great question. Look backward to previous chapters on loops and control structures. The solution is quite simple; simply make a loop that will keep calling the Index(...) function until the end of the string is reached.

3) `Ada.Strings.Unbounded.Index(Example, "x")` – Now the search is for a sub-string that does not even exist. The return value is 0. This is important. In Ada, all arrays and strings start with the index of 1. If you have a return value of 0, then that means that there is no way that this is a legitimate position in the string, but an error return value.

Notice that in the preceding example only one-character search strings were used, although nothing is stopping you from making search strings that have multiple characters.

Think about what you have learned up to now. Think of how you can combine the previous two examples in order to create a function that can grab a sub-string after it finds a specific set of characters. The function should return this sub-string. Furthermore, input the length of the sub-string that you want returned. Even if you do not write the actual code (which would be a fantastic exercise and massively improve your competency in Ada), just thinking about it and writing it out on paper would be beneficial.

More Advanced Text Manipulation Techniques

You have a good grasp of how to do basic things with unbounded strings. But now, let's learn about more advanced concepts:

1) Replacing a slice of text with a different text, even if the size is different

2) Inserting a piece of text at a point in the string

3) Overwriting entirely a certain section of the main text

4) Deleting pieces of text

```
-- replace_string.adb:

with Ada.Text_IO.Unbounded_IO;
with Ada.Strings.Unbounded;
with Ada.Text_IO;
```

```ada
procedure Replace_String is
  Main_String : Ada.Strings.Unbounded.Unbounded_String :=
    Ada.Strings.Unbounded.To_Unbounded_String(
      "Hello there!  We're having very nice weather today!");
  Place_Holder : Ada.Strings.Unbounded.Unbounded_String :=
    Ada.Strings.Unbounded.Null_Unbounded_String;
begin
  Ada.Text_IO.Put(" --===> Original main string:            ");
  Ada.Text_IO.Unbounded_IO.Put_Line(Main_String);
  Ada.Text_IO.New_Line;

  -- delete a value inside of the main string.
  Place_Holder := Ada.Strings.Unbounded.Delete(Main_String, 4, 10);
  Ada.Text_IO.Put(" --===> Main string after deletion:       ");
  Ada.Text_IO.Unbounded_IO.Put_Line(Place_Holder);
  Ada.Text_IO.New_Line;

  -- insert a string inside of the main string.
  Place_Holder := Ada.Strings.Unbounded.Insert(Main_String, 20,
    " [ Well, here is some oddly inserted text! ] ");
  Ada.Text_IO.Put(" --===> Main string after insertion:      ");
  Ada.Text_IO.Unbounded_IO.Put_Line(Place_Holder);
  Ada.Text_IO.New_Line;

  -- flat out overwrite a portion of the string.
  Place_Holder := Ada.Strings.Unbounded.Overwrite(Main_String, 10,
    "'I like cats!'");
  Ada.Text_IO.Put(" --===> Main string after overwriting:    ");
  Ada.Text_IO.Unbounded_IO.Put_Line(Place_Holder);
  Ada.Text_IO.New_Line;

  -- cut out a piece of the main string and replace it with a different
  -- sub-string.
  Place_Holder := Ada.Strings.Unbounded.Replace_Slice(Main_String, 4, 8,
    " [ Random text in this string! ] ");
```

```
Ada.Text_IO.Put(" --===> Main string after replacing slice: ");
Ada.Text_IO.Unbounded_IO.Put_Line(Place_Holder);
Ada.Text_IO.New_Line;
end Replace_String;
```

There are so many cool things that the unbounded string package can do that we are barely scratching the surface:

1) `Ada.Strings.Unbounded.Delete(Main_String, 4, 10);` – This function is for when you just want to cut out a piece of the input text. For example, if you want to cut off the first ten characters of a string that you know is not important, this is the best way to do this.

2) `Ada.Strings.Unbounded.Insert(Main_String, 20, " ... ");` – Insert is useful for sticking in a piece of text in the middle of a string whenever necessary. For example, this can be useful if you know a specific location where the title of an individual needs to be inserted.

Note   If you want to append or prepend a string to an unbounded string, then using "+" is the way to go. Yes, you can "add" fixed size strings and characters to unbounded strings and the result will be an unbounded string.

---

3) `Ada.Strings.Unbounded.Overwrite(Main_String, 10, "'I like cats!'");` – The beauty of this function is that you can easily overwrite a given string with another string at any point. Just make sure that the last input value is a fixed size string.

4) `Ada.Strings.Unbounded.Replace_Slice(Main_String, 4, 8, " [ Random text in this string! ] ");` – The best is for last. This function takes an input of an unbounded string and then permits you to overwrite any portion of the text with a different string (even if the overwritten area is smaller than the secondary string). Think of the insert and delete function combined together, but requiring less typing.

How to Execute Regular Expressions

All of the preceding ideas are great, but when it comes to some very precise string manipulation, the best way to do this is with a regular expression. Just what is a regular expression? This Wikipedia explanation is quite accurate:

> *a regular expression (sometimes called a rational expression) is a*
> *sequence of characters that define a search pattern, mainly for use*
> *in pattern matching with strings, or string matching*

Regular expressions will give you the power to take your string searches to a whole new level. The advantage here is that with a regex (short for regular expression), you will be able to create very robust and easy to maintain code, without hard-coding any sort of complex logic which can be difficult to change and easy to break. This is a fairly advanced technique, and this book is not about to cover this topic in depth.

Regular Expressions

If you are interested in giving regex an honest shot (and you are not proficient with it), then you should consult the following resources:

1) Look online using your favorite search engine for examples of regex to do what you want, since someone has bound to have solved the problem already.

2) Find an online regex tester (such as the one shown in the following), and try various scenarios until you get the result that you want:

    `www.regexpal.com`

Note   Try to find scenarios where your regex will fail and not just the one where it will succeed. This way you will have some assurance that you are not getting false positives.

---

3) If you have tried these steps and are not getting the results that you really want, then I recommend that you ask in a public forum. You still have to do the work in order to be taken seriously and have your question answered, but it does make sense to use to this as a last chance option.

Ultimately you will need to pick up a good book on the topic and read through it. It does not have to happen overnight, but a few pages a day will improve your proficiency over time.

Now, without further ado, let's get coding and create an application that will find all integers in a given piece of text:

```
-- regex_example.adb:

with Ada.Text_IO;
with GNAT.Regpat;

procedure Regex_Example is
  Regex_Pattern   : constant String := "([0-9]+)";
  Sample_Words    : String := "There are 12 cats in the 1 " &
    "large house on the hill!  They are all eating from " &
    "12 bowls 4 meals a day!";
  Found           : Boolean := True;
  String_First    : Positive := Sample_Words'First;
  String_Iterator : Positive := Sample_Words'First;
  String_Last     : Positive := 1;
  Compiled_Exp    : GNAT.Regpat.Pattern_Matcher :=
    GNAT.Regpat.Compile(Regex_Pattern);

  procedure Search_String(
    Compiled_Regex  : in GNAT.Regpat.Pattern_Matcher;
    String_To_Parse : in String;
    First           : out Positive;
    Last            : out Positive) is

    Result : GNAT.Regpat.Match_Array(0 .. 1);
  begin
    GNAT.Regpat.Match(Compiled_Regex, String_To_Parse, Result);
```

```
    if (not GNAT.Regpat."="(Result(1), GNAT.Regpat.No_Match)) then
      First := Result(1).First;
      Last  := Result(1).Last;
    else
      Last := String_To_Parse'Last;
    end if;
  end Search_String;
begin
  loop
    Search_String(
      Compiled_Regex  => Compiled_Exp,
      String_To_Parse => Sample_Words(String_Iterator .. Sample_
      Words'Last),
      First           => String_First,
      Last            => String_Last);

    String_Iterator := String_Last + 1;
  exit when String_Last = Sample_Words'Last;
    Ada.Text_IO.Put_Line(" The number found:    " &
      Sample_Words(String_First .. String_Last));
  end loop;
end Regex_Example;
```

This example is not terribly long. You have seen much longer ones in the part about packages. However, some of the logic can be convoluted; please set aside at least 1 hour of your time to follow this example carefully. If something is still vague or unclear, then come back to this example another day:

1) with GNAT.Regpat; – This will give you access to the libraries to compile and execute regular expressions. If you are wondering what GNAT is, it is a collection of Ada libraries that were designed to make your life easier when you begin to do some serious software development. The following link will provide you with all of the documentation that is available for GNAT:

    http://docs.adacore.com/gnat_rm-docs/html/gnat_rm/gnat_
    rm.html

Note   There is a Regexp package that can also be used to execute regular expressions. Since this is merely a small topic in an introductory book, this will not be discussed beyond a mere mention.

---

2) From line 7 to 16 is where you find all of the variables being declared. These variables are needed in order to make the rest of the example work correctly. Of particular importance is this:

    ```
    Regex_Pattern   : constant String := "([0-9]+)";
    ```

    This is your regular expression pattern that will determine what it is that you are searching for. In this case it will look out for only numbers (one or more times), hence 0–9. Feel free to play around with the Sample_Words variable and this one to see how you can change the output of the application.

3) Continuing from the previous point, have a look at this piece of code (line 15):

    ```
    Compiled_Exp   : GNAT.Regpat.Pattern_Matcher :=
    GNAT.Regpat.Compile(Regex_Pattern);
    ```

    What do you think is going on here? Notice the function called Compile(...) which takes as an input the regular expression. If you are thinking that you are "compiling" the regular expression code, then you are correct. In order to be used, regular expressions need to be processed so that they can be used later in your application.

    First you compile your source code and then your compiled application compiles the regular expressions! Wait... what if the regular expressions begin scheming to compile something else as well? At that point Skynet is up and running, escape is futile! Yikes!

4) Next there is the Search_String procedure. This procedure consumes the compiled regular expression, the string that it needs to search, and provides two outputs that will help you to pinpoint where the sought-after sub-string is located. The Result variable is used to retrieve the start and finish where the sub-string is located.

On line 25, this is where the search actually happens. You pass in the compiled regular expression, the string that is to be searched, and the Result variable which will be populated by result values. If there is a result that is found, then the Result variable is immediately populated with the results of the search.

Line 27 looks a little bit intimidating, but that is not the case when you take your time to understand what is going on. This is a plain if statement, nothing special. Inside of the comparison, you are invoking the "=" operator, which compares the result to the value No_Match; in this context, you are using an overloaded function that is an equal statement, and there will be more on this topic in the advanced object-oriented programming chapter. As long as there is a number – our search term – in the string, then this will never equal a No_Match (since it matches to something). When this happens, the application proceeds to setting the first and last values that are immediately below it. If all numbers have been found, then we go to the code under the else keyword in order to assign the last, which is the last index of the string that is being searched.

5) Now on to the code under the begin keyword on line 35. The loop here is an infinite loop; this is by design. It starts out by calling the Search_String function. This function passes in all of the required inputs and has the last two variables as outputs. After all of this is done – and at this point the application knows whether a matching value was found or not – the variable String_Iterator is updated. String_Iterator is important, since it is the variable that is used to keep track of the character that is immediately after the value that was just located, which is used to cut up the variable Sample_Words; otherwise, the program gets stuck continually finding the same variable over and over, which results in an infinite loop and a useless application.

6) `exit when String_Last = Sample_Words'Last;` – This determines how long the loop can keep going. In this location, there is a comparison of whether the last value that is retrieved is equal to the last index of the string that is to be searched. Once this point is reached, then the code has searched through the entire string and can simply exit.

Assuming that the logical condition was not met, it is safe to say that a matching regular expression was found and it is not the end of the text that is to be searched. As a result, the text at the end of the loop can now be printed out to console.

This is a fairly straightforward little example. What you should do next is re-read the code. Change the Sample_Words variable and then search for other things, such as strings or particular types of strings. Think of ways that you can use this to extract other information that you care about from other strings, such as addresses, phone numbers, zip codes, names, and so on. If you have time, implement such examples.

Lab

Make a series of functions that accomplish the following, with unbounded strings. Each bullet point represents a function that ought to be created:

1) You input a main string and a sub-string. This function should delete all occurrences of the sub-string, and then return the modified copy of the main string to the caller.

2) A way to find the total number of occurrences of a sub-string in a larger string.

Think of how you can use this to create a series of records with different names and addresses, which are unbounded strings. What can you do to manipulate these records as you see fit? If you're feeling particularly adventurous, incorporate regular expressions.

CHAPTER 10

Data Containers

What You Will Get Out of This Chapter

Let's say you are planning a wedding. You plan on inviting at least 100 people. This is something that will not be easy to implement using an array. Some guests will not come, others might ask if they can bring their aunt Annie. You need a solution that can change as your needs change. This is where data containers come into play.

Data containers are a very powerful concept. The central idea is that you do not know in advance how many units of anything you have; you might have a rough estimate, but nothing precise. Data containers will allow you to add and remove elements. This is very handy. In real life, you can never have such precise certainty, and your situation will change from moment to moment. You need tools that will adapt with you as well.

In this chapter, we talk about the following concepts. Each one of them has their advantages and drawbacks:

1) Queue – This gives you the ability to organize the flow of data in order. This will be useful when you are sending out text messages. You want the messages to go out one after another, and a queue is the best way to simulate this.

2) List – A list is the perfect tool for keeping a series of pieces of information that you want to access randomly, but the order of the elements is optional. For example, think of your shopping list. You would go into the store and start going from the top to the bottom. However, if you find milk – an item at the bottom – immediately after entering the store, there is no reason why you should not grab it in order to save some time.

147

© Andrew T. Shvets 2020
A. T. Shvets, *Beginning Ada Programming*, https://doi.org/10.1007/978-1-4842-5428-8_10

3) Hashmap – This is a little database. You can have keys, as well as the values that the keys are associated with. You can use this to store just about anything that you want.

For example, let's say that you created a very complex application and it needs to keep track of various bits and pieces of configuration information in order to function properly. Having hundreds of variables for this task would be a headache. A single source that you can query, and then get the value returned to you would make things more organized.

You have already learned about access types. Each of these data container underpinnings is composed of pointers accessing data. If you ever find yourself searching for a data container that you did not see in this book, first look online and the documentation. If the desired tool is not found, do not be afraid to implement one yourself.

How to Work with a Queue

Conceptually and how they are being used, queues are very easy to work with. You would push values in one end and then pop – remove – the previously entered values from the other end. This is described by the phrase First In, First Out (FIFO).

A vector can be thought of like a queue of people. You have individuals entering from one end and exiting from the other. If you want to have someone placed in the middle of the queue (or remove them), you will need to have others move back and make space for the new person. The upside is that you have everything in a nice and linear fashion. The downside is that if you ever need to place someone in the middle, you need to have others copied over, which can be somewhat time-consuming.

The vector in Ada.Containers is a bit like an array, where you can add or delete elements wherever you want. If you are thinking of using one in place of an array, there are certainly many advantages, especially if you are not sure whether the number of items stored will stay the same.

Let's now get through the example at hand:

```
-- vector_example.adb:

with Ada.Containers.Vectors;
with Ada.Strings.Unbounded;
with Ada.Text_IO;
with Ada.Text_IO.Unbounded_IO;

procedure Vector_Example is
  use type Ada.Strings.Unbounded.Unbounded_String;
  package Software_Companies_Tracker is new Ada.Containers.Vectors(
    Index_Type   => Positive,
    Element_Type => Ada.Strings.Unbounded.Unbounded_String);
  Software_Companies : Software_Companies_Tracker.Vector;

  procedure Populate_Vector(
    Vec : in out Software_Companies_Tracker.Vector) is

  begin
    Vec.Append(New_Item =>
      Ada.Strings.Unbounded.To_Unbounded_String("AdaCore"));
    Vec.Append(New_Item =>
      Ada.Strings.Unbounded.To_Unbounded_String("Google"));
    Vec.Append(New_Item =>
      Ada.Strings.Unbounded.To_Unbounded_String("Yahoo"));
    Vec.Append(New_Item =>
      Ada.Strings.Unbounded.To_Unbounded_String("DuckDuckGo"));
    Vec.Append(New_Item =>
      Ada.Strings.Unbounded.To_Unbounded_String("Oracle"));
    Vec.Append(New_Item =>
      Ada.Strings.Unbounded.To_Unbounded_String("SAP"));
    Vec.Append(New_Item =>
      Ada.Strings.Unbounded.To_Unbounded_String("EA"));
    Vec.Append(New_Item =>
      Ada.Strings.Unbounded.To_Unbounded_String("Id"));
```

```
  Vec.Append(New_Item =>
    Ada.Strings.Unbounded.To_Unbounded_String("Microsoft"));
  Vec.Append(New_Item =>
    Ada.Strings.Unbounded.To_Unbounded_String("BioWare"));
end Populate_Vector;
begin
  Populate_Vector(Software_Companies);

  -- now print out everything using a loop.
  for iter in 1 .. Software_Companies.Length loop
    Ada.Text_IO.Unbounded_IO.Put_Line(
      Software_Companies.Element(Index => Positive(iter)));
  end loop;
end Vector_Example;
```

1) `with Ada.Containers.Vectors;` – This is the package that stores our vector. There is also a package called `Ada.Containers.Indefinite_Vectors` if you need to work with vectors that need to store an enormous number of items; but at that point, it is recommended to look carefully at the problem and determine if another solution would work best.

2) On line 9, we imported the private type of Unbounded_String, so that it could be used later.

3) On lines 10–13, the vector is defined and instantiated. This is what happens:

   a) The package Ada.Containers.Vectors is actually a generic package. This means that you have to define the values that it will store (integers, characters, strings, custom objects, etc.) before you instantiate it for use. This is exactly what is happening by first creating the package Software_Companies_Tracker.

   b) The Index_Type and Element_Type are inputs that you have to specify. What would you specify here? The index type is whatever it is that you will use to iterate over the contents of the vector; in this case the type Positive is used, but feel free to specify the integer type of your choice, but it can only be an integer or a type derived from the Integer type. The one requirement is that the type ought to be something that has a range that permits you to iterate over.

The element type is the other item that will be pointed to by the index in the vector.

c) After all of the work has been done, it is time to create an instance of our declared type, which is done in the form of the variable Software_Companies (Software_Companies_Vector being the type itself).

4) On lines 15–29 is a convenience procedure. The sole purpose of this procedure is to populate the vector with some data that can be used. Notice the "in out" keywords at the top of the procedure. This procedure gets called on line 32 in order for it to do its job.

5) Lines 34–36 are the interesting part. This is where you get the length of the vector so that you can iterate over the entire Software_Companies. Line 35 is a little bit convoluted, so let's have a closer look at what is going on:

a) `Software_Companies.Element(Index => Positive(iter))` – Iter is the variable that we generated by the for loop, and in order to use it as the index of the vector, it needs to be cast to a Positive type, which is what happens; remember, on line 12 we have specified the Index_Type to be a positive value, but iter is an integer by default.

Then, after calling the function Element for the vector instance, iter is passed in which retrieves the string associated with that index.

b) `Ada.Text_IO.Unbounded_IO.Put_Line(...);` – This part of the code is fairly straightforward. The input is an unbounded string and it simply prints it to console.

Arrays or Vectors?

If you remember in Chapter 5, we talked about arrays. Vectors do share one key similarity: You can iterate over both of them.

However, with vectors you can change the number of elements that are being contained without having to re-allocate the new array size and copy over the data from the old version – also add the new item – before proceeding forward. Vectors do indeed make certain things easier for you. So, which one should you use?

1) If you plan on making multiple additions and deletions from your data container, then a simple array is worthless. Going through the hassle by allocating a new array and copying over the data from the old one is a headache. A vector would be the way to go, so let the Ada.Containers.Vectors library do this for you.

2) If you are concerned with being able to just iterate through a bunch of options or the size of the data container is fixed or do not want to import the entire Vectors library into your application, then a simple array is the way to go; you might be working in an embedded application, where you do not have much RAM in the first place.

In the end, if you are still unsure of the best approach, then go with the vector if the extra complexity is not an unnecessary burden.

You are encouraged to read through the *Ada 2012 Reference Manual,* and see all of the functionality that the Vectors package has to offer. One cool feature is that you can pre-allocate the number of elements that a vector is supposed to hold; when you have a very good idea of the number of items that are supposed to be held, then you do not have to allocate a new vector (and copy over the existing data) every time that a new item is added. However, you will still need to do the copying behind the scenes if you insert an item into the middle of the vector, and all of the values on the right-hand side will need to be shifted one by one.

If a vector will not do the job and you expect to have many insertions in the middle of the data container, then a list is a better option.

How to Work with a List

Lists are a little bit easier to digest. Think of them as train wagons. You initially have just the locomotive and then add on wagons as needed. As your application runs, you insert new pieces of data or remove existing data. As a result, the number of wagons can easily vary. This is a linked list in a nutshell.

Deep down in the guts of the linked list, you have a container that has the following three things:

1) An access type to the next container in the sequence

2) An access type to the previous container in the sequence

3) A field that holds the data that you are interested in

The field that holds the data item is what you would normally insert into the list. You can specify a location where you would prefer to have it placed. The actual Ada package name is Ada.Containers.Doubly_Linked_Lists.

The one downside of a list is that if you want to get to a specific position in the middle of the list, you need to iterate over each element from one end until the desired location is reached. This is a downside because it is time-consuming. The upside of a linked list is that it is much easier to insert items in the middle since all that it takes to insert a new item is changing where the respective access types are supposed to point. Now let's get working with an actual example:

```ada
-- list_example.adb:

with Ada.Containers.Doubly_Linked_Lists;
with Ada.Text_IO;

procedure List_Example is
  package Wagon_List is new
    Ada.Containers.Doubly_Linked_Lists(Integer);
  WL : Wagon_List.List;

  procedure Populate_List is
  begin
    WL.Append(New_Item => 23);
    WL.Append(New_Item => 24);
    WL.Append(New_Item => 20);
```

```
    WL.Append(New_Item => 25);
    WL.Append(New_Item => 22);
    WL.Append(New_Item => 23);
    WL.Append(New_Item => 21);
    WL.Append(New_Item => 22);
    WL.Append(New_Item => 24);
    WL.Append(New_Item => 22);

    WL.Insert(Before => WL.Find(21), New_Item => 34);
    WL.Insert(Before => WL.Reverse_Find(24), New_Item => 89);
  end Populate_List;

  procedure Print_List(
    Position : Wagon_List.Cursor) is
  begin
    Ada.Text_IO.Put_Line(
      "Item printed => " & Integer'Image(Wagon_List.Element(Position)));
  end Print_List;
begin
  Populate_List;

  WL.Iterate(Print_List'access);
end List_Example;
```

This is simpler than the vector example. Let's have a look:

1) `with Ada.Containers.Doubly_Linked_Lists;` – This is the
   package that is needed in order to work with doubly linked lists.
   Technically we are dealing with a list called a doubly linked list. It
   is called this way because every item in the list has an access type
   pointing to the node before and after it; hence, it has two links.

2) On lines 7 and 8, we are creating the custom type of a doubly
   linked list that stores an integer. However, in your application, you
   can have just about anything you want in a list, whether a positive,
   boolean, unbounded string, or even a custom record.

   On line 9, the instance of the list is instantiated. This is what will
   be used to store elements as you see fit.

3)   The procedure Populate_List is similar to Populate_Vector; it simply fills up the list of your choice with data that can be used later. Pay close attention to how initially the list is filled up with just an Append, which puts everything at the end of the list. During the last two lines of the procedure, the list has two items inserted in any position that you would like.

4)   Lines 28–33 are something completely new. This procedure is very unique in that it is executed on the actual list itself. The input to the procedure is a Cursor, a small value that is used to indicate a position in the list that the procedure is applied to.

When you look on lines 31 and 32, you are printing to the console. Inside that function call, an element inside of your instance of the Wagon_List is retrieved and then converted to a string (the element in this case is an integer).

At this point, you might be wondering: What are the advantages of a vector over a list? Which should you use more often? The correct answer is that it depends on the situation; however, the list is highly recommended. The reasons for this are the following:

1)   Having a function that will let you execute something on every individual element of the list is very nice. Sure, printing out a single integer might not seem very special, but it becomes more handy if you have a special record and you want to execute a particular function on each one of the elements.

2)   Unless you know roughly how many elements will be in your data structure, a list makes more sense. Adding elements to a list is very easy and computationally cheap. Doing the same to a vector is not the case. When you need to create the vector once and use many times, this would be the case where it will be the superior choice.

3)   The package Doubly_Linked_Lists has more procedures and functions to support various functionality. Look through the *Ada Reference Manual*. Notice that insertion alone has three procedures. This is a much more flexible data structure to work with and easier to grasp for new individuals.

Are vectors completely useless? No. But they are somewhat limited. Keep these differences in mind and draw your own conclusions.

How to Work with a Hashmap

We have worked with arrays, vectors, and lists. Most of these data structures will work just fine for at least 95% of your needs. However, they are quite primitive; in order to retrieve data more quickly, a better approach is needed. With an array, you can easily retrieve the element that you want if you know the exact index; otherwise, you will have to search for it from start to finish. With a list, if you need something, then you will have to iterate through each item in order to get to what you want. There needs to be a better way.

And that solution is a hashmap, also called a hash table or associative array (or a dictionary). In a list and an array, operations on it can be quite expensive computationally. In a hashmap, the amount of time that it takes to modify, insert, or delete an element is always the same, otherwise known as constant time. This makes it an excellent candidate for instances where quick updates are needed.

When you start out with one, you need to keep in mind that you need a key as well as a data item. The key can be any type, and the data item that is associated with the key can be anything that you want: integer, float, string, character, record instance, package instance, custom type, and so on. The key is turned into a hash value and inserted into the hashmap along with the data item of your choice. Let's have a look at an example in order to better make sense of how this is used:

```
-- hashmap_example.adb:

with Ada.Containers.Hashed_Maps;
with Ada.Text_IO.Unbounded_IO;
with Ada.Characters.Handling;
with Ada.Strings.Unbounded;
with Ada.Integer_Text_IO;
with Ada.Strings.Hash;
with Ada.Text_IO;
```

```ada
procedure Hashmap_Example is
  use type Ada.Strings.Unbounded.Unbounded_String;

  function Equivalent_Keys(
    Left  : in Ada.Strings.Unbounded.Unbounded_String;
    Right : in Ada.Strings.Unbounded.Unbounded_String)
      return Boolean is
  begin
    return Left = Right;
  end Equivalent_Keys;

  function Hash_Func(
    Key : in Ada.Strings.Unbounded.Unbounded_String)
      return Ada.Containers.Hash_Type is
  begin
    return Ada.Strings.Hash(Ada.Strings.Unbounded.To_String(Key));
  end Hash_Func;

  function U_To_Lower(
    Key : in Ada.Strings.Unbounded.Unbounded_String)
      return Ada.Strings.Unbounded.Unbounded_String is
  begin
    return Ada.Strings.Unbounded.To_Unbounded_String(
      Ada.Characters.Handling.To_Lower(
        Ada.Strings.Unbounded.To_String(
          Key)));
  end U_To_Lower;

  package Attendance_Tracker is new Ada.Containers.Hashed_Maps(
    Key_Type        => Ada.Strings.Unbounded.Unbounded_String,
    Element_Type    => Boolean,
    Hash            => Hash_Func,
    Equivalent_Keys => Equivalent_Keys);

  Wedding_Attendance : Attendance_Tracker.Map;

  User_Input : Natural := 0;
```

```ada
  String_Input : Ada.Strings.Unbounded.Unbounded_String
    := Ada.Strings.Unbounded.Null_Unbounded_String;
  Confirmation : Ada.Strings.Unbounded.Unbounded_String
    := Ada.Strings.Unbounded.Null_Unbounded_String;

  procedure Populate_Hash_Map is
  begin
    Wedding_Attendance.Insert(
      Key       => Ada.Strings.Unbounded.To_Unbounded_String("Aunt Annie"),
      New_Item => True);

    ...

    Wedding_Attendance.Insert(
      Key       => Ada.Strings.Unbounded.To_Unbounded_String("Quagmire"),
      New_Item => True);
    Wedding_Attendance.Insert(
      Key       => Ada.Strings.Unbounded.To_Unbounded_String("Homer Simpson"),
      New_Item => False);
  end Populate_Hash_Map;

  procedure Print_Hash_Map(
    Position : Attendance_Tracker.Cursor) is
  begin
    Ada.Text_IO.Put_Line(
      "The key: " &
      Ada.Strings.Unbounded.To_String(Attendance_Tracker.Key(Position)) &
      "   the data item: " &
      Boolean'Image(Attendance_Tracker.Element(Position)));
  end Print_Hash_Map;
begin
  -- add people to the list.
  Populate_Hash_Map;

  -- make an infinite loop for further data entry.
  loop
    -- print menu.
    Ada.Text_IO.Put_Line(" - Menu -");
```

```ada
Ada.Text_IO.Put_Line(" - 1 - Enter new value.");
Ada.Text_IO.Put_Line(" - 2 - Delete existing value.");
Ada.Text_IO.Put_Line(" - 3 - Print entire hashmap.");
Ada.Text_IO.Put_Line(" - 4 - Exit application.");
Ada.Text_IO.New_Line;
Ada.Text_IO.Put(" - > ");

-- wait for the user to enter input.
declare
begin
  Ada.Integer_Text_IO.Get(User_Input);
exception
  when Ada.Text_IO.Data_Error =>
    Ada.Text_IO.Put_Line(
      "ERROR: The entered value is not an integer, please try again!");

    -- set this to 0, that way the if-statements right below this will
    --  not process it and the above menu will be printed out again.
    User_Input := 0;
  when others =>
    Ada.Text_IO.Put_Line("ERROR: Another error has been discovered!");

    -- set this to 0, that way the if-statements right below this will
    --  not process it and the above menu will be printed out again.
    User_Input := 0;
end;
Ada.Text_IO.Skip_Line;
Ada.Text_IO.New_Line;

if User_Input = 1
then
  Ada.Text_IO.Put_Line("Enter a new value.");
  Ada.Text_IO.Put("  Name - > ");
  String_Input := Ada.Text_IO.Unbounded_IO.Get_Line;
  Ada.Text_IO.New_Line;

  Ada.Text_IO.Put("  Attending? (yes/y/no/n) - > ");
  Confirmation := Ada.Text_IO.Unbounded_IO.Get_Line;
  Ada.Text_IO.New_Line;
```

159

```
      -- process the confirmation.
      if (U_To_Lower(Confirmation) =
          Ada.Strings.Unbounded.To_Unbounded_String("no"))
          or (U_To_Lower(Confirmation) =
              Ada.Strings.Unbounded.To_Unbounded_String("n"))
      then
        Attendance_Tracker.Insert(
          Container => Wedding_Attendance,
          Key => String_Input, New_Item => False);
      elsif (U_To_Lower(Confirmation) =
              Ada.Strings.Unbounded.To_Unbounded_String("y"))
              or (U_To_Lower(Confirmation) =
                  Ada.Strings.Unbounded.To_Unbounded_String("yes"))
      then
        Attendance_Tracker.Insert(
          Container => Wedding_Attendance,
          Key => String_Input, New_Item => True);
      else
        Ada.Text_IO.Put_Line(
          "WARNING: The confirmation that you entered is not recognized.");
      end if;
    elsif User_Input = 2
    then
      Ada.Text_IO.Put("Delete a value - > ");
      String_Input := Ada.Text_IO.Unbounded_IO.Get_Line;
      Ada.Text_IO.New_Line;

      declare
      begin
        Attendance_Tracker.Delete(
          Container => Wedding_Attendance, Key => String_Input);
      exception
        when Constraint_Error =>
          Ada.Text_IO.Put_Line("The name: '" &
            Ada.Strings.Unbounded.To_String(String_Input) &
            "' is not found.");
```

```
      when others =>
          Ada.Text_IO.Put_Line("ERROR: Another error has been discovered!");
      end;
    elsif User_Input = 3
    then
      Wedding_Attendance.Iterate(Print_Hash_Map'access);
      Ada.Text_IO.New_Line;
    elsif User_Input = 4
    then
      exit;
    end if;
  end loop;
end Hashmap_Example;
```

This is the longest and most complex code example thus far. The number of things that are going on here is not trivial. However, after you are done and understand what is happening here, you can pat yourself on the back that you have achieved some level of mastery of this topic. Let's get started:

1) Everything up to line 12 should be fairly straightforward. You include several packages that will make your life easier. Also, the unbounded string type is mentioned so that it can be used later on.

2) The function Equivalent_Keys compares two unbounded strings and returns the boolean value whether the two strings are the same or not. This becomes more important when dealing with creating the hashmap.

3) The same goes for the Hash_Func. This function simply computes the hash value that is necessary when it comes to generating the key that will be used by the hashmap – an index for our little database.

4) U_To_Lower is simply a convenience function that takes in an unbounded string and makes all of the characters lowercase. It returns the string in all lowercase to the caller as an unbounded string.

5) From line 39 to 43, the hashmap is actually created. Before an instance of it can be created and then used, the type needs to be defined. As a result, all of the various unknowns will need to be fleshed out:

   a) Key_Type – This is the type of the value that will be used to identify a piece of data. It can be just about anything, but in this case it is an unbounded string.

   b) Element_Type – This is the type of the value that is the data. Just like the key, it can be anything.

   c) Hash – This identifies the function that will calculate the hash value of the key (which is the Key_Type). If a record is used for the key type, the application needs to know how to turn this record into a hashed value in order to identify a piece of data. Without this function, the application will be clueless as to how to process this unknown type and your hashmap will not work.

   d) Equivalent_Keys – When the hashmap needs a way to determine whether two keys are the same, this function is used. The reason for specifying the function is the same as for the Hash input. If the key is a record or custom type, then the application will be clueless as to how to compare them.

6) Line 45 is where the instance of the hashmap is created. After all that work specifying this type, it can finally be used.

7) Lines 47–52 are values that are nice to have. They will be used later on to receive inputs from the user.

8) Procedure Populate_Hash_Map does exactly how its name describes it; it populates the hashmap. In the example in the book, the code is shortened simply because this method is very long and only repeats the same action. The full example can be found in the accompanying source code.

9) Looking at the procedure Print_Hash_Map, it looks exactly like the print procedure for a list. A function is called on a data container, and it performs the same action on each element of the data container.

10) On line 127, the hashmap is populated.

11) After the call to populate the hashmap, an infinite loop is created. This will serve as a way to continually interact with the hashmap (add, subtract, and print its contents). A menu inside the loop describes to the user what can be done.

12) From line 141 to 157, this part is very interesting, but has nothing to do with hashmaps. The Get procedure retrieves the input from the user, and make sure that it is an integer. Everything is in a catch block, in case the user enters something that does not make any sense, such as a string. If an error condition is encountered, the User_Input variable is set to 0, so that none of the following conditions will be triggered.

On line 156, the application is instructed to skip a line. This means that after entering an integer at line 143, the user will hit Enter, but this keystroke will not be cleared away until the Skip_Line procedure is called. Without this feature, it could create problems later on where the Enter key is still in play and prevents you from entering text normally.

13) From line 159 to 180, the application gathers input from the user and inserts a new piece of information into the hashmap.

14) Lines 181–197 are where a data item is removed from the hashmap. Keep in mind that keeping a dictionary must always have something inside of it if you want to delete an element.

15) On line 200, the code looks similar from when a list was printed, as in the previous example. Again, using an iterator, a custom procedure is used to print all of the elements one at a time.

16) And lastly, on line 204, if the user enters 4, then the exit keyword is called and the loop is terminated. Keep in mind, exit will not terminate the application, only the infinite loop that is running. Once the application is out of the infinite loop, it will run to the end of the application.

That is all. With this example, there is no reason that you cannot construct your own small database that you use in your applications. These can be used in order to keep track of configuration information, statistics, multiple files, and so on.

It is necessary to note that these three are not the only data containers, there are others. These three are merely the ones that are used the most often. The ARM has even more information on this.

Lab

Re-write the preceding hashmap example, but use a record as a data container. Add information about the guests such as whether they are a vegetarian and how many children they plan to bring along; the kids might need a completely different form of entertainment.

If you are running this application in Windows, it will run best in a Command Prompt and not PowerShell.

PART III

Advanced Topics

CHAPTER 11

Multiprocessing with Tasks

What You Will Get Out of This Chapter

By this point you are probably feeling somewhat confident about your programming skills in Ada. That is good. You can write software that will be able to process files, print data to the screen, accept inputs, and perform some fairly complex logic.

However, there is one small problem. Everything that you can do so far, you are doing one at a time. If you have to do some computationally heavy tasks, write to a file, and ask the user for input, all of this will have to happen in a linear fashion. Sure, you can arrange the methods according to what you think might be the quickest way of doing things, but it is still a terrible way to approach this dilemma.

Enter multiprocessing. Now, if you really need multiple tasks to run independent of one another, then you can create multiple tasks, and have them get together to determine how they will "talk" with one another.

You will learn the following in this chapter:

1) What a task is in Ada.

2) How to start multiple tasks as you see fit.

3) How to share information among tasks and how to do this safely. This is actually a very interesting topic and will be discussed in detail.

The concepts in this chapter are not often easily understood by those new to software development. Do not be alarmed if you fail to accurately grasp the ideas described in this chapter at first, as you are not alone in this. Calmly re-read what you see here again, and think about how all of the conceptual pieces fit together.

© Andrew T. Shvets 2020
A. T. Shvets, *Beginning Ada Programming*, https://doi.org/10.1007/978-1-4842-5428-8_11

What Is a Task

For those who have experience with other programming languages, you might be already acquainted with the concept of threads. Threads are individual and independent execution entities within the same memory space as the process that is running. They can use many of the same resources as the process itself, such as memory, file pointers, and so on. Multiple threads can make use of periods of time when the CPU is waiting for some external work to complete, like waiting for a socket to open up, or a file to load into memory.

Tasks are similar to this. Unlike in C/C++ and Unix, which offer POSIX threads, Ada's tasks are part of the language. The advantages of Ada tasks over regular threads are the following:

1) Multiple entry points – You can begin executing a task at a point of your choosing. This can be beneficial if you want to do some parallel processing, but want the flexibility to choose where to start things off.

2) Built into the language – If there is a need to run multiple tasks, Ada can do this easily since it's part of the actual language. It can do this on several operating systems (macOS, Windows, VxWorks, Linux, etc.) and different processors (x86, ARM, SPARC, etc.), even if libraries for other programming languages do not exist, such as in many embedded environments.

   Think about it this way. You write some code for Linux in Ada, which has tasks. It is a prototype to get buy-in from management. Ultimately, the real application will run on a processor that does not have very good support for threads in other languages. In the Ada application, all of the required task dependencies will be easily migrated over to the new runtime environment without a problem.

3) Performance – You can get performance similar to C/C++ while being able to run your application in Windows, Linux, macOS, and so on.

4) Language support for inter-process communication (IPC) – Ada has internal support for sending either messages (which need to copy information from one task to another) or sharing the same piece of memory (this simply works with the same value and is not copied from among the various tasks). The language goes a long way to make it as easy as possible for developers to build programs that can utilize multiple CPU cores, and have them all communicate with one another.

There are pros and cons to the various topics that are discussed in this chapter; to use tasks or have a single process application and to send messages or share memory. These are important topics that require careful study. All of this will be covered as the chapter progresses. The goal here is to discuss the theory along with examples in a paced manner, so as not to overwhelm the reader.

Hello World Task

To get things going, let's have a look at this very simple example. Right after instantiating the task type, the task begins to run. This is important, because there is no other call that needs to be made in order to begin executing the task:

```
-- hello_world_task.adb:

with Ada.Text_IO;

procedure Hello_World_Task is
  task type Hello_Task;

  task body Hello_Task is
  begin
    for count in 1 .. 15 loop
      Ada.Text_IO.put("Hello world from task!");
      Ada.Text_IO.new_line;

      delay 0.8;
    end loop;
  end Hello_Task;
```

```
  Task_1 : Hello_Task;
begin
  null;
end Hello_World_Task;
```

Let's have a look at this example:

1) `task type Hello_Task;` – This is the specification of our new task. It is very simple.

2) `task body Hello_Task is` – Now, we are getting to the implementation of the body. The syntax is not much different from a package.

3) `for count in 1 .. 15 loop` – A plain for loop. Remember – like a method – this task begins to execute from start to finish. A loop will permit it to keep going as long as necessary.

4) `Task_1 : Hello_Task;` – Up to now, the task's specification was written and the body declared. It was known how the outside world should interact with the task and what it should do. However, up until it was instantiated, this task was not running. The minute that this line is reached, an independent task begins to start executing.

This is the output that you will see:

```
> ./hello_world_task.exe
Hello world from task!
Hello world from task!
Hello world from task!
Hello world from task!
Hello world from task!
Hello world from task!
Hello world from task!
Hello world from task!
Hello world from task!
Hello world from task!
Hello world from task!
```

```
Hello world from task!
Hello world from task!
Hello world from task!
Hello world from task!
```

Look over the preceding example. Change the code inside of the body of the code. What happens when you remove the loop, and just have a very long task? What happens when you put in an infinite loop? How does the task finish executing then?

Infinite Loops and Tasks

An infinite loop inside of a task is often a good idea, even if it seems to be counterintuitive. Tasks need to run for quite some time, and a loop that keeps going without end makes sense.

Tasks Are Limited Types

Tasks are unique types. You cannot do the same things to a running instance of a task.

Tasks cannot be compared to one another. It would not make any sense. Each running instance is unique to itself, and comparing them is absurd. Even if you could, how would you make the comparison? Would it be based on at which point the task is executing? The values of certain variables in the task?

Each task cannot be converted to another type, like a string. If there is an executing thread, how would the application even begin to convert it to a different type? Would a task be a really long string? Double?

Multiple Tasks

An example of just one task has been created. However, most of the time you will need to work with multiple tasks. This example will demonstrate how this is done:

```
-- multiple_tasks.adb:

with Ada.Text_IO;

procedure Multiple_Tasks is
  task type Simple_Task(Input : Integer);
```

```
task body Simple_Task is
begin
  for Count in 1 .. 15 loop
    Ada.Text_IO.put("Task: " & Integer'Image(Input));
    Ada.Text_IO.new_line;

    delay 0.8;
  end loop;
end Simple_Task;

Task_1 : Simple_Task(Input => 1);
Task_2 : Simple_Task(Input => 2);
Task_3 : Simple_Task(Input => 3);
begin
null;
end Multiple_Tasks;
```

As you can see, the outputs do not happen in a clean and orderly fashion. They are not supposed to. After all, the operating system will switch tasks from one to another as it sees fit and you have no control over this. Let's have a closer look:

1) `task type Simple_Task(Input : Integer);` – In this case, the inputs are slightly different; unlike the previous example, an integer is specified. Notice that there is no "in" or "out" keywords specified and this is on purpose. If a variable is passed into the task at the very beginning of its execution, it will always be copied and cannot be passed in by reference.

2) The body of the Simple_Task is the same, but there is one slight difference. You can use the passed in value, Input, by simply naming it in the body of the task. The same can be done for other passed in values. The variable Input does not need to be specified at the top of the body of the task.

   Furthermore, notice that you do not need to specify the flow of information; there is no "in," "out," or "in out" keywords, as you would use in a function or procedure. All information that gets passed in is copied. You could try passing in an access type, but then you run the risk of having multiple tasks working with the same type, which can create problems if this is not handled correctly. This will be delved into greater detail later in this chapter.

3) `delay 0.8;` – The keyword delay has been covered before. This keyword can postpone the execution of an application for a given set of time (here it is 0.8 of a second). However, when it comes to dealing with tasks, it also forces the pausing of the running of a task, giving a chance for other tasks to run on the CPU.

4) Now, please have a look at lines 18–20. These three lines do the actual instantiation of the given tasks. Right after this, the tasks begin to run.

This example is slightly more complex. From this, you now know how to create multiple tasks. This can be even further expanded by having arrays of tasks. This is the output that you should expect (it is not guaranteed to be exactly the same):

```
Task:   1Task:   2Task:   3

Task:   3
Task:   2
Task:   1
Task:   3

....

Task:   2
Task:   1
Task:   3
Task:   2
Task:   1
Task:   3
Task:   2
Task:   1
```

Here you see different tasks printing out seemingly in a chaotic manner. The first line should really be multiple lines. This is to be expected. The scheduler of the operating system will choose at its convenience which tasks to run and when, affecting the output to the command prompt.

Sending Messages to Tasks

Thus far, most of the tasks were very simple. All that they did was start up and print out a few lines of text. Not terribly impressive. Ideally there would be some way that you can communicate with these tasks. After all, if they are running and cannot report on what they have done, tasks are of very limited use. Furthermore, it would be nice to somehow "pause" these tasks until an order is given to keep going:

```
-- simple_messages.adb:

with Ada.Text_IO;

procedure Simple_Messages is
  task type Intro_Task(Serial_Number : Integer) is
    entry Start;
  end Intro_Task;

  task body Intro_Task is
  begin
    accept Start;

    for Count in 1 .. 15 loop
      Ada.Text_IO.Put("Task serial number: " & Integer'Image
      (Serial_Number));
      Ada.Text_IO.New_Line;

      delay 0.5;
    end loop;
  end Intro_Task;

  Task_1 : intro_task(Serial_Number => 1);
  Task_2 : intro_task(Serial_Number => 2);
  Task_3 : intro_task(Serial_Number => 3);
```

```
begin
  Ada.Text_IO.Put_Line("About to begin executing tasks...");
  Task_1.Start;
  Task_2.Start;
  Task_3.Start;
end Simple_Messages;
```

1) `task type Intro_Task(Serial_Number : Integer) is entry Start; end Intro_Task;` – The definition of the task at hand is no longer so simple. The first line still defines the name of the task as well as the input that it will take when it first starts running. However, the "entry" is something completely new. It is a message that gets sent to the running task, giving it instructions on what to do next (and pass in values as well). This can be done by any task so long as it is running in the same memory space.

2) `accept Start;` – The body of Intro_Task is similar to what was observed in previous examples. However, the "accept" keyword is new; it gives the task the ability to take a message out of its queue and process it. Here the message is a simple enumerated type that will give this executing entity the ability to keep going forward.

   Remember the previous statement that when a task is instantiated, it begins running. By putting accept Start at the very beginning, the task is forced to wait for a message in its queue before it can continue forward. In effect, this is a pause functionality that will prevent further execution until specifically told to do so (and that signal is given on lines 27–29).

3) `Task_1.Start;` – This is how a message gets sent. Later we will see how values can be sent to a task and retrieved from it.

Queues and Tasks

One thing that needs to be stated is that tasks have queues. Messages are defined for a given task using the "entry" keyword, and the compiler now knows which ones can be delivered. These messages will be processed in the same order that they were received; think of it as a First In, First Out (FIFO) queue.

Keep in mind that if you specify an entry and then do not use it in the body of the task, the compiler will print a warning. This makes sense, after all, since outside tasks will be able to see the said entry, but if the receiving task does not process the incoming messages, it can potentially lead to a filled up task queue.

Okay, that was a good example. However, as it stands, without an ability to send substantial information, and not just types but integers, floats, strings, and so on, tasks will still be of very limited value to developers.

Let's look at this example. Here, we can send data to tasks and then proceed to retrieve it. This is crucial to ensure that these Ada threads will be able to achieve at least a bare minimum of usefulness. One of the key developments in computing is giving the ability for computers to talk to one another, and doing the same for tasks is just as important:

```
-- tasks_communication.adb:

with Ada.Text_IO;

procedure Tasks_Communication is
  task type Comm_Task is
    entry Input(Value : in Integer);
    entry Retrieve(Value : out Integer);
  end Comm_Task;

  task body Comm_Task is
    Internal_Value : Integer := 0;
  begin
    loop
      accept Input(Value : in Integer) do
        Internal_Value := Value * 2;
      end Input;
```

```
      accept Retrieve(Value : out Integer) do
        Value := Internal_Value;
      end Retrieve;
    end loop;
  end Comm_Task;

  Task_1 : Comm_Task;
  Test_Value : Integer := 10;
begin
  Task_1.Input(Test_Value);
  Task_1.Retrieve(Test_Value);
  Ada.Text_IO.Put_Line("The new test value: " & Integer'Image(Test_Value));

  Test_Value := 23;

  Task_1.Input(Test_Value);
  Task_1.Retrieve(Test_Value);
  Ada.Text_IO.Put_Line("The new test value: " & Integer'Image(Test_Value));

  Test_Value := 83;

  Task_1.Retrieve(Test_Value);

  Task_1.Input(Test_Value);
  Task_1.Retrieve(Test_Value);
  Ada.Text_IO.Put_Line("The new test value: " & Integer'Image(Test_Value));
end Tasks_Communication;
```

At last, an example that will permit you to talk to your tasks in a meaningful way:

1) An explicit start command is not implemented. This can be added, but since the task stops running and waits for a message immediately right after it is instantiated, there is no need for such message. Also, since this task can freely run without having to rely on pre-initialized values, it can run without further intervention; this is not the case all the time, and sometimes you want your task to know extra information before it begins.

2) `entry Input(Value : in Integer); entry Retrieve (Value : out Integer);` – These values are the main new additions. Here it is specified that for the task type Comm_Task, there will be two entries that can be called in order to pass in information to the task at any point and without warning.

   This is called asynchronous message passing. The server, Comm_Task in this case, does not know when the next message will come in and will wait for it to receive the said messages.

3) Looking at lines 15–20, you see how the guts of the messages are implemented. The Input entry takes the integer, multiplies it by 2, and then stores it in its own variable. The Retrieve entry assigns the value of the internal value to the passed in value.

4) Lines 27–43 describe how the interface from the caller looks when data is sent to the task. In each instance, the input and retrieve look like regular function calls to Task_1. Test_Value is reset each time in order to observe variation in how the task operates.

If you run the preceding code and observe carefully, the preceding example has a flaw. This is intentional. Here is the output:

```
> ./tasks_communication.exe
The new test value:   20
The new test value:   46
```

What happened? Where is the third line? The reason for this is that on line 39, the command retrieve has been issued again, and in this case, the message that is expected is input. Refer to lines 15–20 in the preceding example. The way that the task processes these messages is first Input, then Retrieve. After calling Retrieve once on line 34, it is called again on line 39, but Task_1 was expecting Input! As a result, the second Retrieve is sitting in the queue of the task which is waiting on Input. This is clearly a design error that makes a very fragile application.

In the next example, a timeout will be described. The purpose of this timeout is to try to send a message to the task at hand. If the attempt is unsuccessful, then the task will continue to execute. This is quite handy for the following reason: A given task might have a very specific order for processing messages sent, and if any are sent out of order, it will not stall the caller (which can continue to do productive work).

```ada
-- delay_communication.adb:

with Ada.Text_IO;

procedure Delay_Communication is
  task type Comm_Task is
    entry Input(Value : in Integer);
    entry Retrieve(Value : out Integer);
  end Comm_Task;

  task body Comm_Task is
    Internal_Value : Integer := 0;
  begin
    loop
      accept Input(Value : in Integer) do
        Internal_Value := Value * 2;
      end Input;
      accept Retrieve(Value : out Integer) do
        Value := Internal_Value;
      end Retrieve;
    end loop;
  end Comm_Task;

  Task_1 : Comm_Task;
  Test_Value : Integer := 10;
begin
  select
    Task_1.Input(Test_Value);
    Task_1.Retrieve(Test_Value);
```

```
  or
    delay 1.0;
    Ada.Text_IO.Put_Line("ERROR!  The comm task is busy!");
  end select;
  Ada.Text_IO.Put_Line("The new test value: " & Integer'Image(Test_Value));

  Test_Value := 23;

  select
    Task_1.Input(Test_Value);
    Task_1.Retrieve(Test_Value);
  or
    delay 1.0;
    Ada.Text_IO.Put_Line("ERROR!  The comm task is busy!");
  end select;
  Ada.Text_IO.Put_Line("The new test value: " & Integer'Image(Test_Value));

  Test_Value := 83;

  select
    Task_1.Retrieve(Test_Value);
  or
    delay 1.0;
    Ada.Text_IO.Put_Line("ERROR!  The comm task is busy!");
  end select;

  select
    Task_1.Input(Test_Value);
    Task_1.Retrieve(Test_Value);
  or
    delay 1.0;
    Ada.Text_IO.Put_Line("ERROR!  The comm task is busy!");
  end select;
  Ada.Text_IO.Put_Line("The new test value: " & Integer'Image(Test_Value));
end Delay_Communication;
```

This certainly makes everything more robust and resilient. The preceding example is the same as the one before it, with this exception:

1) Please look at lines 27–33. The keyword "select" is used to wrap the sending of messages to Task_1 (Input and Retrieve). The "or" keyword is an alternative should either of the two calls not work. In this case, the application waits for 1 second and then prints out an error message stating that something is wrong.

   The timeout was used during an instance where the lone Retrieve message (line 50) is sent, but the task is expecting an Input. The task cannot process this message and the caller gives up. After 1 second an error message is printed out and the caller goes on its merry way. Furthermore, since the Retrieve message is not processed, the Test_Value variable retains its new value of 83 and is not assigned the internal number of the task.

   This is how the output of the application looks:

   ```
   > ./delay_communication.exe
   The new test value:  20
   The new test value:  46
   ERROR!  The comm task is busy!
   The new test value:  166
   ```

Despite the preceding improvement, the task in question is still very flawed. It is constantly in a paused state and cannot just skip over messages that it does not have in its queue and process the ones that it does. And even if it does not have any messages, it would still be nice to keep going and do productive work. After all, without being able to run in an independent fashion, what is the purpose of multiprocessing that is rarely running?

Also, when the application finishes running, the task has not terminated. In most cases, this would be considered to be either a design flaw or logic error.

This is where the next example comes in. In this case, the Ada task is much more robust and "smart." With these features, it can much more easily process data in a more sane manner:

```
-- selective_wait.adb:

with Ada.Text_IO;
```

```ada
procedure Selective_Wait is
  task type Comm_Task is
    entry Input(Value : in Integer);
    entry Retrieve(Value : out Integer);
    entry End_Task;
  end Comm_Task;

  task body Comm_Task is
    Internal_Value : Integer := 0;
  begin
    Main_Task_Loop :
    loop
      select
        accept Input(Value : in Integer) do
          Internal_Value := Value * 2;
        end Input;
      or
        accept Retrieve(Value : out Integer) do
          Value := Internal_Value;
        end Retrieve;
      or
        accept End_Task;
        Ada.Text_IO.Put_Line("Exiting task!");
        exit Main_Task_Loop;
      else
        null;
      end select;
    end loop Main_Task_Loop;
  end Comm_Task;

  Task_1 : Comm_Task;
  Test_Value : Integer := 10;
begin
  Task_1.Input(Test_Value);
  Task_1.Retrieve(Test_Value);
```

```
Ada.Text_IO.Put_Line("The new test value: " & Integer'Image(Test_Value));
Task_1.End_Task;
end Selective_Wait;
```

This is a much more mature example. In your future, any vanilla task will look like this:

1) Lines 7–9 are the same message declarations. One unique thing about this task is that it has a message that will stop its further execution (called End_Task).

2) The task body (lines 15–32) is the same as what was observed in the past, but there is one distinction. Remember how in Chapter 3 we applied a name to a loop. An approach such as this would be very handy, if you need to terminate the main loop of the task (which is done on line 28), from a deeper point in the task.

3) Look at lines 17, 21, 25, 29, and 31. This is the new structure that is introduced to the body of a task. The select permits the processing of messages sent to the Ada task, with the "or" giving the option to process one after the other. If one message is not detected in the queue, then it is simply ignored and the next one is checked.

   Conceptually, this is similar to an if .. else .. end if statement structure or even a switch case.

   The "else" keyword is a way to run something if none of the sent messages were detected. In this case, no further processing is done because we have the "null" keyword. However, if the task is supposed to do real work, you could put this code right after the else or after the "end select" on line 31.

4) Now let's turn our attention to what is written in the lines between 38 and 41. Here we see a very simple example where the task is already running, a value is sent, and a result is retrieved, which is printed to the console.

   And as a last step, the End_Task message is sent, which causes the task to terminate the main running loop, and it comes to an end. Our simple application makes a clean exit.

The path up to this point might have been somewhat long, but learning all of the ins and outs of tasks is important. This is especially true when it comes to a subject that can very quickly create so many errors that are difficult to catch and debug.

The Select Structure

One thing that is not immediately obvious from the previous example is that right after each "select" and "or," an accept keyword must follow, but is not the case for the "else" keyword. Why is this? This is simply how the language is designed. A design decision such as this was made in order to make the Ada compiler easier.

Add a simple Ada.Text_IO.Put_Line("hello"); after each select/or, and see the compilation errors that are printed out.

Continuing on, there is another way to process messages that are sent to the task. This involves placing "guards" right before a message is used by the task to do some productive work. Accepting certain requests might not be wise unless a specific condition is met. This is the logic that is covered in the following example:

```
-- tasks_guards.adb:

with Ada.Text_IO;

procedure Tasks_Guards is
  task type Comm_Task is
    entry Input(Value : in Integer);
    entry Retrieve(Value : out Integer);
    entry End_Task;
  end Comm_Task;
  task body Comm_Task is
    Internal_Value : Integer := 0;
  begin
    Main_Task_Loop :
    loop
      select
        accept Input(Value : in Integer) do
          Internal_Value := Value * 2;
        end Input;
```

```ada
      or
        when Internal_Value > 10 =>
          accept Retrieve(Value : out Integer) do
            Value := Internal_Value;
          end Retrieve;
      or
        accept End_Task;
        Ada.Text_IO.Put_Line("Exiting task!");
        exit Main_Task_Loop;
      else
        null;
      end select;
    end loop Main_Task_Loop;
  end Comm_Task;

  Task_1 : Comm_Task;
  Test_Value : Integer := 2;
begin
  Task_1.Input(Test_Value);

  select
    Task_1.Retrieve(Test_Value);

    Ada.Text_IO.Put_Line("The new test value: " & Integer'Image(Test_Value));
  or
    delay 0.5;

    Ada.Text_IO.Put_Line("NOTE: Task did not respond for value " &
      Integer'Image(Test_Value) & "!");
  end select;
  Test_Value := 20;

  Task_1.Input(Test_Value);

  select
    Task_1.Retrieve(Test_Value);

    Ada.Text_IO.Put_Line("The new test value: " & Integer'Image(Test_Value));
```

```
  or
    delay 0.5;

    Ada.Text_IO.Put_Line("NOTE: Task did not respond for value " &
      Integer'Image(Test_Value) & "!");
  end select;
  Test_Value := 4;

    Task_1.Input(Test_Value);

  select
    Task_1.Retrieve(Test_Value);

    Ada.Text_IO.Put_Line("The new test value: " & Integer'Image(Test_Value));
  or
    delay 0.5;

    Ada.Text_IO.Put_Line("NOTE: Task did not respond for value " &
      Integer'Image(Test_Value) & "!");
  end select;

  Task_1.End_Task;
end Tasks_Guards;
```

In this example, the concept of a delay will be used again in order to have the caller keep going. This is how the output looks:

```
> .\tasks_guards.exe
NOTE: Task did not respond for value  2!
The new test value:  40
NOTE: Task did not respond for value  4!
Exiting task!
```

1) when Internal_Value > 10 => – This is the only unique piece of code so far. In between the "when" keyword and the arrow "=>", you can put in any expression that evaluates to a boolean type. Whether this is true or not determines if the task proceeds further to process the Retrieve message sent to it.

At this point you might wonder why a plain if statement would not do the job. Refer to a few pages back to the gray box titled "The Select Structure." Right before an accept keyword, you cannot place any other Ada code. However, being able to do some form of logic processing would be very helpful. The compromise is "when ... =>".

How Long Should You Make the Delay?

On average, how long should your delays be? That depends. If you are sending a message to a task and the task needs to make a socket connection and download a large file, then the wait should be quite long to reflect this requirement. But, if you know that the task is local, needs to do a quick computation, and ought to return with a reply near instantly, then having 0.0 or a very small number is sensible.

All of the basics of tasks have been covered. If you have gotten this far and understand the topics discussed here, then you should have no problem with the following example.

Sharing Resources Among Tasks Without Messages

Sending messages to tasks is great. You make a copy of a piece of information and then send it over. If you are careful about how those messages are sent and received, then there is zero chance of there being a problem with having one task put another in a state where it cannot function. However, there is one problem with this approach. What if you have a resource that cannot be copied and sent over? Let's say that it is a piece of hardware, a file, or an external piece of hardware. How will you prevent different tasks from stepping on each other's feet?

You could have a single task devoted to working with just this resource, and all the other tasks would send messages to it. However, there are several problems with this:

1) What if you are working with files or a computer card that inputs/outputs data as a stream? In order to keep up with this throughput, your application will need to copy around a very large amount of data internally in order to process all of it correctly.

2) The layering of responsibilities of which task is supposed to do what and making sure that no other tries to acquire the said resource would be quite complicated. Your application will need to make sure that all of the Ada tasks are not misbehaving or just trust them to be nice. In theory, you would never design software that would misbehave, but errors are inevitable.

Also, if a future developer begins to make changes to the code without knowing how everything fits together, that person could make a task that tries to acquire this resource and cause all sorts of odd errors that are difficult to debug.

For this, a completely different approach is needed. A protected type is required so that tasks can grab a resource and hold on to it, and if there are other tasks, they will not manipulate it until all the work on it is done. Yes, this is another type, and it is also limited because you cannot copy two instances from one to another.

The following example will demonstrate this concept:

```
-- protected_types.adb:

with Ada.Text_IO;

procedure Protected_Types is
  protected type Protected_Value is
    entry Insert(An_Item : in Integer);
    entry Retrieve(An_Item : out Integer);
  private
    Counter : Integer;
    Accessible : Boolean := True;
  end Protected_Value;

  protected body Protected_Value is
    entry Insert(
      An_Item : in Integer)
        when Accessible is
    begin
      Accessible := False;
      Counter := An_Item * 3;
    end Insert;
```

```ada
   entry Retrieve(
     An_Item : out Integer)
       when not Accessible is
   begin
     An_Item := Counter;
     Accessible := True;
   end Retrieve;
end Protected_Value;

Protected_01 : Protected_Value;

task type Access_Protected(Identifier : Integer) is
   entry Start(Input : in Integer);
   entry Quit;
end Access_Protected;

task body Access_Protected is
   Go_Loop : Boolean := True;
   Task_Custom_Value : Integer := 0;
   Task_Return_Value : Integer := 0;
   Serial_Number     : Integer := Identifier;
begin
   accept Start(Input : in Integer) do
     Ada.Text_IO.Put_Line("Task in start entry!");
     Task_Custom_Value := Input;
   end Start;

   while Go_Loop loop
     select
       accept Quit do
         Ada.Text_IO.Put_Line("Task is asked to exit!");

         Go_Loop := False;
       end Quit;
```

```ada
        else
          select
            Protected_01.Insert(Task_Custom_Value);
            delay 1.0;
            Protected_01.Retrieve(Task_Return_Value);
            Ada.Text_IO.Put_Line("The return value: [ " &
              Integer'Image(Task_Return_Value) & " ] in task => " &
              Integer'Image(Serial_Number));
          or delay 0.5;
            Ada.Text_IO.Put_Line(" <=> ERROR! Did not acquire resource!");
          end select;
        end select;
      end loop;
  end Access_Protected;

  Task_01 : Access_Protected(Identifier => 1);
  Task_02 : Access_Protected(Identifier => 2);
  Task_03 : Access_Protected(Identifier => 3);
  Task_04 : Access_Protected(Identifier => 4);
  Task_05 : Access_Protected(Identifier => 5);
begin
  Task_01.Start(1);
  Task_02.Start(2);
  Task_03.Start(3);
  Task_04.Start(4);
  Task_05.Start(5);

  delay 6.0;

  Task_01.Quit;
  Task_02.Quit;
  Task_03.Quit;
  Task_05.Quit;
  Task_04.Quit;
end Protected_Types;
```

1) The first thing that should jump out is the protected type from line 7 to 29. The protected type is how we will keep a resource locked while it is being passed around from task to task. Let's look at the declaration first:

   a) `entry Insert(An_Item : in Integer);` – This is no different than a task. What you are doing here is describing the interface that this protected type has to the outside world. This entry, similar to a function or a procedure, will dictate how the inside of the instance of this protected type will be changed.

      In fact, you can have procedures and functions in place of an entry. This is a matter of personal choice and how you see this protected type being used.

   b) Now look at lines 10 and 11. On line 10, we see the item that we would like to protect from being manipulated in the incorrect manner.

      The variable Empty is what is used to control whether the Buffer can be changed or not.

   c) In the body of the Insert entry, you can see that the code does some processing on the passed in Integer. Also, the variable Accessible is set to False. With Accessible being true, no other task can work with the contents of the protected types. In fact, all other tasks will be blocked until it is set to True.

   d) `Protected_01 : Protected_Value;` – As a last step, an instance of the protected types is needed.

2) Lines 34–37 are the standard declaration of an interface of a task. In this task we specify its serial number as well as entry values.

3) `accept Start(Input : in Integer) do` – In order to initialize this Ada task, it is done by sending a Start message with an Integer. This can be set when the serial number is assigned to the task. It is up to you which method is preferred.

4) All of the code from line 39 to 68 is a standard body of a task. The most interesting part of the code is from line 58 to 65. Let's have a look at the details:

a) The keyword "select" is the start of this code block. With this approach, we will be able to lock down the protected type so that other tasks cannot work with it. However, if the lock does not work, then this Ada task will not block for a period longer than half a second before continuing on.

This way, an effort could be made to acquire a resource and then continue processing.

b) `Protected_01.Insert(Task_Custom_Value);` `delay 1.0; Protected_01.Retrieve(Task_Return_Value); –` This is where the acquisition of the resource happens. When the Insert entry executes successfully, then this task has this instance of the protected type.

Right after that (delay 1.0) is what is called a critical region. This Ada task has complete access to this resource and others cannot work with it. However, make sure that you release this resource; otherwise, the entire arrangement will not work for other tasks. In fact, try to do as much number crunching in the task before trying to acquire this resource so as not to create a bottleneck.

When Retrieve is executed, then others can work with this resource.

c) `or delay 0.5;` – A half a second is all that a task will have to wait for before giving up and then continuing further. When the timeout happens, it will print the error message on line 64.

5) The remainder of the code is something that you have already seen. Instances of tasks are created, started, and then terminated. This is how the output will look:

```
Task in start entry!
Task in start entry!
Task in start entry!
Task in start entry!
Task in start entry!
 <=> ERROR! Did not acquire resource!
 <=> ERROR! Did not acquire resource!
 <=> ERROR! Did not acquire resource!
 <=> ERROR! Did not acquire resource!
The return value: [  3  ] in task =>  1
 <=> ERROR! Did not acquire resource!
 <=> ERROR! Did not acquire resource!
 <=> ERROR! Did not acquire resource!
 <=> ERROR! Did not acquire resource!

...

Task is asked to exit!
 <=> ERROR! Did not acquire resource!
 <=> ERROR! Did not acquire resource!
 <=> ERROR! Did not acquire resource!
 <=> ERROR! Did not acquire resource!
The return value: [  9  ] in task =>  3
Task is asked to exit!
 <=> ERROR! Did not acquire resource!
Task is asked to exit!
The return value: [  12  ] in task =>  4
Task is asked to exit!
```

Look at the preceding example. There are quite a few error messages that are printed out. Think of how these can be reduced by manipulating the delays in the body of the tasks and protected type.

Critical Region

In order to make efficient code with multiple tasks, it is important to reduce the amount of time spent inside of a critical region. This way, one task will not hinder the processing of the entire system. How can you do this? Follow these steps:

1. Do most of the heavy number crunching before you attempt to grab the said resource and then work with it. All unnecessary operations should be moved right outside the critical region and then released immediately the required tasks done. Ideally, you should only be writing or reading data from this resource, nothing more.

2. If you end up working with a very large chunk of data, try to find a way to reduce its size. With a smaller variable, it will be easier to copy it.

3. Avoid writing to files or make any I/O operations once the resource is acquired. These tend to be very time-consuming and will bog down your application.

Lab

Look at the protected types example and make an application that will do to an instance of a record what was done to an unbounded string. Think of different ways that you can update this record.

Advanced Types

What You Will Get Out of This Chapter

This is the chapter that will cover the different custom types that you can create. Other languages do have the ability to do this, but none as successfully as Ada.

The goal is to do the following:

1) Demonstrate the various benefits that specific types bring to the table. Since the programming language is Ada and we want to reduce the chances of getting an error, this chapter is the perfect place to illustrate this.

2) Show the different types that can be created (enumerated, numbers with specific ranges, limited, etc.). Each one brings a functionality with it that will empower you to build robust and predictable applications.

3) Talk about type conversions. This is a potentially dangerous technique that sidesteps some Ada safeguards and can put your program in an uncertain state. At times, this approach makes sense, but be very weary of any type conversions.

It is worth mentioning that this chapter will not give you the whole breadth and depth of the type system in Ada. This topic is quite complex and is beyond the scope of an introductory book. The goal is to build on top of previous chapters so as to give you a well-rounded perspective on the topic and the confidence to explore this topic in greater depth.

© Andrew T. Shvets 2020
A. T. Shvets, *Beginning Ada Programming*, https://doi.org/10.1007/978-1-4842-5428-8_12

In-Depth Look at Ada Types

The most basic of types have been covered. You already know how to represent numbers, strings, boolean values, and individual characters. These types enable you to create simple applications. Let's look at how Ada gives you the ability to create custom integer and float values.

The basic syntax of creating a type can be summarized in the following line of code:

```
type Foo is ...
```

This is the syntax that will be built on top of.

Number Types

Restricting the ranges of certain numbers makes perfect sense at times. For example, if you are making an interface where the user needs to enter an IP address. Each number behind the scenes (and there are four of them) is represented by a range of 0 to 255 (this is a byte – 8 bits – but for a person it makes more sense to have this represented as a decimal). Creating a custom type from 0 to 255 means that no one will ever enter a value that is greater than 255 or less than 0. This can be done without adding on any extra if statements (fewer opportunities to make logic errors) to check the range and the safety of this is handled by the built-in limits in your Ada application. This is done like so:

```
-- custom_number_range.adb:

with Ada.Text_IO;

procedure Custom_Number_Range is
   type Unique_Decimal is range 0 .. 255;
   U_Decimal_1 : Unique_Decimal := 44;
   --U_Decimal_2 : Unique_Decimal := -8;   -- will not compile
   --U_Decimal_3 : Unique_Decimal := 1110; -- will not compile
begin
   Ada.Text_IO.Put_Line("A number: " & Unique_Decimal'Image(U_Decimal_1));
end Custom_Number_Range;
```

1) `type Unique_Decimal is range 0 .. 255;` – This is how a simple type is declared. This is the specification for your type. All that was done was specified that this type name is Unique_Decimal and its range was given. Based on the range, we can safely guess that all valid numbers that can be assigned to such a variable are between 0 and 255.

2) `U_Decimal_1 : Unique_Decimal := 44;` – And this is how you would instantiate this new type. No different than what you have done for an ordinary integer or Boolean type.

3) Look at the lines 8 and 9; you will see that there are two lines of code (commented out), where values exceeding the range of the type Unique_Decimal were assigned to variables. If this code is compiled by an Ada compiler, an error will be returned.

4) `Unique_Decimal'Image(U_Decimal_1)` – Our custom type also has an attribute of Image (a very convenient functionality that Ada provides to all types). In fact, the variables that you have seen applied to integers and other numeric types can be applied to Unique_Decimal as well.

Remember in the beginning of this book, Ada is described as a very type-safe language. You know full well that you cannot compare an integer to a natural or a positive or a float. The same holds true for custom types. Look at the following example:

```
type Unique_Decimal is range 0 .. 255;
type Unique_Integer is range 0 .. 255;

...

Val1 : Unique_Decimal := 5;
Val2 : Unique_Integer := 5;

...

Val1 := Val2; -- ERROR!!
```

So Unique_Decimal and Unique_Integer are exactly the same with the exception of the type name. The ranges are the same. Even the instantiated variables (Val1 and Val2) have the exact same values assigned to them. However, when it comes assigning one to another, your compiler will complain about this. This is a wall that Ada erects among the various types.

But when it comes to numbers, we are not finished. Let's have a look at float values.

Floats can also be customized in Ada. This is helpful if you have a need to represent a value down to a specific level of precision, such as in the financial industry or hardware that is precise up to a certain point, and still utilize the built-in precautions that come with Ada types:

```
-- custom_float_range.adb:

with Ada.Text_IO;

procedure Custom_Float_Range is
   type Custom_Float is delta 0.001 range -1.0 .. 1.0;
   Val1 : Custom_Float := 0.0;
   Val2 : Custom_Float := 0.5;
   Val3 : Custom_Float := -0.5;
   Val4 : Custom_Float := -0.005;
   -- INCORRECT: value has extraneous low order digits
   --Val5 : Custom_Float := 0.0000001;
   -- INCORRECT: range low bound too small for digits value
   --Val6 : Custom_Float := -2.0;
begin
   Ada.Text_IO.Put_Line("Val1: " & Custom_Float'Image(Val1));
   Ada.Text_IO.Put_Line("Val2: " & Custom_Float'Image(Val2));
   Ada.Text_IO.Put_Line("Val3: " & Custom_Float'Image(Val3));
   Ada.Text_IO.Put_Line("Val4: " & Custom_Float'Image(Val4));
end Custom_Float_Range;
```

1) `type Custom_Float is delta 0.001 range -1.0 .. 1.0; -`
   This is the specification for the custom float type. Here new things
   are introduced:

   a. `delta 0.001` – This tells the compiler what the new float type's
      greatest precision will be. This means that if you attempt to
      assign a number such as 0.0001 or 0.2398, all of the digits after
      X.XXX will be ignored.

      The compiler is telling you that it cannot support that level of
      accuracy and your program will not be compiled.

2) Lines 7–10 specify how you would use your new float type. No
   different from a plain Float.

3) The four lines after that illustrate that going outside the range of
   the type will result in incorrect runtime behavior. On line 12, Val5
   will be set to 0. And on line 14, an exception will be thrown when
   it comes time to execute that assignment to Val6.

4) And like the decimal-based type in the previous example,
   Custom_Float also has an 'Image attribute to convert our custom
   float into a string type.

Take a moment to play with the preceding example. What happens when you
increase/decrease the digits count? What about the delta? Change the range without
altering the delta and the digits count.

Array Types

Array types were already covered in Chapter 5. You know that a special type, the type
of the array, needs to be created first. Then you need to instantiate the said type and
proceed to use it.

Enumerated Types

An enumerated type permits the creation of a series of pieces of data that can be used to
describe values that are more self-evident without having to resort to having numbers
mean a particular piece of data. For example, if you have a robot that vacuums the

floor, such as a Roomba, it makes sense to be able to send commands to it to move in a particular direction. With an integer (or positive or natural), you could have 1 mean go forward, 2 turn left, 3 turn right, 4 rotate to the right, 5 rotate to the left, and 6 stop completely. This can be done, but this does not make code legible for others to read. Which numbers are supposed to mean what action can be confusing. With an enumerated type, this problem is easily resolved:

```
--enumerated_type.adb:

with Ada.Text_IO;

procedure Enumerated_Type is
  type Robot_Actions is (forward, turn_left, turn_right, rotate_left,
    rotate_right, stop);
  Vacuum_Bot : Robot_Actions := stop;

  procedure Process_Action(Machine_Action : in Robot_Actions) is
  begin
    if Machine_Action = forward then
      Ada.Text_IO.Put_Line("The robot is moving forward.");
    elsif Machine_Action = turn_left then
      Ada.Text_IO.Put_Line("The robot is turning left.");
    elsif Machine_Action = turn_right then
      Ada.Text_IO.Put_Line("The robot is turning right.");
    elsif Machine_Action = rotate_left then
      Ada.Text_IO.Put_Line("The robot is rotating to the left.");
    elsif Machine_Action = rotate_right then
      Ada.Text_IO.Put_Line("The robot is rotating to the right.");
    else
      Ada.Text_IO.Put_Line("The robot is stopped.");
    end if;
  end Process_Action;
begin
  Process_Action(Vacuum_Bot);
  Vacuum_Bot := forward;
  Process_Action(Vacuum_Bot);
  Vacuum_Bot := turn_left;
```

```
  Process_Action(Vacuum_Bot);
  Vacuum_Bot := rotate_right;
  Process_Action(Vacuum_Bot);
  Vacuum_Bot := forward;
  Process_Action(Vacuum_Bot);
  Vacuum_Bot := turn_right;
  Process_Action(Vacuum_Bot);
  Vacuum_Bot := forward;
  Process_Action(Vacuum_Bot);
  Vacuum_Bot := stop;
  Process_Action(Vacuum_Bot);
end Enumerated_Type;
```

   type Robot_Actions is (forward, turn_left, turn_right, ... – This creates
the specification of this type. Any value within the parentheses can be assigned to
an instance of this type. With an enumerated type, a developer can easily describe a
particular meaning without having to associate the same meaning with a number or
string. Enumerated types make some of this processing much easier and quicker, not to
mention less confusing.

   This is the resulting output of the application:

```
> .\enumerated_type.exe
The robot is stopped.
The robot is moving forward.
The robot is turning left.
The robot is rotating to the right.
The robot is moving forward.
The robot is turning right.
The robot is moving forward.
The robot is stopped.
```

Is It 0 or 1? 4 or 10?

Whenever you have two or more developers, each develops a unique way of thinking and
development style. One unfortunate side effect is when this group of people are working
on different parts of the same system and everyone has their own assumptions as to what

number should be used to represent a state, a piece of data, a control action, and so on. Often these assumptions are made and not communicated, because the developer either forgot or thought that this unique approach was the "logical" one.

When it comes time to integrate the various pieces, and hopefully this is done sooner than later, issues start popping up that no one expected. Using an enumerated type can easily reduce some of this confusion.

Enumerated types do not have a number value associated with them, which C and C++ do, but they just are. So, comparing 0 or 1 to the first enumerated value is absurd and the compiler will not accept this.

Limited Types

Limited types are types that cannot be compared to one another. Recall how a task cannot be compared to one that is exactly the same as the first value. One would think that if they are instantiated from the same task body, then this should work. However, if the issue is carefully analyzed, when would it ever make sense to compare two tasks? Yes, they are of the same type, but if they are compared what will this comparison be based on? Value of internal variables? How long each task was executing? Whether the two Ada tasks are executing at the same instance of the code? How would this information be tracked?

In such cases, it makes sense to restrict such comparisons when possible, hence the limited type. This can make sense when you do not want to give others the ability to compare a certain record type during times when a record is used to represent a resource that cannot be copied or does not make sense to compared, like a piece of physical hardware, like in this example:

```
-- limited_type.adb:

with Ada.Text_IO;

procedure Limited_Type is
  type New_Integer is limited record
    Tracking_Number : Integer := 0;
  end record;

  Val1 : New_Integer;
  Val2 : New_Integer;
```

```
begin
  if Val1 = Val2 then
    Ada.Text_IO.Put_Line("They're equal!");
  end if;
end Limited_Type;
```

The only new thing done is the placement of the keyword "limited" in the specification of the New_Integer record. If this code is compiled, you will see the following error, which is very descriptive of what the problem is:

```
> gnatmake -g limited_type.adb
gcc -c -I.\ -g -I- .\limited_type.adb
limited_type.adb:13:11: there is no applicable operator "=" for type
"New_Integer" defined at line 6
gnatmake: ".\limited_type.adb" compilation error
```

Right away, the compiler is telling you that the comparison is absurd and should not be made.

Subtypes

Up to now, we have been creating brand new types each time. However, we can use the existing types in order to derive subtypes as needed. This is helpful in these instances:

1) You want to limit the input that can be passed to an application from the command line.

2) A quick type is needed in a function or procedure for a specific task and nowhere else in the application.

3) When an existing type works well enough, but you need a detail changed.

Let's have a look at this example:

```
-- limited_integer.adb:

with Ada.Text_IO;

procedure Limited_Integer is
  subtype Menu_Selection_Value is Integer range 1 .. 6;
```

```
  package Menu_Input is new Ada.Text_IO.Integer_IO(
    Num => Menu_Selection_Value);
  Selected : Menu_Selection_Value := 1;
begin
  Main_Menu :
  loop
    Ada.Text_IO.Put_Line(" - Main Menu at Healthy Fast Food(tm) -");
    Ada.Text_IO.Put_Line(" - 1 - Order Apples");
    Ada.Text_IO.Put_Line(" - 2 - Order Pears");
    Ada.Text_IO.Put_Line(" - 3 - Order Asparagus");
    Ada.Text_IO.Put_Line(" - 4 - Order Cauliflower");
    Ada.Text_IO.Put_Line(" - 5 - Order Granola Bar");
    Ada.Text_IO.Put_Line(" - 6 - Quit");
    Ada.Text_IO.Put(" Your selection: ");

    Main_Menu_Input :
    declare
    begin
      Menu_Input.Get(Selected);
    exception
      when others =>
        Ada.Text_IO.New_Line;
        Ada.Text_IO.Put_Line("ERROR: Input incorrect, must be from 1 to 6.");
        Ada.Text_IO.New_Line(2);
    end Main_Menu_Input;

    case Selected is
      when 1 =>
        Ada.Text_IO.Put_Line("Your apples is ready!");
        Ada.Text_IO.New_Line;
      when 2 =>
        Ada.Text_IO.Put_Line("Your pears is ready!");
        Ada.Text_IO.New_Line;
      when 3 =>
        Ada.Text_IO.Put_Line("Your asparagus is ready!");
        Ada.Text_IO.New_Line;
```

```
      when 4 =>
        Ada.Text_IO.Put_Line("Your cauliflower is ready!");
        Ada.Text_IO.New_Line;
      when 5 =>
        Ada.Text_IO.Put_Line("Your granola bar is ready!");
        Ada.Text_IO.New_Line;
      when 6 =>
        exit Main_Menu;
      when others =>
        Ada.Text_IO.Put_Line("ERROR: Unknown type!");
        Ada.Text_IO.New_Line;
    end case;
  end loop Main_Menu;
end Limited_Integer;
```

Let's have a look at what this example does:

1) `subtype Menu_Selection_Value is Integer range 1 .. 6;` – Here you create a subtype that is derived from an Integer, a primitive type that is part of the Ada language. However, in this case, what is really needed is an upper and lower limit to how many options can be selected. In fact, you can easily make this upper limit a variable and create it dynamically. This will make it easier to update just this one variable and have the entire program dynamically reflect this.

2) `package Menu_Input is new Ada.Text_IO.Integer_IO(Num => Menu_Selection_Value);` – The Integer_IO package is a generic one, meaning that it needs to be instantiated with a specific type before it can be further used. In our case, we are using the subtype that we created, Menu_Selection_Value, to create a custom package that will only accept and process this type only.

3) `Selected : Menu_Selection_Value := 1;` – This is the subtype instantiated with a default value assigned to it.

4) `Menu_Input.Get(Selected);` – Within the block of code from line 21 to 30, this is the most important piece. Menu_Input is the derived Integer_IO package; it will wait for an input from the user. When the user inputs something, it will assign that value to the Selected variable and proceed further.

   a) But wait! What if the user puts in a value of 9, instead of 1 to 6? That is what lines 25–29 are for. When the value received is out of range, an exception will be thrown. This exception will be caught and an error message will be displayed. However, it will not cause the entire loop to stop executing and the application will continue.

5) Lines 32–53 have a switch case that executes code based on the user's selection.

You know how to do this for an integer, but the same lower and upper bound limits can be done for a string as well:

```
procedure Limited_String is
  subtype Menu_Selection_Value is String(1 .. 2);
  Value1 : Menu_Selection_Value := (others => ' ');
begin
  null;
end Limited_String;
```

The subtype Menu_Selection_Value will not store a string that has more than two characters in it. If you attempt to store a three-character string, an exception will be thrown. Furthermore, notice that when we initialize an instance of Menu_Selection_Value, we retain the right to use the "others" keyword, just like in a typical string, to set the entire string to a default character. Do not forget about this inherited functionality as you continue to create other subtypes.

Ada Types in Improving Development

As discussed in the previous section, custom types can be used to make your application less prone to encountering an error. You can do this like so:

1) Use enumerated types to mean a specific state or term. This makes it much clearer what it is that you intend to do. Your code becomes much more readable since the string "turn_on_fan" is clearer than "3".

2) Whenever processing any sort of input from the command line or reading information from a socket, use a type that has an upper and a lower limit. This approach prevents other users from putting your application into an undefined state. Furthermore, if you forget to write an if statement to check if this upper or lower limit applies, you do not have to worry since the language itself will catch this error.

   Many bizarre and obscure bugs popped up when some variable would be set to an unknown state and the program will not work as expected.

   In the worst circumstances, these unchecked inputs would generate real-world vulnerabilities that can cause damage. The following article describes when inputs are not checked as they should be:

   https://security.web.cern.ch/security/recommendations/en/codetools/c.shtml

   In this article, in each case, it is recommended that the programmer puts a limit as to how much data can be read. Without this, you could have a potential problem that will come up in an unexpected way or an opening for a hacker. Give only the minimum range that is needed to get the job done. Going above that is simply asking for trouble.

3) Represent your data accurately. Look up the preceding example with a custom float value. In most cases, you can easily get away with having just a float. But when dealing with very specific requirements, such as representing financial information or precise scientific computations, it makes sense having a specific type dedicated for this. Having $23.098202 does not make sense.

The beauty of this language is the fact that it can be easily tailored to represent the world around you. Your inputs could be varied and inconsistent. With some languages, this could be confusing or difficult to enforce. With Ada, one simply creates a new type that matches the outside world perfectly. This saves you time trying to write complex logic that is designed to enforce these rules or custom types that are difficult to work with.

With Ada, there is nothing that you cannot reproduce or simulate in software.

Converting Between Types

This is when things become tricky. There will be times when you need to convert one type into another. Without this, some functionality will be off limits to custom-made types (specific mathematical operations, converting custom strings into generic ones to write out to file, etc.). The act of converting from one type to another is called casting. Casting is part of the Ada programming language, and just as with types, there are certain rules that need to be followed:

1) Normally converting among like types is permitted (Integer to Positive to Natural to a custom derived Integer). But problems can arise when you are casting a variable of a similar type that has its value out of range of the type that it is being cast to. We will look into this in the upcoming example.

2) Converting from a custom string to a standard one, so that the results could be written to a file or manipulated in another manner.

3) Sometimes, a direct conversion is not recommended. As a result, an in-between function would work best. This will be explored in greater detail.

Ada.Unchecked_Conversion

You can also do unchecked conversions. This a copy of all the data – bit by bit – from the source to the destination, without any checks. Think about this for a moment…

If you ever feel that this is justified, it is almost always incorrect. You are taking data, copying it in place somewhere else entirely, doing so without the present Ada type conversions, and using the destination variable with the assumption that nothing went wrong. This is a fantastic recipe for vague and inconsistent bugs that crop up without you expecting them. In order to use unchecked conversions correctly, you would need first that the source is not in an incorrect state and then check (pun intended) that the destination is in a consistent state. Frankly, if you ever need to do this, a superior solution would be to create a custom copy function/procedure. At the very least, there will be complete control over the copying process, and any obvious mistakes will be easily and quickly caught.

In addition, if the input is not checked thoroughly, then it could open up a vulnerability for attackers. After all, an unchecked conversion faithfully copies the data from one location to another, without even making a single glance at what the data is.

One argument in favor of using unchecked conversions is that it will be faster than a function. Doing so might take up less computational resources, but will easily take up software developer resources should problems show up.

There are exceptions to this. Certain low-level system calls might require copying whole bits, but this is beyond the scope of this book. This function will not be covered in this book beyond a mention of it. For someone starting out in Ada, such a function will not add a single iota of value for learning how to write better software, but will add headaches when used improperly, which is easy to do so.

Let's have a look at how conversions for integers work:

```
-- casting_example.adb:

with Ada.Text_IO;

procedure Casting_Example is
   type Custom_Int is range -10 .. 10;
   Val1 : Custom_Int := 0;
   Val2 : Integer    := -9;
   Val3 : Positive   := 1;
   Val4 : Natural    := 0;
begin
   Val1 := Custom_Int(Val2);
   Ada.Text_IO.Put_Line("Val1 now: " & Custom_Int'Image(Val1));
   Val1 := 8;
```

```
Val3 := Positive(Val1);
Ada.Text_IO.Put_Line("Val3 now: " & Positive'Image(Val3));
Val4 := Positive(Val1);
Val4 := Natural(Val1);
Ada.Text_IO.Put_Line("Val4 now: " & Positive'Image(Val4));

-- how to cast when you do not know if the variable is in range.
Test_Block :
declare
begin
  Val1 := 0;

  Val3 := Positive(Val1);
  Ada.Text_IO.Put_Line("Val3 the second time: " & Positive'Image(Val3));
exception
  when Constraint_Error =>
    Ada.Text_IO.Put_Line("ERROR: A value is out of range!");
  when others =>
    Ada.Text_IO.Put_Line("ERROR: An another error was discovered.");
end Test_Block;

Ada.Text_IO.Put_Line("Val3 the second time: " & Positive'Image(Val3));
end Casting_Example;
```

Look through this example and try to trace the flow of logic. Notice how types are being converted – Type(InputVariable) – and think about the results that you should receive. Now let's have a closer look and see if your logic was sound:

1) `Val1 := Custom_Int(Val2);` – Val2 is a plain Integer and Val1 is our custom integer. In this case, it is a simple conversion to the custom one.

2) `Val1 := 8; Val3 := Positive(Val1);` – In this case, our custom integer is set to 8 so that it can be easily converted to a Positive type. Remember, Positive types range from 1 upward. If this is not done, then the compiler will throw a warning stating that when the application runs, a Constraint_Error will be thrown, similar to this:

```
> gnatmake -g casting_example.adb
gcc -c -I.\ -g -I- .\casting_example.adb
casting_example.adb:27:13: warning: value not in range of type
"Standard.Positive"
casting_example.adb:27:13: warning: "Constraint_Error" will be
raised at run time
gnatbind -x casting_example.ali
gnatlink casting_example.ali -g
```

The best way to handle this, if possible, is to never assign a value that is out of range.

3) `Val4 := Positive(Val1);` – This is odd. Val1 is the custom integer. However, Val4 is a Natural type and not a Positive. So why can you just cast Val1 to a different type and then assign it to a Natural?

    Well, for starters, Natural and Positive are both derived from the Integer type. And Val1 is well within the bound of Natural, which starts with 0 and goes upward. This means that you can assign among these three values to each other as you see fit, provided that they are all within their specified ranges.

4) From line 22 to 34, we have a declare block whose job will be to catch an exception that is thrown when an incorrect conversion happens. Val1 is still a Custom_Int, but on line 25, it is set to zero, something that it can handle easily. On line 27, the application attempts to convert a zero to a positive, a value that the Positive type cannot handle. As a result, the Constraint_Error is thrown and the following output is observed:

```
> ./casting_example.exe
Val1 now: -9
Val3 now:  8
Val4 now:  8
ERROR: A value is out of range!
Val3 the second time:  8
```

5) Lastly, pay attention to line 36. When this does the printing, you will see that Val3 is still 8. When that exception was thrown, the assignment did not occur and Val3 retained its original contents.

When it comes to dealing with custom string types, things are much simpler. In fact, no conversion is needed. It is possible to pass a custom string value directly into a function that is expecting a regular String type:

```
-- custom_string_cast.adb:

with Ada.Text_IO;
with Ada.Strings.Fixed;

procedure Custom_String_Cast is
  subtype Currency_String is String(1 .. 3);
  US_Dollar : Currency_String         := "USD";
  Euro : Currency_String              := "EUR";
  British_Pound : Currency_String     := "GPB";
  Japan_Yen : Currency_String         := "JPY";
  Australian_Dollar : Currency_String := "AUD";
  HongKong_Dollar : Currency_String   := "HKD";
  NewZealand_Dollar : Currency_String := "NZD";
  --Dumpling : Currency_String         := "DUMPL";
  Singapore_Dollar : String           := "SGD";
begin
  Ada.Text_IO.Put_Line("US Dollar country code:       " &
    Ada.Strings.Fixed.Head(US_Dollar, 2));
  Ada.Text_Io.Put_Line(" Length of Currency_String: " &
    Natural'Image(US_Dollar'Length));
  Ada.Text_IO.Put_Line("Euro country code:            " &
    Ada.Strings.Fixed.Head(Euro, 2));
  Ada.Text_IO.Put_Line("British Pound country code:   " &
    Ada.Strings.Fixed.Head(British_Pound, 2));
  Ada.Text_IO.Put_Line("Japanese Yen country code:    " &
    Ada.Strings.Fixed.Head(Japan_Yen, 2));
  Ada.Text_IO.Put_Line("Australian Dollar country code: " &
    Ada.Strings.Fixed.Head(Australian_Dollar, 2));
```

```
Ada.Text_IO.Put_Line("Hong Kong Dollar country code:    " &
    Ada.Strings.Fixed.Head(HongKong_Dollar, 2));
Ada.Text_IO.Put_Line("New Zealand Dollar country code: " &
    Ada.Strings.Fixed.Head(NewZealand_Dollar, 2));
Ada.Text_IO.Put_Line("Singapore Dollar country code:    " &
    Ada.Strings.Fixed.Head(Singapore_Dollar, 2));
end Custom_String_Cast;
```

1) From line 7 to 16, we can clearly see the new type being created and instantiated. The instantiation works exactly like a regular string, with the only exception that exactly three characters are allowed (no more and no less).

2) On line 15, we can see a new currency being added, the Dumpling. Since the length of the code is clearly incorrect, you will get the following compilation error should you compile the code (and have it uncommented as well!):

```
> gnatmake -g custom_string_cast.adb
gcc -c -I.\ -g -I- .\custom_string_cast.adb
custom_string_cast.adb:15:42: warning: wrong length for array of
type "Currency_String" defined at line 7
custom_string_cast.adb:15:42: warning: "Constraint_Error" will be
raised at run time
gnatbind -x custom_string_cast.ali
gnatlink custom_string_cast.ali -g
```

The code will compile, and if you try to run it, a Constraint_Error exception will be thrown and the application will stop. So let's not do that.

3) `Ada.Strings.Fixed.Head(US_Dollar, 2)` – Using a standard function that is found in the strings fixed package, we can easily extract the country code portion of the currency. In this case, the US_Dollar variable is a Currency_String, and yet it can be interchangeably used in place of a String.

4) US_Dollar'Length – If that was not enough proof that Currency_ String is a full-fledged string, this type sports the same attributes as a regular string.

There you have it. One can easily create a custom string type while retaining the same comforts of a regular string. The most important of which is that these custom string types are easily plugged into a function that just as well expects the same primitive String type.

Now, let's look at how you could work effectively with custom float types.

An application needs to crunch some weather data. The existing function Display_ Temp represents some legacy code from a previous project that you know works well by outputting the warmth in a location exactly how you need it. However, there is also a piece of hardware that has a different input range from that of a regular float. Let's see how this comes together:

```
-- custom_float_cast.adb:

with Ada.Float_Text_IO;
with Ada.Text_IO;

procedure Custom_Float_Cast is
  type Earth_Temp_C is delta 0.001 range -50.0 .. 100.0;
  New_York_Temp_C : Earth_Temp_C  := 20.23;
  Sahara_Temp_C : Earth_Temp_C   := 35.291;
  Reykjavik_Temp_C : Earth_Temp_C := 9.002;

  procedure Display_Temp(Temp : in Float) is
  begin
    Ada.Text_IO.Put("The temperature is : ");
    Ada.Float_Text_IO.Put(Temp, Fore => 2, Aft => 1, Exp => 0);
    Ada.Text_IO.New_Line;
  end Display_Temp;
begin
  Display_Temp(Float(New_York_Temp_C));
  Display_Temp(Float(Sahara_Temp_C));
  Display_Temp(Float(Reykjavik_Temp_C));
end Custom_Float_Cast;
```

1. `type Earth_Temp_C is delta 0.001 range -50.0 .. 100.0; –`
   This code is nothing new. You have seen it already. Earth_Temp_C is used to represent the temperature that is received from a piece of hardware outside of the computer that this application is running.

2. `procedure Display_Temp(Temp : in Float) is` – This is the function that you would like to keep since it does things how you want them to be done. After all, why fix something if it is already working?

   In reality, Display_Temp would be a much more complex piece of code and have more lines than just three. For this example, it will do just fine.

3. `Display_Temp(Float(New_York_Temp_C));` – This is very straightforward. Float takes the input of an Earth_Temp_C type, converts it to a Float value, and then passes it along to the Display_Temp procedure. Since Float can be much more exact than Earth_Temp_C, the conversion goes through without any loss of data.

Custom Floats

A custom float value, such as in the procedure Custom_Float_Cast, just like its Integer cousins, comes with all of the Attributes as a standard Float value. You can easily make use of this to create logic that takes advantage of the new type just as easily as the primitive type.

Now that we have all of these things covered, let's look into how easy it is to turn integers and floats into strings and vice versa. The language itself has functionality that lets us do this:

```
-- string_int_float.adb:

with Ada.Integer_Text_IO;
with Ada.Float_Text_IO;
with Ada.Text_IO;
```

```
procedure String_Int_Float is
  Sample_Int : Integer := 803;
  Sample_Float : Float := 1.23;

  String_Integer : String := "8915";
  String_Float : String   := "100.0";
  Output3 : Integer := 0;
  Output4 : Float    := 0.0;
begin
  Ada.Text_IO.Put_Line("The converted integer: " &
    Integer'Image(Sample_Int));
  Ada.Text_IO.Put_Line("The converted float:   " &
    Float'Image(Sample_Float));

  -- string to float and integer.
  Output3 := Integer'Value(String_Integer);
  Ada.Text_IO.Put("Output3: ");
  Ada.Integer_Text_IO.Put(Output3);
  Ada.Text_IO.New_Line;
  Output4 := Float'Value(String_Float);
  Ada.Text_IO.Put("Output4: ");
  Ada.Float_Text_IO.Put(Output4, 3, 1, 0);
  Ada.Text_IO.New_Line;
end String_Int_Float;
```

1) Integer'Image(Sample_Int) – This is not new. You take an integer as the input and then proceed to turn it into a string.

2) Output3 := Integer'Value(String_Integer); – Here the variable String_Integer is consumed, and it is attempted to be converted to an integer.

   However, this can be a dangerous operation. What if the contents of the string are not correct? If that is the case, then it makes much more sense to put this operation inside of a declare block and catch any resulting exceptions that are thrown. Without this, if any error is encountered, your application will simply stop executing.

3) `Ada.Float_Text_IO.Put(Output4, 3, 1, 0);` – A put function in this case will limit the output of the float value; this is done so that the float is displayed in non-scientific notation.

At this point, you should have a good grip on the topic of types in Ada. This system is wonderful for getting an easy improvement in reliability in your code. However, there is still much to learn. The goal here was to make you more comfortable with the basics. You are encouraged to explore and learn more about Ada types from the *Ada Reference Manual* and other resources.

Lab

Have a look at the lab in Chapter 5. In that problem you were supposed to create a structure that described a company of ten employees. For things such as age, you used an integer or subtypes. Go through that structure and replace all of the values with a custom type, with the exception of the title and first and last names.

Hint   When trying to create a random type that is based on an integer, review the hint at the end of the lab in Chapter 5.

When making a custom float value type, have a look at the following example:

```
type Custom_Floatie is delta 0.1 range 0.0 .. 100.0;

...

  Seed : Ada.Numerics.Float_Random.Generator;
  Temp : Float := 0.0;
begin
  Ada.Numerics.Float_Random.Reset(Seed);

  Temp := Float(Custom_Floatie'First) +
    (Ada.Numerics.Float_Random.Random(Seed) * Float(Custom_Floatie'Last));
  return Custom_Floatie(Temp);
```

This entire example you have already seen before, the exception being the last two lines:

1) ```
Temp := Float(Custom_Floatie'First) + (Ada.Numerics.
Float_Random.Random(Seed) * Float(Custom_Floatie'Last));
```

   Here you are grabbing the first value of the custom float and then proceed to cast it to an actual float, and the same goes for the last attribute. The reason for this is because Float_Random. Random(Seed) always generates a value of type Float, so this is something that you are required to work with.

2) `return Custom_Floatie(Temp);` – Since a Custom_Floatie type is required, you cast the result of the previous operation to this type.
```

CHAPTER 13

Advanced OOP

What You Will Get Out of This Chapter

This chapter will expand on the topic of object-oriented programming. There are several key concepts that really need more scrutiny if you want to become a competent Ada software developer. With the topics described here, you will be better equipped to package up your code in a logical and sane manner. Furthermore, you will be able to add unique tools to the use of your packages that did not exist before:

1) Inheritance will enable you to create more general packages that then can be extended to suit your needs. Imagine there is an accounting package. When you need to keep track of items in a warehouse, you just create a new package and inherit most of the functionality from the accounting package (customizing what you need). Then, if you want to create a payroll system, the very same accounting package can be easily reused.

2) The topic of polymorphism was covered before, but no advanced OOP topic is complete without at least touching this issue. We will talk about when it makes sense to use this and how.

3) Believe it or not, you can add objects together (or subtract or multiply or divide) as you wish. Yes, this is what you normally do with integers and floats. However, the very same operators can be adapted to manipulating instances of packages. This will be discussed.

4) In the previous chapter, generic packages were used to create a random value from a numeric type. But it needs to be mentioned how these types are actually implemented and when they are useful.

© Andrew T. Shvets 2020
A. T. Shvets, *Beginning Ada Programming*, https://doi.org/10.1007/978-1-4842-5428-8_13

Inheritance

Inheritance is a very useful tool. Used correctly, it can easily reduce the amount of code that you need to create and permit you to reuse existing (which has been proven to work) software as needed. It really is an amazing technique.

Let's have a look how to inherit from one package into another:

```
-- air_vehicle.ads:

package Air_Vehicle is
  type Air_Machine is tagged private;

  procedure Print_Description(
    AM : in Air_Machine);
private
  type Air_Machine is tagged record
    Height : Natural;                   -- meters
    Length : Natural;                   -- meters
    Width : Natural;                    -- meters
    Mass : Natural;                     -- kilograms
    Max_Operating_Height : Natural;     -- meters
    Max_Speed : Float;                  -- kilometers per hour
  end record;
end Air_Vehicle;

-- air_vehicle.adb:

with Ada.Text_IO;

package body Air_Vehicle is
  procedure Print_Description(
    AM : in Air_Machine) is
  begin
    Ada.Text_IO.Put_Line(Ada.Text_IO.Standard_Error,
      "ERROR: You should not be seeing this output!");
  end Print_Description;
end Air_Vehicle;

-- air_vehicle-hotair_balloon.ads:
```

```ada
with Ada.Float_Text_IO;
with Ada.Text_IO;

package Air_Vehicle.Hotair_Balloon is
  type HA_Balloon is new Air_Machine with private;

  function Init_Balloon(
    B_Height : in Natural;
    B_Length : in Natural;
    B_Width : in Natural;
    B_Mass : in Natural;
    B_Max_Operating_Height : in Natural;
    B_Max_Speed : in Float;
    B_Balloon_Volume_M3 : in Positive;
    B_Propane_Volume : in Float)
      return HA_Balloon;

  procedure Print_Description(
    HAB : in HA_Balloon);
private
  type HA_Balloon is new Air_Machine with record
    Balloon_Volume_M3 : Positive; -- cubic meters
    Propane_Volume : Float;       -- liters
  end record;
end Air_Vehicle.Hotair_Balloon;

-- air_vehicle-hotair_balloon.adb:

package body Air_Vehicle.Hotair_Balloon is
  function Init_Balloon(
    B_Height : in Natural;
    B_Length : in Natural;
    B_Width : in Natural;
    B_Mass : in Natural;
    B_Max_Operating_Height : in Natural;
    B_Max_Speed : in Float;
    B_Balloon_Volume_M3 : in Positive;
```

```
  B_Propane_Volume : in Float)
    return HA_Balloon is

  HAB : HA_Balloon;
begin
  HAB.Height := B_Height;
  HAB.Length := B_Length;
  HAB.Width := B_Width;
  HAB.Mass := B_Mass;
  HAB.Max_Operating_Height := B_Max_Operating_Height;
  HAB.Max_Speed := B_Max_Speed;
  HAB.Balloon_Volume_M3 := B_Balloon_Volume_M3;
  HAB.Propane_Volume := B_Propane_Volume;

  return HAB;
end Init_Balloon;

procedure Print_Description(
  HAB : in HA_Balloon) is
begin
  Ada.Text_IO.Put_Line("Height of vehicle:            " &
    Natural'Image(HAB.Height));
  Ada.Text_IO.Put_Line("Length of vehicle:            " &
    Natural'Image(HAB.Length));
  Ada.Text_IO.Put_Line("Width of vehicle:             " &
    Natural'Image(HAB.Width));
  Ada.Text_IO.Put_Line("Mass of vehicle:              " &
    Natural'Image(HAB.Mass));
  Ada.Text_IO.Put_Line("Max operating height of vehicle: " &
    Natural'Image(HAB.Max_Operating_Height));
  Ada.Text_IO.Put("Max speed of vehicle:            ");
  Ada.Float_Text_IO.Put(HAB.Max_Speed, Aft => 2, Exp => 0);
  Ada.Text_IO.New_Line;
  Ada.Text_IO.Put_Line("Balloon volume of vehicle:      " &
    Positive'Image(HAB.Balloon_Volume_M3));
```

```
    Ada.Text_IO.Put("Propane volume of vehicle:       ");
    Ada.Float_Text_IO.Put(HAB.Propane_Volume, Aft => 2, Exp => 0);
    Ada.Text_IO.New_Line;
  end Print_Description;
end Air_Vehicle.Hotair_Balloon;

-- main.adb:

with Air_Vehicle.Hotair_Balloon;

procedure Main is
  Large_Hotair_Balloon : Air_Vehicle.Hotair_Balloon.HA_Balloon;
begin
  Large_Hotair_Balloon := Air_Vehicle.Hotair_Balloon.Init_Balloon(
    50, 20, 20, 2000, 10000, 5.5, 300, 1.2);
  Air_Vehicle.Hotair_Balloon.Print_Description(Large_Hotair_Balloon);
end Main;
```

1) Let's begin with the Air_Vehicle package (in files air_vehicle.ads and air_vehicle.adb):

   a) In here you define the basic record that will be used in all derived packages. This record can be added later on as requirements evolve.

   b) You can also define functions and procedures that can be executed in child packages. For example, a procedure called Sum can be used to calculate the sum of several accounts.

   In our case, Print_Description does not do anything productive other than print out an error message saying no one should be using it. Its purpose here is to illustrate how you can re-define it in a child package and re-write its body. Make a mental note that the record type is called Air_Machine; this will change later.

   c) Keep note of the "tagged" keyword that is used in the record. It is necessary in order to be able to derive new records from this one in subsequent child packages.

2) Moving on to the package Air_Vehicle.Hotair_Balloon (in files air_vehicle-hotair_balloon.ads and air_vehicle-hotair_balloon.adb), this is where things get interesting:

a) First, let's begin with the name of the package. Hotair_Balloon is the child package of the Air_Vehicle package. As a result, in the derived one, you see Air_Vehicle.Hotair_Balloon. Notice the period between the two names. In Ada, this is how inheritance is explicitly specified.

b) Second, the name of the file itself is important. Notice how it is air_vehicle-hotair_balloon.ads (or adb). The "-" sign is used in place of the period. This is just as important. If you were to exclude this, then the compiler would throw an error that the name of the package does not match the name of the file where it is contained.

c) `type HA_Balloon is new Air_Machine with private; -` This is where the new record is created from the one that is in the parent record. Without the bold portion, the compiler will assume that this is merely a new record entirely and completely unrelated with one in the parent package.

`type HA_Balloon is new Air_Machine with record –` Something similar is done when it comes to fleshing out the details of the record. The Air_Machine record is included, along with the new items, and both make up the HA_Balloon record.

The type HA_Balloon is now the type that can be used throughout the entire Air_Vehicle.Hotair_Balloon package (as is done by the Init_Balloon function and Print_Description procedure).

d) Have a look at Init_Balloon in the body of the package. Notice how you just define the package HAB : HA_Balloon; and immediately begin to assign values to it. And HA_Balloon is one record that is a fluid combination of the Air_Machine record and two new values as defined in the child package.

3) Lastly, the Main procedure (in main.adb) is fairly straightforward:

   a) Notice how only the package Air_Vehicle.Hotair_Balloon is imported into this file. When you import it, the Air_Vehicle package is included as well.

   b) `Large_Hotair_Balloon : Air_Vehicle.Hotair_Balloon.` `HA_Balloon;` – The record that was re-defined inside of Hotair_Balloon is referenced. This will serve as our instance of this package (as opposed to Air_Machine inside of the Air_Vehicle package).

   c) Then it is a matter of calling the function Init_Balloon and procedure Print_Description, which are defined in the Air_Vehicle.Hotair_Balloon package.

The way that you would compile this source is by compiling the main.adb file first and let the compiler pull in the rest of the packages (the base one and the one that is created by inheritance). Your output should look similar to this:

```
> gnatmake -g main.adb
gcc -c -I.\ -g -I- .\main.adb
gcc -c -I.\ -g -I- .\air_vehicle.adb
gcc -c -I.\ -g -I- .\air_vehicle-hotair_balloon.adb
gnatbind -x main.ali
gnatlink main.ali -g
```

If inheritance proves to be a complex concept at first, do not be concerned about it. Not knowing this idea inside out will not hamper your software development efforts until you enter the realm of very complex applications.

For the Times That Inheritance Is a Poor Approach

It is difficult to describe inheritance as a bad idea. After all, it will reduce the amount of code that needs to be written and the number errors that are encountered will also fall. What is not to like?

One problem with this is it needs to be used sparingly and in a targeted manner. Incorrectly designed inherited packages will create a maze of code that is difficult to read and comprehend. The goal ought to make your project easier to decipher, not to appear as if you are a know-it-all. After all, sometime in the future (when you have forgotten about this project), you will need to make new features or fix bugs. Since you wrote the original code (and by now do not remember anything), you will be the perfect candidate to make this change!

Or, have someone else make the same updates... and end up with that person abusing your good name for making such a difficult to comprehend application. If your goal is to ruin your professional reputation, then this is a highly recommended approach.

Polymorphism

This has been discussed already. However, it does merit a closer look. One of the key concepts in polymorphism is being able to use the same name for a procedure or a function while differentiating the types of inputs or the number of inputs:

```
procedure Print_To_Serial_Link(
  Telemetry_Value : in Integer);
procedure Print_To_Serial_Link(
  Telemetry_Value : in Natural);
procedure Print_To_Serial_Link(
  Telemetry_Value : in Positive);
procedure Print_To_Serial_Link(
  Telemetry_Value : in Character);
procedure Print_To_Serial_Link(
  Telemetry_Value : in String);
procedure Print_To_Serial_Link(
  Telemetry_Value : in Integer;
  Offset          : in Positive);
procedure Print_To_Serial_Link(
  Telemetry_Value : in Natural;
  Offset          : in Positive);
```

```ada
procedure Print_To_Serial_Link(
  Telemetry_Value : in Positive;
  Offset          : in Positive);
procedure Print_To_Serial_Link(
  Telemetry_Value : in Character;
  Offset          : in Positive);
procedure Print_To_Serial_Link(
  Telemetry_Value : in String;
  Offset          : in Positive);
```

This is pretty much the gist of polymorphism in Ada. The type can be a record, a custom type, or a subtype. It extends to determining which function to call based on the return value of the function. Let's have a look:

```ada
-- return_polymorphism.adb:

with Ada.Text_IO;

procedure Return_Polymorphism is
  function Return_Value
    return Integer is
  begin
    return 5;
  end Return_Value;

  function Return_Value
    return Float is
  begin
    return 21.9;
  end Return_Value;

  Int_Val : Integer := 0;
  Flo_Val : Float := 0.0;
begin
  Int_Val := Return_Value;
  Flo_Val := Return_Value;
```

```
  Ada.Text_IO.Put_Line("Integer: " & Integer'Image(Int_Val));
  Ada.Text_IO.Put_Line("Float:   " & Float'Image(Flo_Val));
end Return_Polymorphism;
```

Notice how the name of the function is exactly the same in both instances. The only difference is the return value. When an integer is needed, then the correct function is called. And in this case, we see that the correct function was selected for the job. This is the output of this app:

```
Integer:  5
Float:    2.19000E+01
```

If the value that was being assigned to was a string, but no Return_Value that returns a string existed, then you would get a compilation error.

Polymorphism in Different Programming Languages

When it comes to C/C++ (and many of the languages that use similar syntax), being able to determine which function to use based on the return value is not possible. Those languages are structured such that if a similar condition is encountered, you will be greeted with a compilation error.

The strict typing system in Ada enables you to pull this off.

Operator/Function Overloading

How would you like to know how to add, subtract, multiply, and so on record instances that are generated by packages? Up until now, if you tried this with a simple record, you would get all sorts of compilation errors. This makes sense. However, if you define a way to do this, then it is feasible.

This is a package that adds and subtracts time:

```
-- time.ads:

with Ada.Text_IO;

package Time is
  type Time_Rec is private;

  procedure Put(
    TR : in Time_Rec);
```

```ada
procedure Put_Line(
  TR : in Time_Rec);

function "+"(
  Val1 : in Time_Rec;
  Val2 : in Time_Rec)
    return Time_Rec;

function "+"(
  Val_Minutes : in Natural;
  Val2 : in Time_Rec)
    return Time_Rec;

function "+"(
  Val1 : in Time_Rec;
  Val_Minutes : in Natural)
    return Time_Rec;

function "-"(
  Val1 : in Time_Rec;
  Val2 : in Time_Rec)
    return Time_Rec;

function "-"(
  Val_Minutes : in Natural;
  Val2 : in Time_Rec)
    return Time_Rec;

function "-"(
  Val1 : in Time_Rec;
  Val_Minutes : in Natural)
    return Time_Rec;

function "="(
  Val1 : in Time_Rec;
  Val2 : in Time_Rec)
    return Boolean;
```

```
private
  type Time_Rec is record
    Hours : Natural    := 0;
    Minutes : Natural := 0;
  end record;

  function Get_Minutes(
    Val : in Time_Rec)
      return Natural;
end Time;
```

This package starts out as a plain declaration. However, let's look closer at the following features:

1) "+" functions. These are not ordinary functions. They are quite unique. Here you are saying that an operator, in this context, is converted into being a function. The same goes for "-" functions.

2) Pay attention to this function:

```
function "+"(
  Val1 : in Natural;
  Val2 : in Time_Rec)
    return Time_Rec;
```

Here you are defining just how the addition operator will be used. You can add just about anything to your record. Two instances of the same record can be added together, with the sum being a combination of the two times. Or a completely different type can be added as well.

In this example, a Natural is being added, but there is no reason to think that a Positive or a Float or an Integer or a String can be summed up... provided you create a way for the addition to happen. You can even add a completely different object, but the addition function needs to create a way to process it.

3) The function Get_Minutes simply takes in a time record and
    returns the total minutes inside (the hours are multiplied by 60
    and the minutes are added for the result). This makes things
    easier in case you want to do basic arithmetic to the record and
    figure out if a certain time is greater or less than another.

```ada
-- time.adb:

package body Time is
  procedure Put(
    TR : in Time_Rec) is

  begin
    Ada.Text_IO.Put("Hours: " & Natural'Image(TR.Hours) & " Minutes: " &
      Natural'Image(TR.Minutes));
  end Put;

  procedure Put_Line(
    TR : in Time_Rec) is
  begin
    Put(TR);
    Ada.Text_IO.New_Line;
  end Put_Line;

  function "+"(
    Val1 : in Time_Rec;
    Val2 : in Time_Rec)
      return Time_Rec is

    Temp : Time_Rec;
    Total_Minutes : Natural := 0;
  begin
    Total_Minutes := Get_Minutes(Val1) + Get_Minutes(Val2);

    Temp.Hours := Total_Minutes / 60;
    Temp.Minutes := Total_Minutes rem 60;

    return Temp;
  end "+";
```

```
function "+"(
  Val_Minutes : in Natural;
  Val2 : in Time_Rec)
    return Time_Rec is

  Temp : Time_Rec;
begin
  Temp.Hours := Val2.Hours + ((Val2.Minutes + Val_Minutes) / 60);
  Temp.Minutes := (Val2.Minutes + Val_Minutes) rem 60;

  return Temp;
end "+";

function "+"(
  Val1 : in Time_Rec;
  Val_Minutes : in Natural)
    return Time_Rec is

begin
  return Val_Minutes + Val1;
end "+";

function "-"(
  Val1 : in Time_Rec;
  Val2 : in Time_Rec)
    return Time_Rec is

  Temp : Time_Rec := Val1;
  Result : Natural := 0;
begin
  if Get_Minutes(Val1) > Get_Minutes(Val2) then
    Result := Get_Minutes(Val1) - Get_Minutes(Val2);

    Temp.Hours := Result / 60;
    Temp.Minutes := Result rem 60;
  else
    Ada.Text_IO.Put_Line(Ada.Text_IO.Standard_Error,
      "ERROR: The number of minutes is not enough!");
  end if;
```

```ada
    return Temp;
end "-";

function "-"(
  Val_Minutes : in Natural;
  Val2 : in Time_Rec)
    return Time_Rec is

  Temp : Time_Rec := Val2;
  Result : Natural := 0;
begin
  if Val_Minutes > Get_Minutes(Val2) then
    Result := Val_Minutes - Get_Minutes(Val2);

    Temp.Hours := Result / 60;
    Temp.Minutes := Result rem 60;
  else
    Ada.Text_IO.Put_Line(Ada.Text_IO.Standard_Error,
      "ERROR: The number of minutes is not enough!");
  end if;

  return Temp;
end "-";

function "-"(
  Val1 : in Time_Rec;
  Val_Minutes : in Natural)
    return Time_Rec is

  Temp : Time_Rec := Val1;
  Result : Natural := 0;
begin
  if Get_Minutes(Val1) > Val_Minutes then
    Result := Get_Minutes(Val1) - Val_Minutes;

    Temp.Hours := Result / 60;
    Temp.Minutes := Result rem 60;
```

```
    else
      Ada.Text_IO.Put_Line(Ada.Text_IO.Standard_Error,
        "ERROR: The number of minutes is not enough!");
    end if;

    return Temp;
  end "-";

  function "="(
    Val1 : in Time_Rec;
    Val2 : in Time_Rec)
      return Boolean is

  begin
    if Get_Minutes(Val1) = Get_Minutes(Val2) then
      return True;
    else
      return False;
    end if;
  end "=";

  function Get_Minutes(
    Val : in Time_Rec)
      return Natural is
  begin
    return Val.Hours * 60 + Val.Minutes;
  end Get_Minutes;
end Time;
```

The Time body is where the actual magic is implemented:

1) The Put and Put_Line procedures are there so that we can see what the values inside of the record are.

2)
```
   function "+"(
     Val_Minutes : in Natural;
     Val2 : in Time_Rec)
```

`return Time_Rec is` – This is an interesting example. In this function, we specify that the inputs are a Natural type and a Time_Rec record. "+" will need to create a way to specify how to add a natural to a Time_Rec record, and this is how it does it:

a) `Temp.Hours := Val2.Hours + ((Val2.Minutes + Val_Minutes) / 60);` – Here we are taking the current minutes that exist in the record, adding them to the natural, and see if we can get a whole hour from this (the operator "/" will return zero if the sum does not add up to 60 or greater). Then, the result of this is added to the hours.

b) `Temp.Minutes := (Val2.Minutes + Val_Minutes) rem 60;` – In this example, the minutes are added up and the remainder of the sum is now the total minutes that we have to work with.

c) And as a last step, the result is returned.

3) `function "+"(`
   `Val1 : in Time_Rec;`
   `Val2 : in Natural)`

`return Time_Rec is` – In this function declaration, since adding two values – irrespective of the order will yield the same result – we can reuse the function that was declared before it.

4) `function "-"(`
   `Val1 : in Time_Rec;`
   `Val2 : in Time_Rec)`

`return Time_Rec is` – In a subtraction, there is a need for more elaborate logic. There needs to be a check to ensure that the amount of time in the first value is not less than the amount in the second value (this check is accomplished by the Get_Minutes function). Otherwise, the operation will not work (the minutes and hours are Natural types, which cannot be less than zero, because –5 minutes does not make any sense).

a) `Result := Get_Minutes(Val1) - Get_Minutes(Val2);` – When it is established that the operation can and should go through, this very subtraction is performed and the value is stored in a temporary variable.

If the math does not line up, then an error message is printed out after the else statement.

b) `Temp.Hours := Result / 60;`
`Temp.Minutes := Result rem 60;` – Lastly, the temporary time record is updated with the result of the operation and it is returned to the caller of the operation.

c) `Temp : Time_Rec := Val1;` – This bears mentioning at least once. The Temp variable immediately has the value of the record that is to the left of the minus operation. The reason for this, if the left value's – the minuend – time is less than the right one's, the subtrahend, then an error printed out and the original value is returned to the top.

If this value was not initialized like so and this error condition was triggered, then the value assigned – which is a result of this subtraction – will have zero hours and minutes (which is what a Time_Rec instance has by default). This would hardly be an ideal operation and illogical.

5) `function "="(`
   `Val1 : in Time_Rec;`
   `Val2 : in Time_Rec)`

`return Boolean is` – This operation is perhaps the easiest. All that you do is take the two records, get their minutes, and see if they are equal to each other. There is no reason why you cannot do the same for comparing a time record to that of a Natural using the same approach.

The following example is a more verbose version of how to use operators:

```
-- time_main.adb:

with Time;
--use Time;

procedure Time_Main is
  Current_Time : Time.Time_Rec;
begin
  Time.Put_Line(Current_Time);

  Current_Time := Time."+"(24, Current_Time);

  Time.Put_Line(Current_Time);

  Current_Time := Time."+"(Current_Time, 293);

  Time.Put_Line(Current_Time);
end Time_Main;
```

Pay attention that the statement just under "with Time;" is commented out. This is on purpose, in order to show you have to call these special functions when you do not import the package using "with":

1) `Time.Put_Line(Current_Time);` – This should be very familiar to you. Using the contents of the package Time, call the function Put_Line.

2) `Current_Time := Time."+"(24, Current_Time);` – Since the Time package did not have the keyword "use" in front of it, its functions, some of them are operators, need to be named explicitly. As a result, you have the preceding code.

However, this example is one that is more concise:

```
-- time_main.adb:

with Time;
use Time;
```

```
procedure Time_Main is
  Current_Time : Time.Time_Rec;
begin
  Put_Line(Current_Time);

  Current_Time := Current_Time + Natural(24);

  Put_Line(Current_Time);

  Current_Time := Current_Time + 293;

  Put_Line(Current_Time);
end Time_Main;
```

In this snippet of code, the entire Time package is included inside of the Time_Main procedure. This permits us to use the functions and procedures in this package more liberally. When adding Time_Rec records to Naturals, the summation can be done by simply adding them and there is no need to reference the Time package. In this case, the code does appear less wordy.

And this is the output of the preceding code:

```
> .\time_main.exe
Hours:  0 Minutes:  0
Hours:  0 Minutes:  24
Hours:  5 Minutes:  17
```

To Use "Use" or Not?

Should you utilize the "use" keyword on some packages and call their methods without having to reference the name of the package? It really depends on your taste.

When you call the packages by name, this makes your code more verbose and removes any sort of ambiguity as to whether a function is from a specific location or not. This can help the readability of your code. However, as in the preceding example, specifying the package for the overloaded operator will make the code somewhat more confusing to read (especially for programmers new to Ada and your application).

When the "use" keyword is invoked, this makes your code more concise. It can improve readability should you have procedures and functions that are difficult to confuse with the standard library ones. And simply adding records to primitive types can make your code easier to read. But in some instances, when your method names are not distinct enough, this can add ambiguity and reduce the readability of your code.

This book errs on the side of not bothering with the "use" keyword since usually without it, the application code can be more vague. However, you will have to decide what is best for you and your project.

Generic Packages

Generic packages are interesting. Should you want to instantiate one, a type will need to be provided for it to indicate what it should be. For example, remember the random number generator for a custom integer that is the lab of Chapter 5? You created first a package (which started out as a generic) that is supposed to generate a random value based on the integer at hand. Then, you created the instance of that type which could now be used to spit out random numbers within a specific range. In Chapter 10, you also created a custom type of a list or vector based on the type of item that it was supposed to store.

In C++ this is called a Template. Let's have a look at how to go about making one:

```
-- gener.ads:

generic
  type Custom_Integer_Type is (<>);
  type Custom_Float_Type is digits <>;
package Gener is
  procedure Swap(
    Val1 : in out Custom_Integer_Type;
    Val2 : in out Custom_Integer_Type);

  function Min(
    Val1 : in Custom_Integer_Type;
    Val2 : in Custom_Integer_Type)
      return Custom_Integer_Type;
```

```
function Max(
  Val1 : in Custom_Integer_Type;
  Val2 : in Custom_Integer_Type)
    return Custom_Integer_Type;

procedure Swap(
  Val1 : in out Custom_Float_Type;
  Val2 : in out Custom_Float_Type);

function Min(
  Val1 : in Custom_Float_Type;
  Val2 : in Custom_Float_Type)
    return Custom_Float_Type;

function Max(
  Val1 : in Custom_Float_Type;
  Val2 : in Custom_Float_Type)
    return Custom_Float_Type;
end Gener;
```

The vast majority of this package is fairly normal. The one exception is the first three lines:

1) generic – Right away, we are letting the compiler know that the one trying to instantiate this package will need to first derive the type before using it. Right after this keyword, the generic types will need to be specified.

2) type Custom_Integer_Type is (<>);
   type Custom_Float_Type is digits <>; – This specifies that the user needs to pass in two types – one an integer-like type and the other a float-like type – in order to create a viable instance of this package. For example, putting a string where an integer-like type is expected will cause your code to not compile.

3) The rest of the package is a series of functions and procedures that make use of these two types. You should have no problem understanding what these methods are supposed to do.

```
-- gener.adb:

package body Gener is
  procedure Swap(
    Val1 : in out Custom_Integer_Type;
    Val2 : in out Custom_Integer_Type) is

    Temp : Custom_Integer_Type;
  begin
    Temp := Val2;
    Val2 := Val1;
    Val1 := Temp;
  end Swap;

  function Min(
    Val1 : in Custom_Integer_Type;
    Val2 : in Custom_Integer_Type)
      return Custom_Integer_Type is
  begin
    if Val1 < Val2 then
      return Val1;
    else
      return Val2;
    end if;
  end Min;

  function Max(
    Val1 : in Custom_Integer_Type;
    Val2 : in Custom_Integer_Type)
      return Custom_Integer_Type is
  begin
    if Val1 > Val2 then
      return Val1;
    else
      return Val2;
    end if;
  end Max;
```

```
procedure Swap(
  Val1 : in out Custom_Float_Type;
  Val2 : in out Custom_Float_Type) is

  Temp : Custom_Float_Type;
begin
  Temp := Val2;
  Val2 := Val1;
  Val1 := Temp;
end Swap;

function Min(
  Val1 : in Custom_Float_Type;
  Val2 : in Custom_Float_Type)
    return Custom_Float_Type is

begin
  if Val1 < Val2 then
    return Val1;
  else
    return Val2;
  end if;
end Min;

function Max(
  Val1 : in Custom_Float_Type;
  Val2 : in Custom_Float_Type)
    return Custom_Float_Type is

begin
  if Val1 > Val2 then
    return Val1;
  else
    return Val2;
  end if;
end Max;
end Gener;
```

The body of this procedure is exactly the same as you have seen before. None of the preceding code should be a surprise to you.

```ada
-- generic_main.adb:

with Ada.Text_IO;

with Gener;

procedure Generic_Main is
   type Some_Int is range 0 .. 5000;
   type Some_Float is new Float range -5.0 .. 125.0;
   package Generic_Package_Test is new Gener(Some_Int, Some_Float);

   procedure Put_Line_Int(
     Val1 : in Some_Int;
     Val2 : in Some_Int) is

   begin
     Ada.Text_IO.Put_Line("Val1: " & Some_Int'Image(Val1) &
       " Val2: " & Some_Int'Image(Val2));
   end Put_Line_Int;

   procedure Put_Line_Int(
     Val : in Some_Int) is

   begin
     Ada.Text_IO.Put_Line("Val: " & Some_Int'Image(Val));
   end Put_Line_Int;

   procedure Put_Line_Flo(
     Val1 : in Some_Float;
     Val2 : in Some_Float) is

   begin
     Ada.Text_IO.Put_Line("Val1: " & Some_Float'Image(Val1) &
       " Val2: " & Some_Float'Image(Val2));
   end Put_Line_Flo;
```

```
  procedure Put_Line_Flo(
    Val : in Some_Float) is

  begin
    Ada.Text_IO.Put_Line("Val: " & Some_Float'Image(Val));
  end Put_Line_Flo;

  Int_Test1 : Some_Int     := 10;
  Int_Test2 : Some_Int     := 20;
  Int_Temp : Some_Int      := 0;
  Float_Test1 : Some_Float := -1.0;
  Float_Test2 : Some_Float := -2.0;
  Float_Temp : Some_Float  := 0.0;
begin
  Put_Line_Int(Int_Test1, Int_Test2);
  Generic_Package_Test.Swap(Int_Test1, Int_Test2);
  Put_Line_Int(Int_Test1, Int_Test2);

  Ada.Text_IO.Put("Min value: ");
  Put_Line_Int(Generic_Package_Test.Min(Int_Test1, Int_Test2));

  Ada.Text_IO.Put("Max value: ");
  Put_Line_Int(Generic_Package_Test.Max(Int_Test1, Int_Test2));

  Put_Line_Flo(Float_Test1, Float_Test2);
  Generic_Package_Test.Swap(Float_Test1, Float_Test2);
  Put_Line_Flo(Float_Test1, Float_Test2);

  Ada.Text_IO.Put("Min value: ");
  Put_Line_Flo(Generic_Package_Test.Min(Float_Test1, Float_Test2));

  Ada.Text_IO.Put("Max value: ");
  Put_Line_Flo(Generic_Package_Test.Max(Float_Test1, Float_Test2));
end Generic_Main;
```

This is where all of the bits and pieces are pulled together, and you can see how everything works:

1) On lines 8–10, two types (one integer and the other float) are created and a static package Generic_Package_Test is derived from Gener.

2) Lines 12–42 are helper functions. They will be used to print out and display the values after certain operations are performed to them.

3) And from line 44 to 49, we have our variables declared.

4) Generic_Package_Test.Swap(Int_Test1, Int_Test2); and Generic_Package_Test.Swap(Float_Test1, Float_Test2); – These are interesting. Here we are using both the custom floats and integers interchangeably. As a result of polymorphism – as discussed in Chapter 11 – the compiler knows which Swap function to call for which set of values.

The same can be said about every function that is used in the Generic_Main procedure.

Please Do Not Make Every Package Generic

As was have stated in Chapter 11, talking about inheritance, when it does make sense to use certain object-oriented programming features, you should use them. However, they must be used judiciously.

Generic packages make sense when you know you have a bunch of functions that can provide the same benefit across multiple types, and this can be accomplished without making major changes to each generic package for a given type (otherwise there is no point in using a generic package and a custom one for each type is needed).

The preceding example shows you how to have two or more types in a generic package (this is done purely as an illustration). However, most of the time you will need just one. In fact, the Gener package could easily do without having an extra set of the same functions and instead makes use two different derivations of the Gener package.

How to Better Specify Different Format Types

In order to be able to instantiate the type that you want, there are some rules that need to be followed. For example, if you would like to have a custom Float type, a specific set of keywords is necessary, which is different from that of an Integer or a String. This table will help you in deciding which keywords will be needed for which purpose.

Generic Type Syntax	Matching Type
`type T (<>) is limited private;`	This is used for just about any type that you want. This is a limited type, so that means you cannot make copies of this type but you can assign a value to it. You need to provide an initial range for this type.
`type T (<>) is private;`	Same as above, but you can now make copies of this type.
`type T is private;`	Same as above, but an initial range is no longer obligatory.
`type T (<>) is tagged private;`	A type that represents a tagged record, meaning that this type can be enhanced using inheritance.
`type T is (<>);`	Any discrete type, such as an integer or an enumerated type.
`type T is range <>;`	Any signed integer, applies only to numbers and nothing else.
`type T is delta <>;`	This refers to any type that is a float that has a specific level of precision (e.g., 0.001 or 0.1). This type will work only if the precision is equal or less than the type specified here.
`type T is digits <>;`	An example such as this will represent any floating type, but will concern itself with only so many significant decimal digits. For example, if the number of significant decimal digits is 4, then numbers 4.249 and 982.3 are both acceptable. However, all numbers after the decimal that do not fit into the total number of significant digits will not be considered to be accurate.

This type is not discussed in great detail in this book. |

(continued)

Generic Type Syntax	Matching Type
`type T is delta <>` `digits <>;`	Same as above – the 4th row from the bottom of this table – on account of precision, but this now limits the number of significant decimal digits that this type keeps track of. This is for a type where you only care for so many values inside the float to be accurate and want to keep a certain level of precision in regard to the decimal value; all other numbers after the decimal digit are assumed to be imprecise.
`type T is access` `Some_Obj;`	This is an access to the object Some_Obj. This is not radically different from what you have learned about access types.

It must be noted that the preceding table shows the types that you would most likely use, especially as you are starting out. The Ada language has many more. But for the sake of brevity and not overwhelm a new reader, these were selected.

Generic Functions and Procedures

Having generic functions and procedures is very useful. However, creating a package and then the type only if you want just a few generic functions is a poor investment of effort. The time to create something so simple and small is wasted and adds unnecessary complexity to your application, impacting its ability to be read and understood by others (most likely you, in the future, after you have forgotten how the code works). So, what can one do? In this case, an individual generic function can help:

```
-- generic_methods.adb:

with Ada.Text_IO;

procedure Generic_Methods is
  generic
    type T is range <>;
  procedure Print_Int(
    Val : in T);
```

```
generic
  type T is range <>;
function Compute_Sum(
  Val1 : in T;
  Val2 : in T)
    return T;

procedure Print_Int(
  Val : in T) is
begin
  Ada.Text_IO.Put_Line(T'Image(Val));
end Print_Int;

function Compute_Sum(
  Val1 : in T;
  Val2 : in T)
    return T is

begin
  return Val1 + Val2;
end Compute_Sum;

procedure Print_Integer is new Print_Int(Integer);
procedure Print_Positive is new Print_Int(Positive);

function Sum_Integer is new Compute_Sum(Integer);
function Sum_Positive is new Compute_Sum(Positive);

Result_I : Integer := 0;
Result_P : Positive := 1;
begin
  Ada.Text_IO.Put_Line("Adding some integer values together.");
  Result_I := Sum_Integer(22, -9);
  Print_Integer(Result_I);

  Ada.Text_IO.Put_Line("Adding some positive values together.");
  Result_P := Sum_Positive(49, 73);
  Print_Positive(Result_P);
end Generic_Methods;
```

This is what the preceding example does:

1)  ```
    generic
       type T is range <>;
    function Compute_Sum(
       Val1 : in T;
       Val2 : in T)
    ```

    `return T;` – First thing, declare the function. In here, you will
    specify just what types it will process so that others can easily see
    it. Without this step, the function will not know what sort of inputs
    it should expect and the results it needs to return.

2)  ```
    function Compute_Sum(
       Val1 : in T;
       Val2 : in T)
    ```

    `return T is` – The implementation is pretty straightforward. It is
    no different from the declaration, aside from body of the function
    that needs to be filled in.

    Keep in mind, this function is still not instantiated. You have
    the inputs, the output, and the logic of this method figured out.
    However, the type that will be processed is still unknown. This last
    hurdle will be cleared in the next line.

3) `function Sum_Integer is new Compute_Sum(Integer);` – Now
    is the part that this function's generic type needs to be specified.
    By executing this line of code, you are telling the compiler that the
    generic function Compute_Sum will use Integer as the generic
    type and that its new name will be Sum_Integer.

Comparing Records Inside Generic Packages

This is all well and good, but what if you have a generic package and would like to
pass in a record for the type? Easy enough, just look at the preceding table and use
the private type:

```
generic
  type Some_Record is private;
package Funky_Pack is

  ....
```

But, what if you would like to use a record that is part of a package that has overloaded operators, such as ">," "<," and "="? You might think that you can just use these operators. This is incorrect; the compiler will immediately complain that it has no idea what you are doing. You see, the comparison function that you have defined in a different package is not visible from this one. With Integer, Positive, Natural, Boolean, etc. types, it is part of the language itself and the compiler immediately knows what is going. So, how do you go about informing the compiler that this record can be compared? Like so:

```
generic
  type Some_Record is private;
  with function ">" (
    L : in Some_Record;
    R : in Some_Record)
      return Boolean is <>;
  with function "<" (
    L : in Some_Record;
    R : in Some_Record)
      return Boolean is <>;
  with function "=" (
    L : in Some_Record;
    R : in Some_Record)
      return Boolean is <>;
package Funky_Pack is

  ....
```

This way, you are importing the relevant functions as well as the unique record type. Look at the functions themselves; they look no different from how you declared them. This is on purpose. Now the compiler has all of the tools that it needs in order to understand how to use this function. Just remember – as before – to include the "use" keyword as well.

Lab

1) Have a look at the Time package earlier in this chapter and add functionality to multiply and divide the time, as well as a greater or less than comparison.

2) Create a generic package that will be a queue. The representation of the queue can be an array, and it should have the functions to push values from one end, pop them off of the other, and get the length of the queue. If more values are entered into the queue than it can hold, an error message should be displayed.

CHAPTER 14

Contracts and Proofs

What You Will Get Out of This Chapter

This chapter will dive into a very powerful technique of "proving" that your code works. This is something very unique to Ada 2012. None of the previous versions have them. They are used to ensure that certain conditions are met before executing a method, and certain changes were made after the execution has stopped.

They are absolutely brilliant. Every time that you need to double-check that some conditional value is met before running that function, you would need to put it in an if statement. This can turn problematic if your logic ever changes, or you need to be sure that a change you wanted to make indeed has been done. For example, if you have an application that opens a door, that door better be closed before anything begins to open up; having the hardware that opens the door be damaged means that the software was poorly thought out. The same goes for closing the door.

This becomes especially crucial when you need to build a secure and reliable application. You can verify that a list has one extra element after executing a method, when you expect this to happen. Or if a range of values have been created. Even how to include other methods when necessary.

Contracts on Functions and Procedures

You have seen custom types and how they can be used to reduce the range of possible inputs. Contracts can do that as well. However, in addition they can double-check the logic of a given method. If it can be verified that a given condition is met, then all the better in order to reduce possible problems down the road.

© Andrew T. Shvets 2020
A. T. Shvets, *Beginning Ada Programming*, https://doi.org/10.1007/978-1-4842-5428-8_14

Let's look at the following example of a simulation of bottles being packaged at a bottling plant. The goal with this code is to illustrate how this could possibly work:

```
-- contracts.ads:

pragma Assertion_Policy(Check);

package Contracts is
  procedure Simulate;
private
  Bottles_Finished : Natural       := 0;
  Boxes_Packed : Natural           := 0;
  Bottles_In_Box : constant Natural := 16;

  procedure Label_Bottle;

  procedure Package_Bottles
    with Pre  => (Bottles_Finished >= Bottles_In_Box),
         Post => (Bottles_In_Box - Bottles_Finished = Bottles_Finished'Old);

  procedure Print_Report;
end Contracts;
```

The most salient part of the example are the following points:

1. `pragma Assertion_Policy(Check);` – This part is crucial. It tells the compiler that all of the contracts in the file must be enforced.

   You can also enable the checking of contracts, but passing in the "-gnata" flag when compiling your code and not bothering with the preceding pragma. The command will look like this:

   ```
   $ gnatmake -g -gnata contracts_main.adb
   ```

   However, the pragma is preferred. The reason for this is that you can forget the compiler flag, and you do not have the same problem with a pragma.

2. "Pre" dictates what conditions must be met before the execution of the procedure can proceed. In this case, the number of bottles that are finished has to be equal to or greater than the number of bottles that can fit in a box.

3. "Post" ensures that certain conditions are met after the execution of this procedure in order to count this as a successful finish.

Whatever happens in "Pre" or "Post," it has to evaluate to a boolean type of True. For example, if you are checking the length of an array to ensure that it meets a certain length, that check has to evaluate to a boolean True.

All of the Aspects

In this book, we will be using only Pre and Post aspects. However, they are not the only ones and you can certainly create far more complex logic, assuming you need to. Here is a list of all aspects:

`www.ada-auth.org/standards/12rm/html/RM-K-1.html`

However, what will happen if the Pre or Post conditions are not met? You will get an exception thrown and will have to deal with this. You see, if the conditions are not true, then the contract is in violation, and Ada will do everything to ensure that you are aware of this problem. And all of this happens at runtime. How is that for a language when it comes to looking out for your interests?

```
-- contracts.adb:

with Ada.Text_IO;

package body Contracts is
  procedure Simulate is
  begin
    for iter in 1 .. 423 loop
      Label_Bottle;

      if iter rem Bottles_In_Box = 0 then
        Packaging_Block :
        declare
        begin
          Package_Bottles;
```

```
        exception
          when Constraint_Error =>
            Ada.Text_IO.Put_Line("CONSTRAINT ERROR!");
          when others =>
            Ada.Text_IO.Put_Line("ERROR: Unknown!");
        end Packaging_Block;
      end if;
    end loop;

    Print_Report;
  end Simulate;

  procedure Label_Bottle is
  begin
    Bottles_Finished := Bottles_Finished + 1;
  end Label_Bottle;

  procedure Package_Bottles is
  begin
    Bottles_Finished := Bottles_Finished - 16;
    Boxes_Packed := Boxes_Packed + 1;
  end Package_Bottles;

  procedure Print_Report is
  begin
    Ada.Text_IO.Put_Line(" - Current Report -");
    Ada.Text_IO.Put_Line(" Bottles finished: " &
      Natural'Image(Bottles_Finished));
    Ada.Text_IO.Put_Line(" Boxes packed:      " &
      Natural'Image(Boxes_Packed));
    Ada.Text_IO.New_Line;
  end Print_Report;
end Contracts;
```

Let's take this package body apart:

1. `procedure Simulate is` – This is a procedure that symbolizes the process of packaging bottles, with the loop going through the packaging of individual bottles:

   a) `if iter rem Bottles_In_Box = 0 then` – The first thing to keep in mind is this if statement. It is here to symbolize the 16 bottles that go into a box.

   b) From line 11 to 13, we call the Package_Bottles procedure. This procedure has our Pre and Post contractual obligation.

   But do not forget that the method that has the contract is inside of a declare block. This is done on purpose. If a contract is not satisfied, an exception will be thrown. And on lines 15–18 you can see the catching of this exception; this is the Constraint_ Error exception. Most of the time, it will be a constraint violation.

2. `procedure Label_Bottle is` – This is a simple function that only increments the number of bottles that were completed.

3. `procedure Package_Bottles is` – Package_Bottles represents the action of putting all bottles into a box and accounting for this change.

4. `procedure Print_Report is` – This procedure is here purely to print out the result of the computation.

```
-- contracts_main.adb:

with Contracts;

procedure Contracts_Main is
begin
   Contracts.Simulate;
end Contracts_Main;
```

Since no instance of a private record is ever created, the Simulate function can be called as it is.

Verifying a Range of Values

You know how to verify just one value to ensure it is correct. However, what if you want to be sure that an array was correctly changed? The best part is that you could update the array and then verify the result.

The following example is trivial, but the goal is to show you how to do this:

```
-- multiply_array.ads:

pragma Assertion_Policy(Check);

package Multiply_Array is
  type Int_Array is array(Positive range <>) of Integer;

  procedure Init_Array(Arr : in out Int_Array);

  procedure Multiply_By_Two(Arr : in out Int_Array)
    with Post => (for all Item in Arr'Range =>
                    Arr(Item) = Arr'Old(Item) * 2);

  procedure Print_Array(Arr : in Int_Array)
    with Pre => (for some Index in Arr'Range =>
                    Arr(Index) /= 0);
end Multiply_Array;
```

Let's have a look at how the array variables are checked:

1. `pragma Assertion_Policy(Check);` – As before, tell the compiler that we need to enable the checking of contracts.

2. The first two lines inside of the package are very straightforward and were covered in previous parts of the book.

3. `procedure Multiply_By_Two(Arr : in out Int_Array)`
   `with Post => (for all Item in Arr'Range =>`

   `Arr(Item) = Arr'Old(Item) * 2);` – First, the aspect Post tells us immediately that all of the checking will be done after the function finished executing.

Next, have a look at the keyword "for all". This means that each and every one of those array elements that are being iterated over need to meet the condition outlined in this aspect in order for the result to be correct.

Lastly, the comparison of the arrays – Arr(Item) = Arr'Old(Item) * 2); – is verification being performed.

4.
```
procedure Print_Array(Arr : in Int_Array)
  with Pre => (for some Index in Arr'Range =>
```

Arr(Index) /= 0); – In this instance, the Pre aspect tells us that the check will happen before the procedure is called.

Notice the text "for some". This is different from before. This tells the compiler that if we go through the array Arr, the goal is to verify that at least one of the values of the array meets the requirement. If all of the values in the array fail to meet the requirement, only then is an exception raised:

```
-- multiply_array.adb:

with Ada.Text_IO;

package body Multiply_Array is
  procedure Init_Array(
    Arr : in out Int_Array) is

  begin
    for iter in Arr'Range loop
      Arr(iter) := iter + 5;
    end loop;
  end Init_Array;

  procedure Multiply_By_Two(
    Arr : in out Int_Array) is
```

```
begin
  for iter in Arr'Range loop
    Arr(iter) := Arr(iter) * 2;
  end loop;
end Multiply_By_Two;

procedure Print_Array(
  Arr : in Int_Array) is

begin
  Ada.Text_IO.Put_Line("The contents of the current array:");

  for iter in Arr'Range loop
    Ada.Text_IO.Put(" " & Integer'Image(Arr(iter)));
  end loop;

  Ada.Text_IO.New_Line(2);
end Print_Array;
end Multiply_Array;
```

Most of this code you should be able to easily understand. Let's go through a few points in the context of the contracts that we discussed in the preceding example:

1. The code written here does not have any of the checks as they were when the package was declared.

2. The body of the package is where you can relax and go about writing the code that will create the computation that meets the requirements of the Post aspect, if there is one.

```
-- multiply_array_main.adb:

with Multiply_Array;

procedure Multiply_Array_Main is
  use type Multiply_Array.Int_Array;
  MA_Array : Multiply_Array.Int_Array(1 .. 40) := (others => 0);
begin
  Multiply_Array.Init_Array(MA_Array);
```

```
      Multiply_Array.Multiply_By_Two(MA_Array);

      Multiply_Array.Print_Array(MA_Array);
   end Multiply_Array_Main;
```

Once the code is written, it is time to make use of it. And that is done in the preceding example.

Using Custom Methods in Verification

Now, what if you have a set of conditions that need to be met, but the logic for this verification is complex? How would you deal with this? How would you describe this logic? You could separate a method into smaller pieces so that the contracts for the different parts can be created correctly. But what if this is either very difficult or would make the code less readable? For this instance, a custom verification function is in order.

Let's say that you were given a task to verify passed in values to an interpreter that is supposed to work every time. How would you do this? Here is one approach:

```
-- function_check.ads:

pragma Assertion_Policy(Check);

package Function_Check is
   function Is_Formatted_Correctly(
     Command : in String)
       return Boolean;

   function Evaluate(Command : in String) return Boolean
     with Pre => Is_Formatted_Correctly(Command);
end Function_Check;
```

The preceding code is different from what was shown before. Let's have a closer look:

1. `pragma Assertion_Policy(Check);` – As before, this tells the compiler that the contracts that are created in this application need to be enforced.

2. `function Is_Formatted_Correctly(` – This is the function that we will need to use in order to verify the other one.

3. function Evaluate(Command : in String) return Boolean

    with Pre => Is_Formatted_Correctly(Command); – This is
    the most interesting part. Whether the aspect is Pre or Post, it
    has to evaluate to a Boolean value. In our case, the function Is_
    Formatted_Correctly returns a Boolean.

    ```
    -- function_check.adb:

    with Ada.Strings.Fixed;

    package body Function_Check is
       function Evaluate(
         Command : in String)
           return Boolean is

       begin
         return Ada.Strings.Fixed.Index(Command, "command:") > 0;
       end Evaluate;

       function Is_Formatted_Correctly(
         Command : in String)
           return Boolean is

       begin
         return Ada.Strings.Fixed.Index(Command, "command:") > 0;
       end Is_Formatted_Correctly;
    end Function_Check;
    ```

The implementation of the Function_Check package is very straightforward. You will
easily notice that the code of Evaluate and Is_Formatted_Correctly is very similar. The
goal of doing this was to better illustrate how to use a function to verify the functionality
of another method and not create extra confusion by using a more complex example:

```
-- function_check_main.adb:

with Ada.Text_IO;

with Function_Check;
```

```
procedure Function_Check_Main is
  Result : Boolean := False;
begin
  Result := Function_Check.Evaluate("command: remove --dir \temp");

  if Result then
    Ada.Text_IO.Put_Line("The command was formatted correctly.");
  else
    Ada.Text_IO.Put_Line("The command was formatted incorrectly.");
  end if;
end Function_Check_Main;
```

And this is where everything is tied together.

In the next chapter, we will dive into networking examples. This is where you can make your code "talk" to other applications.

Lab

Create an application that uses contracts in order to control a high-tech and humane mousetrap. Imagine that the mousetrap has a weighted platform and if a rodent were to step on it, the door would shut. Afterward, the mouse would be transferred to a holding area and the trap would be reset.

## CHAPTER 15

Networking and Advanced I/O

What You Will Get Out of This Chapter

We will discuss the basics of how to form socket connections. Examples will be shown of clients and servers. Two protocols will be covered, TCP and UDP, and their individual nuances will be discussed from a high level. The focus will be on how to work with sockets.

What this chapter will not do is explain in detail the nuts and bolts of computer networking. That is beyond the scope of this book. There are many technologies and different approaches to various problems, and each topic could be turned into a book by itself. Instead, a section is included in this chapter that will list resources that you can use to further your knowledge of networking, if you find the topic interesting. The goal is to give you a starting point and good direction of where to go next.

TCP Protocol

TCP stands for Transmission Control Protocol. In order to work correctly, this protocol needs to establish a connection. Furthermore, when packets – small pieces of information that your data is split up into – are sent, the receiver talks to the sender and ensures that each one of them has arrived successfully and correctly. Here is more information on TCP:

```
https://en.wikipedia.org/wiki/Transmission_Control_
Protocol
```

© Andrew T. Shvets 2020
A. T. Shvets, *Beginning Ada Programming*, https://doi.org/10.1007/978-1-4842-5428-8_15

The benefit of this protocol is that there are plenty of checks to ensure that all of the information arrives as it should. Furthermore, if there is a problem, an exception will be thrown. However, when sending information across networks, the rate of sending data is slower when compared to UDP, due to checking with the sender making sure that every value arrived successfully. Despite this, a significant portion of communication online is dependent on this protocol.

The original TCP server example was obtained from this link; improvements were made as needed:

https://rosettacode.org/wiki/Echo_server#Ada

Now let's have a look at how it works:

```
-- tcp_server.adb:

with Ada.Text_IO;
with Ada.IO_Exceptions;

with GNAT.Sockets;

procedure TCP_Server is
   Receiver    : GNAT.Sockets.Socket_Type;
   Connection  : GNAT.Sockets.Socket_Type;
   Client      : GNAT.Sockets.Sock_Addr_Type;
   Channel     : GNAT.Sockets.Stream_Access;

   Server_Data : constant String := "I like cake!";
   Server_Data2 : String := "               ";
begin
   GNAT.Sockets.Create_Socket(Receiver, GNAT.Sockets.Family_Inet,
     GNAT.Sockets.Socket_Stream);
   GNAT.Sockets.Set_Socket_Option(Receiver, GNAT.Sockets.Socket_Level,
     (GNAT.Sockets.Reuse_Address, True));
   GNAT.Sockets.Bind_Socket(Receiver, (GNAT.Sockets.Family_Inet,
     GNAT.Sockets.Inet_Addr("127.0.0.1"), 50000));
   GNAT.Sockets.Listen_Socket(Receiver);

   Ada.Text_IO.Put_Line(" !! TCP Server started !!");
```

```
loop
  GNAT.Sockets.Accept_Socket(Receiver, Connection, Client);

  Ada.Text_IO.Put_Line("Client connected from " &
    GNAT.Sockets.Image(Client));
  Channel := GNAT.Sockets.Stream(Connection);

  begin
    loop
      String'Read(Channel, Server_Data2);
      String'Write(Channel, Server_Data);
    end loop;
  exception
    when Ada.IO_Exceptions.End_Error =>
      null;
  end;

  GNAT.Sockets.Close_Socket(Connection);
  end loop;
end TCP_Server;
```

Let's see what this application does exactly:

1. `with GNAT.Sockets;` – This is the library that is needed in order to make it possible use sockets for sending and receiving information. Here is an excellent source of reference information on this topic:

   `https://en.wikibooks.org/wiki/Ada_Programming/Libraries/ GNAT.Sockets`

2. In lines 9–12, variables are declared so that a connection can be established:

   a) `Receiver : GNAT.Sockets.Socket_Type;` – This is the object that is used to receive information from clients to this server program. Look at it as a handle on a file descriptor.

   b) `Connection : GNAT.Sockets.Socket_Type;` – This is the same as the Receiver variable, but it will be used to send information to the client after the required processing has been complete.

    c) `Client : GNAT.Sockets.Sock_Addr_Type;` – This object will be used to reference the object of the application that is sending data to our server. With this, we can find information such as the IP address of the sender and display it to the command line. This can be vital information if you are debugging connectivity issues in your program, such as making sure that the connection was established in the first place.

    d) `Channel : GNAT.Sockets.Stream_Access;` – This is an access type that we will use to read information from the sender and respond back to it.

3. The variables Server_Data and Server_Data2 were made so that received data could be captured and new data sent to the client.

4. `GNAT.Sockets.Create_Socket(Receiver);` – What this procedure does is configure the Receiver socket so that it uses an IPv4 protocol so you can use the IP address of 127.0.0.1 and use the Socket_Stream. Socket_Stream indicates that we want to use the TCP protocol; for UDP, this will change to something else.

5. `GNAT.Sockets.Set_Socket_Option(Receiver, GNAT.Sockets. Socket_Level, (GNAT.Sockets.Reuse_Address, True));` – Here we set socket options for our Receiver socket:

    a) The first variable passed to the procedure is the Receiver; that way, it knows what it is working with.

    b) The second variable is an indicator at which level we want to set the option. In our case, we want to set it for the entire object. We can be more specific about this, and set it for just TCP, IP, or UDP.

    c) Next is what we want the option to be. For GNAT.Sockets.Reuse_Address, the server can reuse the local address when using it for communication. The boolean True indicates that it should be enabled.

6. `GNAT.Sockets.Bind_Socket(Receiver, (GNAT.Sockets.Family_ Inet, GNAT.Sockets.Inet_Addr("127.0.0.1"), 50000));` – The receiving address now needs to have an address bound to it; in this case, it is localhost (127.0.0.1).

7. `GNAT.Sockets.Listen_Socket(Receiver);` – This is where the application begins to listen to the socket for any incoming requests. After this line, we can begin to start accepting requests and that will be done in a loop.

8. `GNAT.Sockets.Accept_Socket(Receiver, Connection, Client);` – Accept a connection. This procedure queries a queue in order to accept from a list of requests. The Client variable will be filled with information about the sender such as IP. The Connection variable will be populated with information on how to write back to the client.

9. On line 25, the client's information is displayed.

10. `Channel := GNAT.Sockets.Stream(Connection);` – This is a bidirectional source of communication that is opened up between the client and the server.

11. From line 28 to 36, this is where the actual "talking" happens. A block is used to do this. Let's break this down further:

    a) `String'Read(Channel, Server_Data2);`
       `String'Write(Channel, Server_Data);` – The incoming information is read from the stream (Channel) as a string in the first line. This is done via "String'Read(Channel, Server_Data2);". This will fill up the variable Server_Data2 with whatever the client sent us.

       Then, by using the Write attribute, different information is written back using the same stream. The client will send us "Hello world!" and will receive the message "I like cake!".

    b) The way that this loop works is that it depends on having the exception Ada.IO_Exceptions.End_Error being thrown. Otherwise, this will be an infinite loop. And indeed, that is what happens after all of the characters from the request have been read, and there is no more information. The exception is thrown; it is caught but nothing happens, and the loop is exited.

12. `GNAT.Sockets.Close_Socket(Connection);` – This is where the
request is closed. However, remember how on line 18 we decided
to reuse the same address as often as needed? Even after the
socket is closed, it can be easily reused the next time that the loop
runs and accepts a new request on line 23.

This is the output that you should see:

```
> ./tcp_server
Client connected from 127.0.0.1:39026
Client connected from 127.0.0.1:39028
Client connected from 127.0.0.1:39030
Client connected from 127.0.0.1:39032
```

You will need to manually kill the server process by Ctrl + C.

The client process is much simpler. It only needs to open up a socket to the same
port where the server is listening (50000), and write a string to it:

```
-- tcp_client.adb:

with Ada.Text_IO;

with GNAT.Sockets;

procedure TCP_Client is
  Address : GNAT.Sockets.Sock_Addr_Type := (GNAT.Sockets.Family_Inet,
    GNAT.Sockets.Inet_Addr("127.0.0.1"), 50000);
  Socket  : GNAT.Sockets.Socket_Type;
  Channel : GNAT.Sockets.Stream_Access;

  Data : String := "Hello world!";
begin
  GNAT.Sockets.Create_Socket(Socket);
  GNAT.Sockets.Connect_Socket(Socket, Address);
  Channel := GNAT.Sockets.Stream(Socket);

  String'Write(Channel, Data);
  String'Read(Channel, Data);
  Ada.Text_IO.Put_Line(Data);
```

```
GNAT.Sockets.Close_Socket(Socket);
end TCP_Client;
```

Let's quickly go through the preceding example:

1. On lines 8–12, the same types of variables are created. The one difference is the lack of a second Socket_Type that is used to query the server about it. The string that will be sent (Data) is also included.

   Fun fact, if you try to send a string that is longer than "Hello world!" to the server, your client will stop and wait for a reply. The reason for this, the longer string will cause the client to keep waiting for the server to send a string that is longer than 12 characters to completely fill it up. The client will keep waiting forever (unless a timeout is set) until the string has been received. You might be wondering what the server process is doing with the excess characters; the server will grab only the things that it needs, and the rest are simply ignored.

2. `GNAT.Sockets.Create_Socket(Socket);` – As before in the server, the socket value needs to be created using the same Create_Socket procedure.

3. `GNAT.Sockets.Connect_Socket(Socket, Address);` – This is where the client app actually tries to make a connection to the server. Should this call fail, an exception will be thrown.

4. `Channel := GNAT.Sockets.Stream(Socket);` – As before, create a bidirectional stream to be used to send and receive data.

5. `String'Write(Channel, Data);`
   `String'Read(Channel, Data);` – On the first line, the contents of Data are written to the server. On the second line, the same contents that were sent were received, and now it gets stored in the variable Data.

6. GNAT.Sockets.Close_Socket(Socket); – Just as in the server,
    this socket is closed. Unlike in the server, where the socket was
    configured to be reused as necessary, the same will not hold true
    here.

This is the output that you should expect to see:

```
> ./tcp_client
I like cake!
```

UDP Protocol

UDP stands for User Datagram Protocol. Unlike TCP, a connection is not necessary for
this protocol to operate. The information is split up into datagrams. It is very lightweight
when it comes time to use it. Furthermore, there is no guarantee that the datagrams will
arrive in the order that they were received, and some may not even arrive at all! UPD
relies on checksums in order to verify that it has received all information that was sent
to it. If any information is missing, then the receiver asks the sender to re-send it. Here is
more information on UDP:

https://en.wikipedia.org/wiki/User_Datagram_Protocol

The following example is a modification of the TCP server/client examples; let's
have a look:

```
-- tcp_server.adb:

with Ada.Text_IO;
with Ada.IO_Exceptions;

with GNAT.Sockets;

procedure UDP_Server is
   Receiver   : GNAT.Sockets.Socket_Type;
   Channel    : GNAT.Sockets.Stream_Access;

   Server_Data : String := "              ";
begin
   GNAT.Sockets.Create_Socket(Receiver, GNAT.Sockets.Family_Inet,
     GNAT.Sockets.Socket_Datagram);
```

```
GNAT.Sockets.Set_Socket_Option(Receiver, GNAT.Sockets.Socket_Level,
  (GNAT.Sockets.Reuse_Address, True));
GNAT.Sockets.Bind_Socket(Receiver, (GNAT.Sockets.Family_Inet,
  GNAT.Sockets.Inet_Addr("127.0.0.1"), 50000));

Ada.Text_IO.Put_Line(" !! UDP Server started !!");

loop
  Channel := GNAT.Sockets.Stream(Receiver);

  begin
    loop
      String'Read(Channel, Server_Data);
      Ada.Text_IO.Put_Line(" The data received: " & Server_Data);
    end loop;
  exception
    when GNAT.Sockets.Socket_Error =>
      exit;
  end;
end loop;
end UDP_Server;
```

This is a much simpler example, but let's look at what was changed and why:

1. `Receiver : GNAT.Sockets.Socket_Type;`
   `Channel : GNAT.Sockets.Stream_Access;` – This is much
   simpler in a connectionless protocol so the server will simply
   begin listening and consuming any and all information that
   comes across on the socket.

2. `GNAT.Sockets.Create_Socket(Receiver, GNAT.Sockets.`
   `Family_Inet, GNAT.Sockets.Socket_Datagram);` – The type
   of socket used is different. In the previous example, we could
   accept the default setting, GNAT.Sockets.Socket_Stream, for the
   Create_Socket procedure. In this case, the Datagram enumerated
   type needs to be used. The Family_Inet is saying that we want to
   use the IPv4 IP address and it is there to fill in the 2nd parameter
   position in the Create_Socket procedure.

3. GNAT.Sockets.Set_Socket_Option(Receiver, GNAT.Sockets. Socket_Level, (GNAT.Sockets.Reuse_Address, True)); – As before, we are specifying that this address will be reused in the future.

4. GNAT.Sockets.Bind_Socket(Receiver, (GNAT.Sockets.Family_ Inet, GNAT.Sockets.Inet_Addr("127.0.0.1"), 50000)); – Again, this is saying which port and IP address will be used in the connection.

   One key difference is the lack of the Listen_Socket procedure call. UDP does not need to connect and immediately will begin reading the incoming information from the specified socket.

5. Channel := GNAT.Sockets.Stream(Receiver); – Again, as in the previous point, there is no need to call the Accept_Socket function as it happens in the TCP example. Right away, we can start streaming the data coming from the specified socket and reading it. When the server is done, it will simply stop running and terminate. Since no connection needs to be established, there is no need to terminate it as well.

When the server runs, this is the output that you should expect to see:

```
> ./udp_server
 !! UDP Server started !!
 The data received: Hello world!
 The data received: Hello world!
 The data received: Hello world!
 The data received: Hello world!
 The data received: Hello world!

-- udp_client.adb:

with Ada.Text_IO;

with GNAT.Sockets;
```

```
procedure UDP_Client is
  Address : GNAT.Sockets.Sock_Addr_Type := (GNAT.Sockets.Family_Inet,
    GNAT.Sockets.Inet_Addr("127.0.0.1"), 50000);
  Socket  : GNAT.Sockets.Socket_Type;
  Channel : GNAT.Sockets.Stream_Access;

  Data : String := "Hello world!";
begin
  GNAT.Sockets.Create_Socket(Socket, GNAT.Sockets.Family_Inet,
    GNAT.Sockets.Socket_Datagram);
  GNAT.Sockets.Connect_Socket(Socket, Address);
  Channel := GNAT.Sockets.Stream(Socket);

  String'Write(Channel, Data);

  GNAT.Sockets.Close_Socket(Socket);
end UDP_Client;
```

This client is even simpler:

1. `Address : GNAT.Sockets.Sock_Addr_Type := (GNAT.Sockets.`
   `Family_Inet, GNAT.Sockets.Inet_Addr("127.0.0.1"),`
   `50000);` – As in the UDP server, instantiate an address that can be
   used to send data over to the server.

2. Lines 9 and 10 are the basic types that are needed in order to
   establish a connection.

3. `GNAT.Sockets.Create_Socket(Socket, GNAT.Sockets.Family_`
   `Inet, GNAT.Sockets.Socket_Datagram);` – You have seen the
   exact same code in the UDP server. A socket is established with
   an IPv4 address type, and datagrams will be used to transmit
   information.

4. `GNAT.Sockets.Connect_Socket(Socket, Address);`
   `Channel := GNAT.Sockets.Stream(Socket);` – The exact same
   code is used in the TCP client example. The address is associated
   with the protocol, and a stream is created so that data can be read.

5. `String'Write(Channel, Data);` – And this is where the actual text is written to the socket. Yes, that is all that you need to do.

6. `GNAT.Sockets.Close_Socket(Socket);` – Just to be tidy, the socket is closed.

The example does not output anything. In order to write data to the server, all that it needs to do is simply write the string over the data stream.

Further Networking Reading

If you are interested in learning more about networking, here are some resources that you can use to improve your knowledge. This is a very complex and broad topic that requires a massive investment of time and effort.

Networking Theory Resources

Here are books that you can use to further your understanding of computer networking.

1. Computer Networks 5th Edition

   ```
   ISBN-10:    9332518742
   ISBN-13: 978-9332518742
   ```

2. Computer Networking: A Top-Down Approach (6th Edition)

   ```
   ISBN-10:    0132856204
   ISBN-13: 978-0132856201
   ```

3. Computer Networking: A Top-Down Approach (7th Edition)

   ```
   ISBN-10:    0133594149
   ISBN-13: 978-0133594140
   ```

Practical Networking Resources

Theory is great. But if there is no way to put those ideas into action, then they are worthless. This list of books will provide more practical examples of how to work with networks:

1. TCP/IP Illustrated, Volume 1: The Protocols (2nd Edition)

    ```
    ISBN-10:    0321336313
    ISBN-13: 978-0321336316
    ```

2. Unix Network Programming, Volume 1: The Sockets Networking API

    ```
    ISBN-10:    0131411551
    ISBN-13: 978-0131411555
    ```

3. Network Programming for Microsoft Windows, Second Edition

    ```
    ISBN-10:    0735615799
    ISBN-13: 978-0735615793
    ```

Reading the numerous tutorials, articles, and other materials online will also help you, and most of it is free!

Lab

You now know how to make a simple TCP server. Now, modify the preceding code so that instead of a plain String, an unbounded string is used. Writing back to the client an answer is not required.

If you are more comfortable working with UDP, you can try that. However, the lab example has been written with TCP in mind.

Modify the TCP client to send the unbounded string.

Modify the TCP server to receive the message no matter how long it is. To accomplish this, have a look at the following link:

```
https://en.wikibooks.org/wiki/Ada_Programming/Libraries/
GNAT.Sockets_examples
```

And the following is the documentation for GNAT.Sockets and Ada.Streams:

```
https://en.wikibooks.org/wiki/Ada_Programming/Libraries/
GNAT.Sockets
```

```
https://en.wikibooks.org/wiki/Ada_Programming/Libraries/
Ada.Streams
```

CHAPTER 16

Project Organization

What You Will Get Out of This Chapter

Up to now, you have learned more and more about how to write code in Ada and what the different forms of syntax are for. This book has taken on you a small journey through the world of this wonderful language. And it would not be a surprise if you were slowly developing ideas of your own that you want to create. This is good. This chapter will not cover anything specific to Ada itself.

The goal of this chapter is to start you off on the right track of improving your software development skills. Certain topics will be briefly introduced, and it will be up to you to think about how to use this knowledge. You will begin to become a genuine software engineer and not just someone who throws lines of code together without much planning.

The following three topics will be covered:

1) So far, your source code and binary files were mixed in with each other when you created them. It is convenient to just run them from the same directory that you were in. However, as the number of files grows, the resulting mess is simply annoying. What if you wanted to delete a binary file and deleted your source code instead by mistake? Bringing some order to the chaos via a project specific directory layout is a must when the number of packages and lines in your software grows.

2) Not far behind your directory structure, a project file will come in handy in order to build all of your code in a consistent manner. When you compile a file that pulls in other packages, only that file is compiled how you want it, meaning that it has the same compilation flags passed the compiler. Tools to make the compilation of your code more procedural will be introduced.

© Andrew T. Shvets 2020
A. T. Shvets, *Beginning Ada Programming*, https://doi.org/10.1007/978-1-4842-5428-8_16

3) Last, but equally important, is source control. What is source control? It is when you have an application, outside of the one that you are developing, that keeps track of the changes that you make to your code. Whenever you make a change that breaks your application and you wonder what you did wrong, having some way to diff the changes made to the file will become a lifesaver.

Application Folder Structure

First and foremost, the folder layout suggested in the following is a recommendation and is not any standard. Having your source code and the generated binaries in separate directories will make it much easier to be able to understand what is going on based purely by going to the directory where you expect things to be.

If you want to lay out your development directories differently or make a unique one for each project that you do, this is purely a matter of taste and the requirements of each project.

".hidden" Files in Project Directories

When writing this book and the accompanying code, all of it was dutifully checked into a Mercurial version control system.

One thing that must be mentioned, Mercurial does not keep track of created and committed directories if they do not have a file inside of them, which also will need to be committed. As a result, if you ever pull or clone your repository to a different location, then those empty directories will be pruned. This is something that is done by design by Mercurial.

In order to get around this, all Chapter 16 empty directories have a file called ".hidden" in them. The reason for this has to do with Mercurial and not Ada or Ada project build utility. You see, a file with a period in front of it, at least in Linux, means that that file is hidden and will not be displayed unless specifically sought out. Combined with its unrelated name, a seemingly empty directory structure can now be preserved and will not interfere with any of your builds.

In short, if you are looking at the accompanying code that you downloaded for Chapter 14, do not be concerned if you see any ".hidden" files. They are not related to Ada in any way (or Ada's build utilities) and will not interfere with your project:

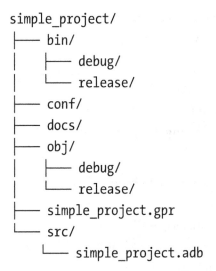

```
simple_project/
├── bin/
│   ├── debug/
│   └── release/
├── conf/
├── docs/
├── obj/
│   ├── debug/
│   └── release/
├── simple_project.gpr
└── src/
    └── simple_project.adb
```

Keep in mind that every time that you see a "/" at the end of any name, it means that that is a directory; otherwise, it is a file:

1) some_project – This is the name of our project and the main directory.

2) bin – This contains all of the executable binaries. These binaries are the built applications that can be run:

   a) debug – In this directory, you have the runnable binaries that have debug information. What is this exactly? This is a set of extra data stuffed into your binary that make it possible for a debugger to hook into this binary. With a debugger, you can more easily see what it is that your application is doing while it runs. The debugger, and how to use it, is discussed in Appendix D.

   This executable is useful most for your testing and debugging. You would normally perfect your product using a debug binary and get it ready to be released into the world, but it is not something that would be considered to be a finished product.

   b) release – This contains the binary of what is considered to be the final product. This is what would normally be used to either do late-stage testing or be released into the wild (sold or distributed as part of an open source application).

The release build does not have the debug information, which means it cannot be debugged in the traditional way that a debug build can.

3) `conf` – This directory holds your application's configuration information. You put your XML, JSON, and conf files here. Settings for things such as an IP address, or a path to a logging directory, would be put into a text file and stored in conf.

4) `doc` – Whenever a project is released, it makes sense to include some documentation with it. This can range from a simple text file to an HTML or PDF file. This is entirely up to you, as this directory can be left blank. However, giving others the ability to learn non-obvious features is often helpful and contributes greatly to your esteem in the eyes of users.

5) `obj` – This holds the object files that are generated as part of the compilation process. These are the $*$.o and $*$.ali files that you have seen whenever any Ada code was compiled. It makes sense to put them somewhere so that they do not clutter your source location.

   There are debug and release sub-directories so that these intermediate files will have a place to stay for each of the compilation processes.

6) `src` – This is where all of the source will reside. Here you can put all of your source files in one location or organize them further into library-like sub-directories. This will depend on the project at hand.

7) `simple_project.gpr` – This is the project file that is discussed in greater detail in the next section. The organization of this project at the folder level is closely tied to this file.

Again, the layout of this directory structure is purely dependent on the project at hand. If you had tests to verify the functionality of your application, it makes sense to place those in a "tests" directory in simple_project. If you are making a video game, a media directory might be helpful in order to place image and audio files.

Project File

The layout of a sample project is sufficiently obvious. However, a project file is needed to control all of this. This is where the simple_project.gpr file comes in. Again, the following project file is a recommendation, and you are free to modify it as you see fit for your project. In the accompanying code, Chapter 13 generic package project is compiled using this project file:

```
-- simple_project.gpr:

project Simple_Project is
  type Mode_Type is ("debug", "release");
  Mode : Mode_Type := external ("mode", "debug");

  for Source_Dirs use ("src");
  for Object_Dir use "obj/" & Mode;
  for Exec_Dir use "bin/" & Mode;
  for Main use ("generic_main.adb");

  package Builder is
  end Builder;

  package Compiler is
    case Mode is
      when "debug" =>
        for Switches ("Ada")
          use ("-g", "-gnatwa");
      when "release" =>
        for Switches ("Ada")
          use ("-O2", "-gnatwa");
    end case;
  end Compiler;

  package Binder is
  end Binder;

  package Linker is
  end Linker;
end Simple_Project;
```

The syntax of this project and that of an Ada package are remarkably alike, and this is by design. Let's take this file apart line by line:

1) `project Simple_Project is` – Just as you would with a package, you would create a project with the same name as the file. The only difference is the file has an ending of *.gpr.

2) `type Mode_Type is ("debug", "release");` – For our purposes, an enumerated type will be declared. Well, perhaps calling this an enumerated type is generous, but it is a close cousin to an Ada enumerated type.

   If you are wondering why this Mode_Type is needed, just remember that in the bin and obj directories there are release and debug sub-directories. This type will be used to switch from one to another.

3) `Mode : Mode_Type := external ("mode", "debug");` – Based on the type Mode_Type, a variable Mode is created. The external(…) function is basically saying that the command line needs to be checked if something was passed in. If something was passed in, then that argument is used to set the Mode variable. If this is not provided, then the value of "debug" is assigned by default.

   In short, if the Mode variable is not invoked at the command line, then it has the string "debug" assigned to it by default.

4) `for Source_Dirs use ("src");` – Here the Source_Dirs variable is used to point to the directory where our project should expect to find source code for our application. If the source is located in the same directory as the project file, then the string should be "".

   Furthermore, if you want to add any sub-directories, then specify them in another string that is separated by a comma:

   `for Source_Dirs use ("src", "src/lib");`

5) `for Object_Dir use "obj/" & Mode;` – This line is particularly interesting. Here the project file is saying to put all of the objects, the intermediate files that are part of the compilation process, into the obj folder.

However, there is that ampersand and the variable Mode. Remember how on line 23 the variable Mode was created and filled in based on what the caller of the project file passed in (or nothing at all) as a command-line argument? From that point, the Mode variable had either debug or release assigned to it. And in this case, the directory path to either "obj/release" or "obj/debug" was created dynamically.

So, when you compile your application, this information will be carried inside the project file and used to place the relevant binary products into its own location.

6) `for Exec_Dir use "bin/" & Mode;` – This is the same as the preceding obj folder example. The only difference is that the variable Exec_Dir will contain the finished application.

7) `for Main use ("generic_main.adb");` – The Main variable in our project will hold the name of the file that represents the entry point of the application.

8) `package Builder is` – This package is unique in this context. It is not a traditional package. Basically, what it does is enable the developer to specify how the application should be built. If you look down the file, you will see similar packages for the Linker and the Binder.

As the size and scope of your software systems grows, you might encounter instances where to get a unique form of functionality, and you would need to include certain flags or inputs for the build process.

9) `package Compiler is` – In this case, we want to do something precise when compiling. When the software is being compiled, a series of flags need to be set in order to tell the compiler to either build a release version or a debug version.

A case statement is used (not that different from an Ada one) to check whether the compilation process should make the build with debug information in the binary or not. This is demonstrated in the switches variable being set:

```
for Switches ("Ada")
use ("-g", "-gnatwa");
```

Pay attention to the string "Ada" in the Switch variable. Although project files were developed primarily in mind to build Ada applications, they can be used also to compile C and C++ code. However, this is beyond the scope of this book.

For the record, here is what each flag means:

a) "-g" – This is the debug flag. Build the code so that the debug information is part of the binary and the software can be hooked into by a debugger when it runs. Normally, this is done for the debug build.

b) "-O2" – This is the flag that is used to tell the compiler to optimize the binary to be very efficient and quick to execute. Normally, this is done for the release build.

c) "-gnatwa" – A compilation flag of this nature tells our compiler to treat all warnings and info messages as errors. This is done in order to make the compiler be even more strict about the type of code that is allowed to be turned into an executable. You are basically doing some form of static checking by having the compiler have a good look at the code to see if there are any silly mistakes beforehand, in order to ensure that there will be fewer problems when the application is created.

Including this flag is very much worth the effort up-front. It will save you a headache later on.

You can get at this information and more by running gnatmake --help in the command line. You will see hundreds of flags with an explanation as to what each does. The documentation for this tool is quite extensive.

Making Builds

Okay, the project structure is laid out and you have your project file, but how do you use it? As described in Appendixes A and B for Linux and Windows, respectively, you need to invoke the gprbuild command, like so:

```
> gprbuild
using project file simple_project.gpr
Compile
   [Ada]         generic_main.adb
   [Ada]         gener.adb
Bind
   [gprbind]     generic_main.bexch
   [Ada]         generic_main.ali
Link
   [link]        generic_main.adbgcc -c -g -gnatwa generic_main.adb
```

Remember as you go through the following explanation, based on how the project file was written, your application will compile with debugger information inside of it:

1) Notice the first line, where it prints out the exact project file that is being used; this is done on purpose so that there is no guessing about what *.gpr file is used.

2) gcc -c -g -gnatwa – Count the three lines that begin with this string. Notice how the same flags are being applied by the compiler to each of the *.adb files. In Chapter 13, when you did "gnatmake -g generic_main.adb", the -g flag was applied to the generic_main file, but not gener.adb. In this case, the same flag is applied to each *.adb file the same way.

   The beauty of using projects is being able to apply the same build rules to each of your source files. This is difficult and tedious to do by hand.

3) The rest of the lines are the commands of compiler and linker as it puts together the final application. At the very end, the generic_main object file is turned into an actual executable, like so:

   ```
   gcc generic_main.o -o generic_main
   ```

And now, how the application would be compiled for a release build:

```
> gprbuild -Xmode=release
using project file simple_project.gpr
Compile
   [Ada]          generic_main.adb
   [Ada]          gener.adb
Bind
   [gprbind]      generic_main.bexch
   [Ada]          generic_main.ali
Link
   [link]         generic_main.adb
```

1) `gprbuild -Xmode=release` – Remember how in our project file we specified the "mode" string for the Mode variable? It comes into play again.

   The "mode" string specified that in order to be able to set the Mode variable, at the command line, it would be "-Xmode=release". If you were to change the string to "comp", then you will need to write "-Xcomp=release".

   Furthermore, when the mode is specified, the external(…) function in the project is run, and the "release" string is grabbed and stored in the project's Mode variable.

   If, in place of "release", you specified "debug", then that would run the default compilation of making a debug build. No different from the first example of how the code was built.

2) `gcc -c -O2 -gnatwa gener.adb` – Here it is clearly illustrated that the compilation went exactly how it was supposed to. Based on the selection of the mode, the correct compilation flag ("-O2") was selected and used to build the release binary.

Command Arguments

If the "-Xmode=release" was mistyped and "-Xmode=cat" was used, then you would get an error message saying that "cat" is illegal for the variable Mode. The project building tool will ensure that you enter the right variable. And should a command-line argument of "cat" be needed, it can be added to the line where the Mode_Type is defined.

There is one more command-line argument that needs to be shown for the sake of completeness. It specifies the actual project file that is being used for the build:

```
> gprbuild -Xmode=release -Psimple_project
...
gcc generic_main.o -o generic_main
```

Wait a minute, what is "-Psimple_project"? That is the project file explicitly included. You would normally not need to be so explicit. The only time this would come in handy is when there are multiple project files to build different programs that are very similar in terms of functionality and the source code that they share, or they are part of a script that jumps from directory to directory in order to compile Ada projects.

And if you were to run the preceding command without the release specified, the debug version of the application would be built (the same as if no arguments were passed in).

Cleaning Up Builds

Creating binaries and placing them into their respective directories is all well and good. However, just as important, it is necessary to clean out these files once in a while. There is a different tool for this that also uses our simple_project.gpr file. That tool is called gprclean. Go into your repository and run it, like so:

```
> gprclean
using project file simple_project.gpr
"simple_project/obj/debug/gener.o" has been deleted
"simple_project/obj/debug/gener.ali" has been deleted
"simple_project/obj/debug/generic_main.o" has been deleted
"simple_project/obj/debug/generic_main.ali" has been deleted
"simple_project/bin/debug/generic_main" has been deleted
"simple_project/obj/debug/b__generic_main.o" has been deleted
"simple_project/obj/debug/b__generic_main.ads" has been deleted
"simple_project/obj/debug/b__generic_main.adb" has been deleted
"simple_project/obj/debug/b__generic_main.ali" has been deleted
"simple_project/obj/debug/generic_main.bexch" has been deleted
```

Let's have a closer look at what has happened:

1) `using project file simple_project.gpr` – As in gprbuild, gprclean tells us just which project file is being used.

2) `simple_project/obj/debug/` and `simple_project/bin/debug/` – Pay attention to the file path. The removal of generated files is done in both the bin and the obj directories.

And you can just as easily specify if you want to clean out the products of the build process from the release directory. All you need to do is name the mode:

```
> gprclean -Xmode=release
using project file simple_project.gpr
"simple_project/obj/release/gener.o" has been deleted
"simple_project/obj/release/gener.ali" has been deleted
"simple_project/obj/release/generic_main.o" has been deleted
"simple_project/obj/release/generic_main.ali" has been deleted
"simple_project/bin/release/generic_main" has been deleted
"simple_project/obj/release/b__generic_main.o" has been deleted
"simple_project/obj/release/b__generic_main.ads" has been deleted
"simple_project/obj/release/b__generic_main.adb" has been deleted
"simple_project/obj/release/b__generic_main.ali" has been deleted
"simple_project/obj/release/generic_main.bexch" has been deleted
```

And as with gprbuild, you can just as easily specify the project file should you be dealing with multiple projects, like so:

```
> gprclean -Psimple_project
"simple_project/obj/debug/gener.o" has been deleted
"simple_project/obj/debug/gener.ali" has been deleted
"simple_project/obj/debug/generic_main.o" has been deleted
"simple_project/obj/debug/generic_main.ali" has been deleted
"simple_project/bin/debug/generic_main" has been deleted
"simple_project/obj/debug/b__generic_main.o" has been deleted
"simple_project/obj/debug/b__generic_main.ads" has been deleted
"simple_project/obj/debug/b__generic_main.adb" has been deleted
"simple_project/obj/debug/b__generic_main.ali" has been deleted
"simple_project/obj/debug/generic_main.bexch" has been deleted
```

Or:

```
> gprclean -Psimple_project -Xmode=release
"simple_project/obj/release/gener.o" has been deleted
"simple_project/obj/release/gener.ali" has been deleted
"simple_project/obj/release/generic_main.o" has been deleted
"simple_project/obj/release/generic_main.ali" has been deleted
"simple_project/bin/release/generic_main" has been deleted
"simple_project/obj/release/b__generic_main.o" has been deleted
"simple_project/obj/release/b__generic_main.ads" has been deleted
"simple_project/obj/release/b__generic_main.adb" has been deleted
"simple_project/obj/release/b__generic_main.ali" has been deleted
"simple_project/obj/release/generic_main.bexch" has been deleted
```

Why "clean" a project? Simple. You might need to zip up the contents in order to e-mail it to a colleague, and making the source as compact as possible is the best option.

Advantages of Using Project Files

At this point, you might be thinking if the extra complexity of this tool is worth it. After all, simply compiling the starting function and letting the compiler pull in the rest of the packages does seem easy. While going without a project file might be very simple in a short amount of time, there are some serious benefits that should not be ignored:

1) Better organization, less cruft, and more control over what files go where. A project gives you the ability to place any of the generated files in their respective directories. This will make cleanup much easier and reduce the clutter of files in your project directory.

2) Improved control over how files are compiled and gives you the ability to make debug/release binaries or even custom builds with their own compilation flags for particular performance configurations. As mentioned before, if the generic_main.adb file was compiled with the debug flag, only that file will have debug information, gener.adb will not. However, with a project, each source file is compiled with the exact same flags.

Furthermore, this utility enables the developer to create parallel builds as needed. In this example, there are debug and release builds (or more).

3) Include other projects in order to make your application take advantage of already developed and tested code. To make use of AWS that has many useful tools to send e-mail and interact with the World Wide Web or AUnit used for a test-driven development framework, the project files from each of these will need to be used. Both are collections of libraries, so a different strategy is needed in order to build software with them. For this, you would simply include it in your project like so:

```
with "aws";
with "aunit";
```

Further Documentation

If you would like to know more about project files, here is an excellent piece of documentation that will describe every piece of this utility:

```
https://docs.adacore.com/gprbuild-docs/html/gprbuild_ug.html
```

Source Control

If you already know about source control and have a favorite tool in mind, feel free to skim through this section, or skip it entirely. If you know little about source control, then read through it. Source control is not a requirement in order to do software development, but it is extremely helpful.

Being able to store your source code in an organized manner that lets you track changes will become essential with any non-trivial application. Sure, a developPop Tubeser might implement a small prototype that works. However, the minute that you want to add any extra functionality to your product, the complexity will grow. It will become impossible to keep track of every code change in your head, and recall all of it perfectly without forgetting a single detail.

In this section, three source control tools will be described. Each has its own advantages and disadvantages. The goal is to give the reader an overview of what each does. When it comes to installing and configuring each utility, this is beyond the scope of this book. Fortunately, each program has plenty of useful and accurate documentation online to help you should a problem arise.

Lastly, all of the tools described here are open source and you can acquire them without paying a dime. There are proprietary applications that can do the job, but the availability of open source solutions makes it much easier to get started.

Is It Source Control or Configuration Management or Something Else?

The term that will be used in this book is source control. In other books or web sites, such an application might be referred to as Configuration Management (CM) or Software Configuration Management (SCM), among many other terms. For the purposes of this discussion, these all refer to the same concept of keeping track of changes that are made in your application.

If there are any conceptual differences among these acronyms, then they are beyond the scope of this book:

1) Mercurial – This is a distributed source control application. Distributed means that when you check out someone's repository, you have all of the tools to be able to diff or commit to your local repository. At some point, you will need to push or pull your changes to a more centralized repository if you are working with others on a project:

   a) Pros: Mercurial is fairly easy to get started with, since the learning curve is not too steep. Furthermore, the distributed nature of Mercurial permits you to have your own repository wherever you want, even when not connected to a network. Getting started with this tool is very easy. There is plenty of documentation describing how to best use it. It can handle binary files, even large ones.

b) Cons: A distributed source control application can be difficult to understand for those that are coming from a centralized source control one such as Subversion and CVS. If you have very large projects, like a Linux kernel, then certain operations will not be very quick and performance could suffer; keep in mind that the existing code base needs to be massive.

c) Documentation: The main web site of Mercurial is this:

www.mercurial-scm.org/

And here is a good book that will get you started:

http://hgbook.red-bean.com/read/

2) Git – This is also a distributed source control solution. The primary difference between Git and Mercurial is that Git tends to be much faster at working with large code bases:

a) Pros: Faster than Mercurial when it comes to working with large sets of code. Like Mercurial, Git lets you work on your repository wherever you want, even if no Internet connection is available. Also, the documentation is plentiful. Git has become much more popular than Mercurial in the past 5 years and has become the de facto distributed source control tool.

b) Cons: Slightly steeper learning curve than Mercurial. This is even more so for someone who has mostly worked with CVS or Subversion.

c) Documentation: The main web site of Git is this:

https://git-scm.com/

And here is a good book to begin:

https://git-scm.com/book/en/v2

3) Subversion – This is a centralized source control application. This means that it needs to be hosted on a server, and others need to be granted access. Unfortunately, if the server is down or cannot be

reached, no one can commit or check out each other's work. One benefit of Subversion is that it is easy to grasp the concept behind this tool:

a) Pros: Easy to understand for someone who is new to source control. Has plenty of documentation. It works well for projects that do not become massive; you would not want to manage the source of the Linux kernel with Subversion.

b) Cons: It is a centralized solution and will be useless when you lose your network connection, or you are working offsite and do not have a connection back to your office. It requires more planning on topics such as administration and hosting. If your project grows to include dozens of developers and they are all over the world, then performance could very well suffer.

c) Documentation: This is the main web site of Subversion:

`https://subversion.apache.org/`

And here is a good book to get a newbie started:

`http://svnbook.red-bean.com/en/1.7/`

One recommendation for those starting out with source control, do not think that you must read each and every one of those books cover to cover if you want to get something done. First, get a small repository going, and then use your favorite search engine to look online for various blog posts and tutorials on basic functionality. The books are mentioned so that you have a reference point, and then look up the non-trivial topics.

Now, we will move on to the last topic that you will need as your proficiency in Ada improves.

Lab

Like what you have seen done for the generic package in Chapter 13, do the same for the Air_Vehicle package (and its descendants).

CHAPTER 17

Libraries

What You Will Get Out of This Chapter

Libraries are unique containers in that they permit you to package up your code and then simply reuse it elsewhere without needing the original source by simply including them. The advantage here is not having to compile a library from scratch (even more beneficial if the compilation process is very time-consuming) and not needing to have the source code that you want to leverage. We will make use of a very simple library and then see how we can use it in Windows and Linux.

The differences between shared and static libraries will be discussed. When should you use one over the other? How would you include an existing library built for you?

Library Source

The following example is very trivial. The purpose is to have something that can serve as a library:

```
-- calc_time.ads:

package Calc_Time is
  type Mins is private;

  function Init
    return Mins;

  function Init(
    Minutes : in Natural)
      return Mins;
```

© Andrew T. Shvets 2020
A. T. Shvets, *Beginning Ada Programming*, https://doi.org/10.1007/978-1-4842-5428-8_17

```
   function Init(
     Hours : in Natural;
     Minutes : in Natural)
       return Mins;

   function Add_Hours(
     Val : in Mins;
     Hours : in Natural)
       return Mins;

   function Add_Minutes(
     Val : in Mins;
     Minutes : in Natural)
       return Mins;

   function Subtract_Hours(
     Val : in Mins;
     Hours : in Natural)
       return Mins;

   function Subtract_Minutes(
     Val : in Mins;
     Minutes : in Natural)
       return Mins;

   procedure Put(
     Val : in Mins);

   procedure Put_Line(
     Val : in Mins);
private
  type Mins is record
    Hours : Natural   := 0;
    Minutes : Natural := 0;
  end record;
```

```ada
  function Get_Minutes(
    Val : in Mins)
      return Natural;
end Calc_Time;

-- calc_time.adb:

with Ada.Text_IO;

package body Calc_Time is
  function Init
    return Mins is

    Min : Mins;
  begin
    return Min;
  end Init;

  function Init(
    Minutes : in Natural)
      return Mins is

    Min : Mins;
  begin
    if (Minutes > 59)
    then
      Min.Minutes := Minutes;
    else
      Min.Hours := Minutes / 60;
      Min.Minutes := Minutes;
    end if;

    return Min;
  end Init;

  function Init(
    Hours : in Natural;
    Minutes : in Natural)
      return Mins is
```

```
    Min : Mins;
  begin
    Min.Hours := Hours;
    Min.Minutes := Minutes;

    return Min;
  end Init;

  function Add_Hours(
    Val : in Mins;
    Hours : in Natural)
      return Mins is

    Temp_Val : Mins;
  begin
    Temp_Val.Hours := Val.Hours + Hours;
    Temp_Val.Minutes := Val.Minutes;

    return Temp_Val;
  end Add_Hours;

  function Add_Minutes(
    Val : in Mins;
    Minutes : in Natural)
      return Mins is

    Temp_Hours : Natural := 0;
    Temp_Mins : Mins;
  begin
    if (Minutes + Val.Minutes) > 59
    then
      Temp_Hours := (Val.Minutes + Minutes) / 60;
      Temp_Mins.Minutes := (Val.Minutes + Minutes) rem 60;
      Temp_Mins.Hours := Val.Hours + Temp_Hours;

      return Temp_Mins;
    else
      Temp_Mins.Hours := Val.Hours;
      Temp_Mins.Minutes := Temp_Mins.Minutes + Minutes;
```

```
      return Temp_Mins;
   end if;
end Add_Minutes;

function Subtract_Hours(
   Val : in Mins;
   Hours : in Natural)
      return Mins is

   Temp_Mins : Mins := Val;
begin
   if Hours > Val.Hours
   then
      return Val;
   else
      Temp_Mins.Hours := Temp_Mins.Hours - Hours;

      return Temp_Mins;
   end if;
end Subtract_Hours;

function Subtract_Minutes(
   Val : in Mins;
   Minutes : in Natural)
      return Mins is

   Total_Minutes : Natural := Get_Minutes(Val);
   Temp_Mins : Mins;
begin
   if Minutes > Total_Minutes
   then
      return Val;
   else
      Total_Minutes := Total_Minutes - Minutes;

      Temp_Mins.Hours := Total_Minutes / 60;
      Temp_Mins.Minutes := Total_Minutes rem 60;
```

```ada
      return Temp_Mins;
    end if;
  end Subtract_Minutes;

  procedure Put(
    Val : in Mins) is

  begin
    Ada.Text_IO.Put("Hours: " & Natural'Image(Val.Hours) & " Minutes: " &
      Natural'Image(Val.Minutes));
  end Put;

  procedure Put_Line(
    Val : in Mins) is

  begin
    Put(Val);
    Ada.Text_IO.New_Line;
  end Put_Line;

  function Get_Minutes(
    Val : in Mins)
      return Natural is

  begin
    return Val.Hours * 60 + Val.Minutes;
  end Get_Minutes;
end Calc_Time;

-- geometry_shapes.ads:

package Geometry_Shapes is
  function Circle_Area(
    Radius : in Float)
      return Float;

  function Circle_Circumference(
    Radius : in Float)
      return Float;
```

```ada
   function Rectangle_Area(
     X : in Float;
     Y : in Float)
       return Float;

   function Square_Area(
     Side : in Float)
       return Float;

   function Sphere_Volume(
     Radius : in Float)
       return Float;
end Geometry_Shapes;

-- geometry_shapes.adb:

with Ada.Numerics;

package body Geometry_Shapes is
   function Circle_Area(
     Radius : in Float)
       return Float is

   begin
     return Radius * Radius * Ada.Numerics.Pi;
   end Circle_Area;

   function Circle_Circumference(
     Radius : in Float)
       return Float is

   begin
     return Radius * 2.0 * Ada.Numerics.Pi;
   end Circle_Circumference;

   function Rectangle_Area(
     X : in Float;
     Y : in Float)
       return Float is
```

```
begin
  return X * Y;
end Rectangle_Area;

function Square_Area(
  Side : in Float)
    return Float is

begin
  return Rectangle_Area(Side, Side);
end Square_Area;

function Sphere_Volume(
  Radius : in Float)
    return Float is

begin
  return (4.0 / 3.0) * Ada.Numerics.Pi * Radius * Radius * Radius;
end Sphere_Volume;
end Geometry_Shapes;
```

The preceding code is very straightforward, and there is no need to provide any detailed explanation.

Having seen the code, we will make two types of libraries, static and shared. A static library must be included in your application when you compile it, meaning it will be embedded in the resulting binary file. A shared library is included in the application when it begins to execute. There are a number of advantages and disadvantages between the two types, and let's look into those:

- Using a shared library gives you the option to add it to your application only when you need it, consuming less memory and other resources when it executes.

- On the other hand, having a static library means that you have everything that you need immediately when it begins executing. If the dynamic library cannot be found or is the wrong version, this could result in an exception being thrown, and your program needs to be able to handle this, or subtle errors happen that are not self-evident right away.

- Depending on the size of the library, your application could take a performance hit as a result of it locating and loading the library. If this happens often enough, then it can result in a sluggish product.

At this point, you might be wondering, which one should I choose? Here are some some recommendations (these are not rules, merely suggestions):

- Create a static library when you are working in an embedded environment or when performance can be an issue during execution time. Also, when you are not sure that the deployed environment will have your library, including your library in your application at compile time is the way to go.

- Create a dynamic library when it is quite large and you are not certain that you will make use of it. You might be tasked with creating an application that interfaces with a piece of hardware. First it would be wise to check if the hardware is installed before proceeding to work with it; only after your code has verified that the item is there, will it make sense to begin loading all of the supporting binaries into RAM.

Building the Library Object

In order to build a library, a project file becomes indispensable. It is possible to do without one, but the number of hoops that you will need to jump through will be needlessly tedious. As a result, the following project file will be used for this chapter to compile the previously mentioned code:

```
-- lib_build.gpr

library project Lib_Build is
  type Mode_Type is ("debug", "release");
  Mode : Mode_Type := external("mode", "debug");

  for Library_Name use "simpleLibs";
  for Source_Dirs use ("src");
  for Object_Dir use "obj/" & Mode;
  for Library_Dir use "bin/" & Mode;
  for Library_Kind use "static"; --"static/dynamic";
```

```
   for Library_ALI_Dir use "ali/" & Mode;
   --for Library_Interface use ("Calc_Time", "Geometry_Shapes");

   package Builder is
   end Builder;

   package Compiler is
     case Mode is
       when "debug" =>
         for Switches("Ada") use ("-g", "-gnatwa");
       when "release" =>
         for Switches("Ada") use ("-O2", "-gnatwa");
     end case;
   end Compiler;

   package Binder is
   end Binder;

   package Linker is
   end Linker;
end Lib_Build;
```

This project is much different from what we have seen before. Let's take it slow and digest everything carefully:

1) `library project Lib_Build is` – Notice the word "library" right before project. This tells the Ada building tool that we are dealing with something other than a plain application. This keyword is required if you want to build libraries.

2) Lines 23 and 24 are the same as you have seen in the previous example of project files.

3) `for Library_Name use "simpleLibs";` – Instead of specifying the name of the application, the library's name is mentioned.

4) `for Library_Dir use "bin/" & Mode;` – This next new line again calls out the library explicitly and indicates where it will be placed when compiled. It is the same as Exec_Dir in the previous project file example.

5) `for Library_Kind use "static"; --"static/dynamic";` – This is where you specify which library you would like to see created. In this instance, it will be a static library. However, in the future, we will reuse this same project file to create a dynamic library out of the same code; in Windows it is a "Dynamically Linked Library" and in Linux it is a "Shared Object," hence the "dynamic" keyword.

6) `for Library_ALI_Dir use "ali/" & Mode;` – ALI files are needed in order to create a library. They are created during the compilation process, and you have to place them somewhere. ALI stands for "Ada Library Information" and contains dependency information about the compiled code.

7) `--for Library_Interface use ("Calc_Time", "Geometry_Shapes");` – This will be used later on when we talk about shared libraries. For now, it is commented out.

8) Note that there is a distinct lack of a main file where the code should begin to execute. In a library, this does not make any sense. A library has a bunch of functions together, and you can run whichever chunk of code that you need.

If you want to learn more about ALI, please visit this web page:

```
https://gcc.gnu.org/onlinedocs/gnat_ugn/The-Ada-Library-
Information-Files.html
```

Using the Library Object
Static Library

Let's first look into how we can build an application using just static libraries. Note, the following examples for static libraries work the same in Windows and Linux. This is how we can simply include the preceding project file and build our application. First is the project file that assumes we know the source code for the file:

```
with "../../../lib_build.gpr";
```

```
project Main_Static is
  for Source_Dirs use (".");
  for Object_Dir use ".";
  for Main use ("main_static.adb");
  for Languages use ("Ada");

  package Builder is
  end Builder;

  package Compiler is
    for Switches("Ada") use ("-g", "-gnatwa");
  end Compiler;

  package Binder is
  end Binder;

  package Linker is
  end Linker;
end Main_Static;
```

The file is located in the directory ch17/library/main/static/project:

1) with "../../../lib_build.gpr"; – First, we make sure that the library project that we need is included.

2) The rest of the file specifies just how the resulting application should be compiled. The compiler flags and the main function are specified. In this case, it is very much stripped down to the basics that you need.

3) Linking the library into the binary and compiling all of the code is handled by the gprbuild utility. You just have to ensure that there are no syntax errors in your project file.

And here is the application that makes use of the static library:

```
-- main_static.adb:

with Ada.Text_IO;

with Geometry_Shapes;
with Calc_Time;
```

```ada
procedure Main_Static is
  Radius_Val : constant Float := 4.5;
  X_Side : constant Float     := 8.0;
  Y_Side : constant Float     := 13.5;

  Curr_Time : Calc_Time.Mins := Calc_Time.Init(4, 25);
begin
  Ada.Text_IO.Put_Line(" The current radius that is being used: " &
    Float'Image(Radius_Val));
  Ada.Text_IO.Put_Line("   The area of a circle:            " &
    Float'Image(Geometry_Shapes.Circle_Area(Radius_Val)));
  Ada.Text_IO.Put_Line("   The circumference of a circle:     " &
    Float'Image(Geometry_Shapes.Circle_Circumference(Radius_Val)));
  Ada.Text_IO.Put_Line("   The volume of a sphere:          " &
    Float'Image(Geometry_Shapes.Sphere_Volume(Radius_Val)));
  Ada.Text_IO.New_Line(2);

  Ada.Text_IO.Put_Line(" The current X side of a rectangle:    " &
    Float'Image(X_Side));
  Ada.Text_IO.Put_Line(" The current Y side of a rectangle:    " &
    Float'Image(Y_Side));
  Ada.Text_IO.Put_Line("   The area of a square with X size:   " &
    Float'Image(Geometry_Shapes.Square_Area(X_Side)));
  Ada.Text_IO.Put_Line("   The area of a square with X size:   " &
    Float'Image(Geometry_Shapes.Rectangle_Area(X_Side, Y_Side)));
  Ada.Text_IO.New_Line(2);

  -- print the currrent time.
  Ada.Text_IO.Put_Line(" The current time:");
  Calc_Time.Put_Line(Curr_Time);
  Ada.Text_IO.New_Line;

  -- add hours and print it out.
  Ada.Text_IO.Put_Line(" The current time after 12 hours added:");
  Curr_Time := Calc_Time.Add_Hours(Curr_Time, 12);
  Calc_Time.Put_Line(Curr_Time);
  Ada.Text_IO.New_Line;
```

```
 -- add minutes and print it out.
 Ada.Text_IO.Put_Line(" The current time after 12 minutes added:");
 Curr_Time := Calc_Time.Add_Minutes(Curr_Time, 12);
 Calc_Time.Put_Line(Curr_Time);
 Ada.Text_IO.New_Line;

 Ada.Text_IO.Put_Line(" The current time after 67 minutes added:");
 Curr_Time := Calc_Time.Add_Minutes(Curr_Time, 67);
 Calc_Time.Put_Line(Curr_Time);
 Ada.Text_IO.New_Line;

 -- subtract hours and print it out.
 Calc_Time.Put_Line(Curr_Time);
 Ada.Text_IO.Put_Line(" The current time after 2 hours subtracted:");
 Curr_Time := Calc_Time.Subtract_Hours(Curr_Time, 2);
 Calc_Time.Put_Line(Curr_Time);
 Ada.Text_IO.New_Line;

 -- subtract minutes and print it out.
 Ada.Text_IO.Put_Line(" The current time after 6 minutes subtracted:");
 Curr_Time := Calc_Time.Subtract_Minutes(Curr_Time, 6);
 Calc_Time.Put_Line(Curr_Time);
 Ada.Text_IO.New_Line;

 Ada.Text_IO.Put_Line(" The current time after 39 minutes subtracted:");
 Curr_Time := Calc_Time.Subtract_Minutes(Curr_Time, 39);
 Calc_Time.Put_Line(Curr_Time);
 Ada.Text_IO.New_Line;
end Main_Static;
```

Most of this example is very straightforward. Most of the code you see is something that you have learned back in Chapter 5. However, there are some points of interest that need to be covered:

1) `with Geometry_Shapes; with Calc_Time;` – Notice how these packages were simply included without doing anything special. Since the static libraries are included right at the beginning of the compilation process, the build tools resolve these issues right away.

2) `Curr_Time : Calc_Time.Mins := Calc_Time.Init(4, 25);` – Once everything is included in our code as it should be, any package can be instantiated at will, and any method inside of it can be easily called.

The preceding example was very simple. However, in time, you are bound to encounter instances where you will have just the static library and not the source code. For example, you might be asked to use a library that is part of some proprietary software. What do you do then? The preceding project file will not work, since you do not have the source code! For that, you will need to create a brand new project file, a wrapper that will smooth the compilation and linking process.

This is the output that you should see when you run the preceding program:

```
> ./main_dynamic
  The current radius that is being used:  4.50000E+00
    The area of a circle:                 6.36173E+01
    The circumference of a circle:        2.82743E+01
    The volume of a sphere:               3.81703E+02

  The current X side of a rectangle:      8.00000E+00
  The current Y side of a rectangle:      1.35000E+01
    The area of a square with X size:     6.40000E+01
    The area of a square with X size:     1.08000E+02

  The current time:
Hours:  4 Minutes:  25

  The current time after 12 hours added:
Hours:  16 Minutes:  25

  The current time after 12 minutes added:
Hours:  16 Minutes:  12
```

```
  The current time after 67 minutes added:
Hours:   17 Minutes:   19

Hours:   17 Minutes:   19
  The current time after 2 hours subtracted:
Hours:   15 Minutes:   19

  The current time after 6 minutes subtracted:
Hours:   15 Minutes:   13

  The current time after 39 minutes subtracted:
Hours:   14 Minutes:   34
```

Using the Ada code that was shown previously in main_static.adb and the following custom project file, you will be able to link in just the static library. Let's first look at the file that will wrap around just the static library:

```
-- use_project.gpr:

library project Use_Project is
  for Languages use ("Ada");
  for Externally_Built use "true";
  for Source_Dirs use ("src");
  for Library_Dir use "bin/debug";
  for Library_Name use "simpleLibs";
  for Library_Kind use "static"; --"static/dynamic";
  for Library_ALI_Dir use "ali/debug";
end Use_Project;
```

This project file is unclear, given the role that it plays in the entire compilation process. Let's take it slow and pick it apart:

1) `for Externally_Built use "true";` – This tells the Ada compiler that the binary is built outside of this project, and it needs to be connected to whoever needs to use it. This will also stop any compilation that might need to be done; after all, we are supposed to make use of a binary that is already created.

2) `for Source_Dirs use ("src");` – This is where the source code is located. At this point, you might remember that in this instance the goal is to make use of a binary to which the source is not available. So why bother with the source? Great question.

   In any instance where you want to make use of a library, you need header files. Header files in C/C++ are usually *.h and *.hpp files. In our case, it is the definition file *.ads. For this to work, the header files are necessary, as it is for some other compiled programming languages, and the Source_Dirs variable points to their location.

3) `for Library_Dir use "bin/debug";` – Now the actual location of the static library – the *.a file – is needed. Here you specify the directory of this file, but not its actual name, for that you will do so in the next line of use_project.gpr.

4) `for Library_Name use "simpleLibs";` – This is which binary library that we need. Note that it only says "simpleLibs". The actual file is called "libsimpleLibs.a". The "lib" and ".a" are assumed by the build tools, and you do not need to specify them.

5) `for Library_ALI_Dir use "ali/debug";` – The ali files are needed as well. Here we specify their location. They specify certain details for the Ada build tools in order to compile your application successfully. If you want to learn more about what role ALI files play, please see the link right before the section "Using the Library Object."

And now is the project file that will compile main_static.adb while making use of the preceding use_project.gpr:

```
-- main_static.gpr:

with "../../../use_project.gpr";

project Main_Static is
  for Source_Dirs use (".");
  for Object_Dir use ".";
  for Main use ("main_static.adb");
  for Languages use ("Ada");
```

```
  package Builder is
  end Builder;

  package Compiler is
    for Switches("Ada") use ("-g", "-gnatwa");
  end Compiler;

  package Binder is
  end Binder;

  package Linker is
  end Linker;
end Main_Static;
```

The only thing that you need to keep in mind is this:

```
with "../../../use_project.gpr";
```

On this line, you are referencing the use_project.pgr, the middle layer between your static binary file and the program that wants to use it.

Do not forget that it will compile the exact same main_static.adb file as mentioned previously.

Shared Library

Now we will look into making a program that uses a shared library. Right away, we will make use of the same top-level use_project.gpr and lib_build.gpr files. Let's first talk about the latter.

Here is the lib_build.gpr again, but this time modified for building shared libraries:

```
-- lib_build.gpr:

library project Lib_Build is
  type Mode_Type is ("debug", "release");
  Mode : Mode_Type := external("mode", "debug");

  for Languages use ("Ada");
  for Library_Name use "simpleLibs";
  for Source_Dirs use ("src");
  for Object_Dir use "obj/" & Mode;
```

```
for Library_Dir use "bin/" & Mode;
for Library_Kind use "static"; --"static/dynamic";
for Library_ALI_Dir use "ali/" & Mode;
for Library_Interface use ("Calc_Time", "Geometry_Shapes");

package Builder is
end Builder;

package Compiler is
  case Mode is
    when "debug" =>
      for Switches("Ada") use ("-g", "-gnatwa");
    when "release" =>
      for Switches("Ada") use ("-O2", "-gnatwa");
  end case;
end Compiler;

package Binder is
end Binder;

package Linker is
end Linker;
end Lib_Build;
```

Let's go through some key points:

1) for Library_Kind use "dynamic"; --"static/dynamic"; –
This tells the compiler that the resulting binary will be a shared
one and needs to be included at runtime and not when the
application is compiled. With this change, when you compile the
library code, you will see a libsimpleLibs.dll for Windows and
libsimpleLibs.so for Linux in the bin directory.

2) for Library_Interface use ("Calc_Time", "Geometry_
Shapes"); – This code is no longer commented out. For a shared
library, it needs to export the packages that outside applications
should have access to. You could look at it as a crude form of data
hiding as was discussed in the OOP chapter. If you fail to do this,
then your code will not be able to make use of this functionality.

When you compile everything, you should see a libsimpleLibs.dll (or libsimpleLibs.so for Linux) file in bin/debug.

use_project.gpr will need changes as well. We can use the same project file to specify to our program where the DLL is located and how it can be accessed:

```
-- use_project.gpr:

library project Use_Project is
  for Languages use ("Ada");
  for Externally_Built use "true";
  for Source_Dirs use ("src");
  for Library_Dir use "bin/debug";
  for Library_Name use "simpleLibs";
  for Library_Kind use "dynamic"; --"static/dynamic";
  for Library_ALI_Dir use "ali/debug";
end Use_Project;
```

The only thing that needs to be modified is the following line:

```
for Library_Kind use "dynamic";
```

This is necessary in order to ensure that the shared library will be used during the compilation and linking process.

One thing that you need to do is copy the generated DLL to the same location where the binary is located. This seems to be only the case for Windows. When your binary begins to execute, it will immediately begin to look for the library. It first searches in its local directory before trying to find it in the various system directories. If it is not found, then it throws an exception saying so and will not continue to execute. This has to do with how the Windows OS searches for libraries when an application runs. In Linux, you can just run the program and you will see the same results as when you compiled your program with a static library.

Another Option

There is a different way to solve this problem. You can load the shared libraries from inside of the application explicitly:

```
http://rosettacode.org/wiki/Call_a_function_in_a_shared_
library#Ada
```

You can try this by yourself.

One disadvantage to the preceding method is that much of the underlying work that goes into linking the shared library correctly will not be handled for you. You can certainly try to use this method if there is no other solution available.

Conclusion

Hopefully, you now understand the benefits that Ada brings and have a few of your own ideas on how to put together a given application. This programming language has the power to create incredibly robust software that is more reliable and has fewer bugs and errors.

If you have an idea in your head, write it down on paper. Then, proceed to gradually build up to that idea by making small additions over time. If you get stuck, look back at this book or experiment with alternative implementations; rarely is there a "one" and "true" way to make something work.

Lab

Use the preceding code for a library and add a class to simulate a passenger automobile. Give it the ability to specify the motor, transmission, horsepower, and so on.

However, instead of simply adding the package to the existing library, have it compile into a completely new binary alongside "simpleLibs". You will need to create a separate source directory and put the new package files there; otherwise, the build tools will create two exactly the same libraries with different filenames. Look at the previous examples in this chapter as a guide.

APPENDIX A

Installing GNAT in Linux and Unix

When it comes to installing the Ada compiler on a Linux (or Unix) machine, first check to see if you can install it via your package manager. Do the following in the command line; you might need root privileges:

1) Debian/Ubuntu/LinuxMint:

   ```
   $ sudo apt install gnat
   $ sudo apt install gprbuild
   ```

2) Gentoo:

   ```
   $ emerge dev-lang/gnat
   ```

3) Fedora/CentOS:

   ```
   $ yum install fedora-gnat-project-common gprbuild
   ```

4) For FreeBSD, do the following in the command line (you might need root privileges):

   ```
   $ pkg install gps-ide
   ```

Once the install finishes successfully, open a terminal with non-privileged user permissions and run the "gnatmake –version" command, like so:

```
> gnatmake --version
GNATMAKE 6.2.1 20160830
Copyright (C) 1995-2016, Free Software Foundation, Inc.
```

© Andrew T. Shvets 2020
A. T. Shvets, *Beginning Ada Programming*, https://doi.org/10.1007/978-1-4842-5428-8

```
This is free software; see the source for copying conditions.
There is NO warranty; not even for MERCHANTABILITY or FITNESS FOR A
PARTICULAR PURPOSE.
```

And run the gprbuild utility as well:

```
> gprbuild --version
GPRBUILD GPL 2016 (20160515) (x86_64-pc-linux-gnu)
Copyright (C) 2004-2016, AdaCore
This is free software; see the source for copying conditions.
There is NO warranty; not even for MERCHANTABILITY or FITNESS FOR A
PARTICULAR PURPOSE.
```

If you see output similar to what is shown, then you are finished and can go on with the rest of the book.

If you do not see the version of either gnatmake or gprbuild, check to make sure that your install was successful. Connectivity issues as well as installation conflicts can stop this process.

However, if you did all of the above and still do not see the version of the utility printed out (or your OS does not have the above package to install), then do the following:

1) Go to the AdaCore web site from where you will get the correct binaries:

   `www.adacore.com/community`

2) Click the picture with the words "GNAT Community Download."

3) Locate the link that is just below the title "GNAT GPL Ada," click it, and download the executable. The link will look similar to this: gnat-gpl-2017-x86_64-linux-bin.tar.gz.

4) Create an install location. In our case it will be located in the home directory:

   `$ mkdir ~/ada_install`

5) After the download is complete, move the file to a location where you can open it up, if you have not done this already; you can create a temporary directory where the download is residing.

6)   In that directory run the binary that you downloaded:

   `$ ./gnat-community-2019-20190517-x86_64-linux-bin`

Now follow these steps to complete the install:

a)   When you run the script, on the first printout of text, simply press Enter.

b)   On the second printout, specify the directory where you want to have your Ada compiler installed. If the directory is not created, then go create one now.

   Once this directory is made, enter the direct path to it, meaning **DO NOT** type this:

   `~/ada_install`

   But type this:

   `/home/adadeveloper/ada_compiler`

   Take care to enter the path correctly, since there is no auto-complete for filenames when you hit the Tab key.

c)   Hit the Enter key when ready to proceed.

d)   On the next text printout, you will be asked if you want to proceed with the install; enter "Y" and hit the Enter key. If prompted again to verify that you are certain that you want to proceed, enter "Y" and hit the Enter key again.

   The install can take some time to complete; feel free to grab more tea or coffee.

e)   In your ~/.bashrc file (or whichever configuration file corresponds to the shell that you use), insert the following text at the bottom:

   `$PATH=/home/adadeveloper/ada_compiler:$PATH; export $PATH`

   In a new terminal, reload the file in question:

   `$ source ~/.bashrc`

f) Once the install finishes successfully, open a non-privileged terminal and run the "gnatmake –version" command:

```
> gnatmake --version
GNATMAKE 6.2.1 20160830
Copyright (C) 1995-2016, Free Software Foundation, Inc.
This is free software; see the source for copying conditions.
There is NO warranty; not even for MERCHANTABILITY or FITNESS
FOR A PARTICULAR PURPOSE.
```

You should see output similar to what is displayed above.

And run the gprbuild utility as well:

```
> gprbuild --version
GPRBUILD GPL 2016 (20160515) (x86_64-pc-linux-gnu)
Copyright (C) 2004-2016, AdaCore
This is free software; see the source for copying conditions.
There is NO warranty; not even for MERCHANTABILITY or FITNESS
FOR A PARTICULAR PURPOSE.
```

You should see similar output.

7) gprbuild is necessary for Chapters 16 and 17. The lack of this toolset will not hinder you for the preceding chapters.

APPENDIX B

Installing GNAT in Windows

To install on Windows, follow these steps:

1) Go to the AdaCore web site where you will get the correct binaries:

   `www.adacore.com/community`

2) Click the picture with the words "GNAT Community Download."

3) Locate the link that is just below the title "GNAT GPL Ada," click it, and download the executable. The link will look similar to this: gnat-gpl-2017-x86-windows-bin.exe.

4) When prompted, save the executable at the place of your choosing.

5) In Windows Explorer, navigate to the location where the download is saved.

6) Double-click the file to begin the install.

7) In the window "GNAT GPL 2017," click "Next".

8) Click "Next" in order to accept the default destination folder.

9) Click "Next" in order to accept the default Menu Folder location.

10) Click "Install" in order to start the install. This might take some time to finish.

11) Click "Finish" when the install is done.

© Andrew T. Shvets 2020
A. T. Shvets, *Beginning Ada Programming*, https://doi.org/10.1007/978-1-4842-5428-8

12) Now, it is time to run a test. Open the command prompt. How you get to it depends on the version of Windows that you are running. If you do not know how to open this window, please consult Microsoft's web site or search for it online.

13) Now execute the "gnatmake --version" command, and you should see the following:

```
C:\Users\ada>gnatmake --version
GNATMAKE GPL 2017 (20170515-49)
Copyright (C) 1995-2017, Free Software Foundation, Inc.
This is free software; see the source for copying conditions.
There is NO warranty; not even for MERCHANTABILITY or FITNESS FOR
A PARTICULAR PURPOSE.
```

If you do not see the preceding data, please re-trace the install procedure and ensure that all steps were executed successfully.

14) Also, do the same for the gprbuild utility and you should see the following:

```
C:\Users\ada>gprbuild --version
GPRBUILD GPL 2017 (20170515) (i686-pc-mingw32)
Copyright (C) 2004-2017, AdaCore
This is free software; see the source for copying conditions.
There is NO warranty; not even for MERCHANTABILITY or FITNESS FOR
A PARTICULAR PURPOSE.
```

If you do not see the output, please re-trace the install procedure and ensure that all steps were executed successfully.

gprbuild is necessary for Chapters 16 and 17. The lack of this toolset will not hinder you for the preceding chapters.

Reserved Keywords

Here is a list of words that you cannot use as a name for a package, procedure, function, or variable. These words are reserved by the compiler for its own purposes. Avoid them standalone, but feel free to use them as parts of variables, packages, and so on.

abort	else	null	select
abs	elsif	of	separate
abstract	end	or	some
accept	entry	others	subtype
access	exception	out	synchronized
aliased	exit	overriding	tagged
all	for	package	task
and	function	pragma	terminate
array	generic	private	then
at	goto∗	procedure	type
begin	if	protected	until
body	in	raise	use
case	interface	range	when
constant	is	record	while
declare	limited	rem	with
delay	loop	renames	xor

(*continued*)

© Andrew T. Shvets 2020
A. T. Shvets, *Beginning Ada Programming*, https://doi.org/10.1007/978-1-4842-5428-8

delta	mod	requeue
digits	new	return
do	not	reverse

*The only "bad" keyword that is in the entire bunch. It is here because of legacy code reasons. It's easy to start using this keyword and it easily creates some very confusing spaghetti code.

Also, when you do use them as part of other names, do so where they stand out from the original keywords. This would be a poor example of a name using a keyword:

```
arrayb
```

However, this is a much better way of doing things:

```
InventoryArray
```

Debugging Ada Applications

Many problems that you encounter in your software development adventures will be easy to figure out by simply printing out the variable name in the command line. This way, it will be immediately obvious if something is wrong and why. However, this is not always the case, and for those particular issues, a debugger is a must. The goal of this appendix is to walk you through a very simple program and view its execution in a debugger. When you are finished, you will be equipped with basic knowledge of how to use the gdb debugger and how to delve inside of your applications.

All of the following commands that are shown can be executed in Windows (in a command prompt) and in a Linux or Unix operating system. The debugger that will be used is called "gdb" and is installed in Windows when you install the Ada compiler. In Linux (and other Unix-based operating systems), you will need to install it via your package manager.

As you go about in your debugging session, keep the source code of your application open in your favorite editor. gdb does offer you the ability to better view your source code during your session in the debugger, but only small snippets of it. Being able to just view the entire function or package is that much easier.

One point must be made, when compiling the source code, the "-g" flag is a must. Without this compilation flag, the correct debug information will not be included in the executable and the debugger will not be able to help you. It is done like so:

```
$ gnatmake -g source_file.adb
```

© Andrew T. Shvets 2020
A. T. Shvets, *Beginning Ada Programming*, https://doi.org/10.1007/978-1-4842-5428-8

An Overview of GDB and Its Commands

The gdb debugger was originally developed to run on Unix and Linux operating systems. However, it will run in Windows if your install was successful. It is a general debugger and runs from the command line. In order to do its work, gdb needs the required binaries to be compiled with debugging information in them. If you try to put an executable without such information, an error will be displayed saying that these pieces are missing.

In the command line (or command prompt in Windows), just start it up and something like the following should appear; writing "quit" and hitting Enter will exit you back to the command line.

```
> gdb
GNU gdb (GDB) 7.11.1
Copyright (C) 2016 Free Software Foundation, Inc.
License GPLv3+: GNU GPL version 3 or later <http://gnu.org/licenses/gpl.
html>
This is free software: you are free to change and redistribute it.
There is NO WARRANTY, to the extent permitted by law.  Type "show copying"
and "show warranty" for details.
This GDB was configured as "x86_64-pc-linux-gnu".
Type "show configuration" for configuration details.
For bug reporting instructions, please see:
<http://www.gnu.org/software/gdb/bugs/>.
Find the GDB manual and other documentation resources online at:
<http://www.gnu.org/software/gdb/documentation/>.
For help, type "help".
Type "apropos word" to search for commands related to "word".
(gdb) quit
```

This is what you should see. The (gdb) that shows up at the bottom is where you would interact with gdb and control your application. Typing "quit" and hitting Enter will terminate your debugging session; you might be asked if you are sure if you are in the middle of debugging an application.

Debugger Commands

These are the commands that you would execute when you start your debugging session with your application. In Linux (or Unix), it should be started like so:

```
$ gdb your_application
```

And in Windows command prompt:

```
> gdb your_application.exe
```

1) **break** – This will set a breakpoint, a point where the debugger should stop the execution of your application and give you a chance to see what is going on. A breakpoint can be set by specifying the line number in a file or the function that needs to be debugged. If the breakpoint needs to be in a package (which is located in a different file entirely), then the package's filename needs to be used:

```
(gdb) break 10
(gdb) break some_package.adb:30
(gdb) break print_procedure
(gdb) break some_package.adb:print_procedure
```

When a method is specified, the execution of the program will always stop whenever that function is reached.

2) **run** – This will start the execution of your program. If you have set a breakpoint, then the program will stop when it is reached.

If command-line arguments are needed, then a command needs to be executed like so:

```
(gdb) run --arg1=foo --path=/opt
```

3) **backtrace** – This will output the backtrace of your current application. A backtrace is a list (or stack) of functions and procedure that were called ever since the debugging session began.

The shorthand for this command is "**bt**".

4) **continue** – This indicates the debugger should keep running the application and not wait on the programmer to do anything. This will keep going until the application either encounters another breakpoint or finishes executing.

   The shorthand for this command is "**c**".

5) **next** – This will execute the next line. However, if the next line is a function or a procedure, then the debugger will not bother to step into it and see how it runs its code. It will simply execute that method and wait for it to return a value, if any. This can be a time saver when you know that a procedure works, and there is no need to further dive into its guts.

   The shorthand for this command is "**n**".

6) **step** – This will tell the debugger to execute the next line. Unlike "next," if a function or a procedure is encountered, then it will go into the method to step through the logic inside it. This is more useful if you are not sure where an error could be and want to look closer.

   The shorthand for this command is "**s**".

7) **quit** – This tells the debugger to terminate this debugging session. If there is a program that is running and actively being debugged, you will be asked if you are sure that you want to do this.

8) **help** – This displays all of the commands that gdb has to offer. Furthermore, you can get more in-depth information on the command if you specify it with the help command, like so:

   (gdb) help run

9) **shell** – A shell will be started, giving you access to the environment that is outside of the debugger.

10) **clear** – This is used to clear a breakpoint that has been set.

11) **info break** – This shows information about breakpoints.

12) **list** – This shows the next ten lines of code inside of your debug session. Putting a "-" right after this command will display the previous ten lines of code.

LLDB Debugger

There is a new debugger released. It can use most of the commands that gdb has. You should be able to work with it the same way as you do with gdb. However, it is beyond the scope of this book.

A Debugging Session

This section will serve as a short illustration of how a simple debug session looks. The example in Chapter 16 will be dissected for our purpose. Programmer inputs are the bold text:

```
> gdb generic_main
GNU gdb (GDB) 7.11.1
Copyright (C) 2016 Free Software Foundation, Inc.
License GPLv3+: GNU GPL version 3 or later <http://gnu.org/licenses/gpl.
html>
This is free software: you are free to change and redistribute it.
There is NO WARRANTY, to the extent permitted by law.  Type "show copying"
and "show warranty" for details.
This GDB was configured as "x86_64-pc-linux-gnu".
Type "show configuration" for configuration details.
For bug reporting instructions, please see:
<http://www.gnu.org/software/gdb/bugs/>.
Find the GDB manual and other documentation resources online at:
<http://www.gnu.org/software/gdb/documentation/>.
For help, type "help".
Type "apropos word" to search for commands related to "word"...
Reading symbols from generic_main...done.
(gdb) break 44
```

```
Breakpoint 1 at 0x40250d: file /.../simple_project/src/generic_main.adb,
line 44.
```
(gdb) break Put_Line_Flo
```
Breakpoint 2 at 0x402e01: Put_Line_Flo. (2 locations)
```
(gdb) break gener.adb:45
```
Breakpoint 3 at 0x4027c1: file /.../simple_project/src/gener.adb, line 45.
```
(gdb) run
```
Starting program: /.../simple_project/bin/debug/generic_main

Breakpoint 1, generic_main () at /source_code/ch16/simple_project/src/
generic_main.adb:44
44          Int_Test1 : Some_Int      := 10;
```
(gdb) n
```
45          Int_Test2 : Some_Int      := 20;
```
(gdb) n
```
46          Float_Test1 : Some_Float := -1.0;
```
(gdb) print Int_Test2
```
$1 = 20
```
(gdb) print Float_Test1
```
$2 = 5.94943123e-39
```
(gdb) continue
```
Continuing.
Val1:  10  Val2:  20
Val1:  20  Val2:  10
Min value: Val:  10
Max value: Val:  20

Breakpoint 2, generic_main.put_line_flo (val1=-1.0, val2=-2.0)
    at /.../simple_project/src/generic_main.adb:33
33          Ada.Text_IO.Put_Line("Val1: " & Some_Float'Image(Val1) &
```
(gdb) n
```
34            "  Val2: " & Some_Float'Image(Val2));
```
(gdb) n
```
33          Ada.Text_IO.Put_Line("Val1: " & Some_Float'Image(Val1) &
```
(gdb) n

```
34              "   Val2: " & Some_Float'Image(Val2));
(gdb) n
33          Ada.Text_IO.Put_Line("Val1: " & Some_Float'Image(Val1) &
(gdb) n
Val1: -1.00000E+00   Val2: -2.00000E+00
35      end Put_Line_Flo;
(gdb) n
generic_main () at /.../simple_project/src/generic_main.adb:60
60      Generic_Package_Test.Swap(Float_Test1, Float_Test2);
(gdb) continue
Continuing.

Breakpoint 3, generic_main.generic_package_test.swap (val1=-1.0, val2=-2.0)
    at /.../simple_project/src/gener.adb:45
45          Temp := Val2;
(gdb) list -
40          Val1 : in out Custom_Float_Type;
41          Val2 : in out Custom_Float_Type) is
42
43          Temp : Custom_Float_Type;
44      begin
45          Temp := Val2;
46          Val2 := Val1;
47          Val1 := Temp;
48      end Swap;
49
(gdb) list
50      function Min(
51          Val1 : in Custom_Float_Type;
52          Val2 : in Custom_Float_Type)
53          return Custom_Float_Type is
54      begin
55          if Val1 < Val2 then
56              return Val1;
```

```
57          else
58            return Val2;
59          end if;
```
(gdb) print Val1
```
$3 = -1.0
```
(gdb) print Val2
```
$4 = -2.0
```
(gdb) s
```
46          Val2 := Val1;
```
(gdb) s
```
47          Val1 := Temp;
```
(gdb) s
```
48        end Swap;
```
(gdb) s
```
generic_main () at /.../simple_project/src/generic_main.adb:61
61        Put_Line_Flo(Float_Test1, Float_Test2);
```
(gdb) continue
```
Continuing.

Breakpoint 2, generic_main.put_line_flo (val1=-2.0, val2=-1.0)
    at /.../simple_project/src/generic_main.adb:33
33          Ada.Text_IO.Put_Line("Val1: " & Some_Float'Image(Val1) &
```
(gdb) quit
```
A debugging session is active.

Inferior 1 [process 13348] will be killed.
```

Quit anyway? (y or n) y

This output will be challenging to digest for individuals that have never done this before. If you do not understand something the first time, then simply go back at a later time and re-read this portion:

```
  1)  (gdb) break 44
      (gdb) break Put_Line_Flo
      (gdb) break gener.adb:45
```

Three breakpoints have been set. The first is simply a line breakpoint in the file generic_main.adb. The second one is breaking on the function Put_Line_Flo in the same file. The third is a line breakpoint in the gener.adb file (the *.ads is a specification and it would not make sense to break somewhere without any executable code).

Pay attention to how, after setting each breakpoint, the filename and its path are printed out. This is very useful feedback in order to ensure that you know exactly where a breakpoint has been set.

2) (gdb) run
Starting program: /.../bin/debug/generic_main

The program begins executing...

Breakpoint 1, generic_main () at /.../src/generic_main.adb:44
44   Int_Test1 : Some_Int   := 10;

The debugger stops right where it was told to do so.

3) (gdb) n
45   Int_Test2 : Some_Int := 20;

Using the "n" command, short for next, the debugger keeps going forward line by line.

4) 45   Int_Test2 : Some_Int := 20;
(gdb) n
46   Float_Test1 : Some_Float := -1.0;
(gdb) print Int_Test2
$1 = 20
(gdb) print Float_Test1
$2 = 5.94943123e-39

Pay attention as to what is going on here. Right where the variable Float_Test2 is shown, the debugger has stopped where the Float_Test1 has been declared, but not assigned a value. As a result, you get something nonsensical such as "5.94943123e-39" and Int_Test2 has "20" assigned to it. If you were to run commands step or next, Float_Test1 will now have –1.0 assigned to it.

In case you are ever bewildered as to why you have such an absurd value, this is because when the program begins to execute for the first time, its variables do not have anything assigned to them by default and simply have the data of what is in RAM where that variable points. So when you view that piece of memory through your variable, it can be just about anything.

5) ```
(gdb) continue
Continuing.
Val1: 10 Val2: 20
Val1: 20 Val2: 10
Min value: Val: 10
Max value: Val: 20

Breakpoint 2, generic_main.put_line_flo (val1=-1.0, val2=-2.0)
    at /.../src/generic_main.adb:33
33   Ada.Text_IO.Put_Line("Val1: " & Some_Float'Image(Val1) &
```

When the continue command is issued to the debugger, it keeps running until either the next breakpoint is encountered or the end of the program is reached. In this case, the next breakpoint is the function Put_Line_Flo, and when this breakpoint is set, the debugger goes to the first line of the function after the "begin" keyword.

Notice the printout about min and max values; that is the printout of previous functions that ran when continue was issued, but before the next breakpoint was reached.

6) ```
(gdb) list
50      function Min(
51      Val1 : in Custom_Float_Type;
```

The list command prints out the source code itself. When you compile your binary with debug information (using "-g" as a flag to the compiler), your source code is included in the resulting binary as well. When you make changes to your source code, compile it with the debug information; these changes will be displayed in the new executable.

However, as you can see, it is only a very small snippet.

7) `(gdb) quit`

```
A debugging session is active.

    Inferior 1 [process 13348] will be killed.

Quit anyway? (y or n) y
```

And this is how things look when an attempt is made to exit while debugging a program. gdb asks if this is a wise decision and acts on the developer's input.

This is a simple example of how to debug a program. Feel free to re-run the debugger and try different commands to see what happens. Hands-on learning works best.

Index

A, B

Access Types, 82–84
Ada Reference Manual (ARM), 6, 217
Arrays, records and access types
    access types, 82–84
    array of records, 80–82
    concepts of, 69
    integers/floats, 70–73
    lab working, 89
    record (*see* Records)
    run time allocation, 75–77
    strings of, 73–75

C

Command-line arguments, 129, 130
Configuration Management (CM), 293
    git based code, 294
    mercurial project, 293
    subversion, 294
Contracts
    aspects of, 255–257
    functions and
        procedures, 253–255
    verify range, 258
Control structure, 39
    case statement, 42–45
    for loop, 48, 49
    if statement, 40–42
    infinite loop, 49

    goto, 51
    simple loops, 50
    lab application, 51
    parentheses, 42
    while loop, 45–48

D

Data containers, 147
    Ada.Containers.Indefinite_Vectors, 150
    advantages and drawbacks, 147
    arrays/vectors, 152
    Element_Type, 162
    Equivalent_Keys, 162
    hashmap, 148, 156–164
    list of, 147
    lists, 153–157
    queue, 147–152
    vector, 148
Debugger
    commands, 329–331
    debug session, 331–337
    GDB commands, 328
    LLDB, 331

E

Exception handling
    catching exceptions
        Constraint_Error, 114
        ever-helpful compiler, 114–116

339

© Andrew T. Shvets 2020
A. T. Shvets, *Beginning Ada Programming*, https://doi.org/10.1007/978-1-4842-5428-8

N

O

U

W, X, Y, Z

Printed in the United States
By Bookmasters